2022-2023
Middle School
Contest Materials

ISBN-978-1-312-70047-5

2022-2023 Middle School
Contest Materials
Table of Contents

Thank you for purchasing the 2022-2023 mathleague.org contest set series. Good luck to you and your students as you prepare for this year's math contests! Upcoming tournament information and the latest mathleague.org policies and information can be found at our website, https://mathleague.org, and you can reach us at customercare@mathleague.org.

mathleague.org is eager to help bring local math contests and championship meets to areas where such opportunities do not currently exist. Feel free to contact us if you would like more information on hosting a local contest or setting up a mathleague.org championship in your state or province.

Please be sure to let us know if you find typographical or mathematical errors. All tests are copyright 2022 and/or 2023 by mathleague.org and may be photocopied for practice within your school but may not be distributed outside your school.

Creating an entire year's worth of math contests takes a village. Our village this year consisted of Ava Brown, Brian Liu, Chinmay Krishna, David Sun, Doug Keegan, Edward Wu, Eugene Chiou, Freya Edholm, Hannah Wang, Isaac Li, Jimmy Ying, Kyle Lee, Michael Chen, Owen Yang, Paul Hamrick, Ryoko Kitadai, Silas Johnson, Taiki Aiba, Taman Truong, Thinula De Silva, Tim Sanders, and Wentinn Liao. Thanks to everyone who contributed to this effort!

This page intentionally left blank.
[*sic*]

Sprint Round
12310

Place ID Sticker
Inside This Box

Name _____

Grade _____

School _____

1.

2.

3.

4.

5.

6.

7.

8.

9.

10.

11.

12.

13.

14.

15.

16.

17.

18.

19.

20.

21.

22.

23.

24.

25.

26.

27.

28.

29.

30.

1. What is the greatest number of right interior angles that a triangle can have?

2. Patrick has a twenty-dollar bill and 2 one-dollar bills. If he earns $2 per week for his allowance, how many weeks will it take Patrick to have enough money to buy a new construction set worth $30?

3. In water polo, a fair coin is flipped to determine which team goes first. If the coin lands on heads, then Lily's team gets the ball first. Otherwise, Natalie's team gets the ball first. What's the probability that Natalie's team gets the ball first? Express your answer as a common fraction.

4. In football, the "completion percentage" is the percent of the passes that are completed. Chase attempted 15 passes, and his completion percentage, when rounded to the nearest percent, is 73%. How many passes did Chase complete?

5. A triangle and a square have the same perimeter and share a side of length 6. The triangle also has a side of length 10. What is the length of the longest side of the triangle?

6. After a casual game of golf, Connor and Elise each made a dot plot shown below that represents the number of strokes done per hole. What is the mode of the list of numbers representing the number of strokes Connor or Elise did for a hole?

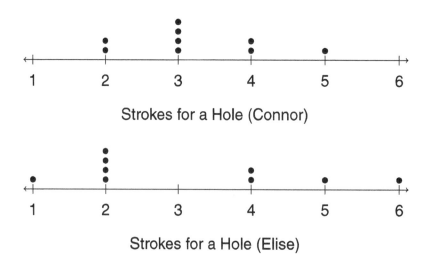

Strokes for a Hole (Connor)

Strokes for a Hole (Elise)

7. Mark's goal is to plant 900 trees. He pilots a drone that can plant trees at a rate of 5 trees per minute. However, once he is halfway done, another drone that also plants trees at a rate of 5 trees per minute starts to work. How many minutes elapses from the time Mark starts planting trees to the time his goal is reached?

8. Rohan measures the three distances between one vertex of a rectangle and the other three vertices. If his shortest measurement is 5 inches and his longest measurement is 13 inches, how many inches are in Rohan's remaining measurement?

9. Amelia is working out a subtraction problem where she subtracts a three-digit number from 1624. Among the two numbers in the subtraction problem, no digits are repeated. Amelia always forgets to carry and borrow when she subtracts, but fortunately she does not need to borrow at any point when doing this subtraction problem and gets the correct answer. What answer does Amelia get?

10. A number is selected uniformly at random from the set $\{1, 2, 3, 4, 5, 6, 7, 8, 9\}$. What is the probability that the number is odd or a multiple of 3? Express your answer as a common fraction.

11. Brian is getting stronger! His power level is currently at 300, and every hour, his power level doubles. What is the smallest whole number of hours it would take for Brian's power level to go over 8000?

12. Thomas has a robot that can use a powerful gear technique, where each use lasts 5 seconds, but after each use, the robot needs to cool down before activating again. The cool down time for the first use is 10 seconds, but each subsequent cool down time is 10 seconds longer than that of the previous cool down time. How many times could the robot activate the gear technique within 3 minutes, assuming the robot first uses the gear technique as the timer starts?

13. At a party, there are 8 people. Each pair of people shakes hands with each other once, except for one pair, who are best friends and refuse to shake hands with anyone else other than themselves. In total, how many handshakes take place?

14. Trunan now has 110 batteries available. An RC toy requires 4 batteries, which last for 30 days before they all need to be replaced, while an RC controller requires 2 batteries, which last for 40 days. If Trunan puts in all batteries at once for the RC toy and the RC controller on the first day, and he replaces batteries as soon as any batteries need to be replaced, how many days will the RC toy and the RC controller last before Trunan runs out of batteries?

15. Point A is at $(21, -12)$, point B is at $(40, 4)$, point C is at $(-78, -42)$, and point D is at $(66, -5)$. There is only one way to select two of the four points such that the slope of the line passing through the two points is negative. What is the sum of the coordinates of those two points? Note that you will be adding four whole numbers to get your answer.

16. Let x and y be real numbers such that $x^3 + y^3 = 12$ and $2x^3 + 3y^3 = 12$. What is the value of x^3?

17. What is the 6th smallest positive multiple of 6 that is divisible by neither 2^3 nor 3^3?

18. What is the probability that a randomly chosen divisor of 324 is both a multiple of 6 and a multiple of 9? Express your answer as a common fraction.

19. Collin is sketching an arch bridge below, where he draws an upward-facing semicircle with diameter 10 centimeters, then a straight horizontal line with length 2 centimeters, then another upward-facing semicircle with diameter 6 centimeters, and finally another horizontal line with length 2 centimeters going back to the starting point. To the nearest whole number, how many square centimeters is the area of Collin's arch bridge?

20. Audrey and her friends plan to visit Heaven's Park and Sakura Mountain, but they have to travel by vehicle, where each vehicle can have up to four passengers. The entrance fee for Heaven's Park is a fixed amount per vehicle, while the entrance fee for Sakura Mountain is a fixed amount per passenger. Audrey finds that the minimum cost if a group of 3 travels to both places is $60 while the minimum cost if a group of 8 travels to both places is $140. How many dollars does Audrey need if she, Melody, Lily, Jaedyn, and Madison all plan on travelling as a group to both places?

21. Jon has two 52-card decks where each deck has the positive whole numbers from 1 to 52, inclusive. One deck has all cards red while another deck has all cards blue. He is playing a modified version of Survival, where two of the 104 cards are marked as "harm cards". Jon knows that if A and B denote the values of the two harm cards, $AB = 90$, A is prime, and B is greater than 26. Based on this information, how many possible harm card configurations are there?

22. A positive number a is selected so that the equation $(3x+2)(4x+7) = (ax+3)(x+5)$ has exactly one solution. What is a?

23. Right triangle ABC with right angle at B has area 9. The lengths of both AB and BC are whole numbers, and the altitude from B to $\overline{AC}$ has length strictly greater than 2. What is AC^2?

24. Luke does a 2-minute street workout where he punches a speed bag. At first, he hits the bag at a rate of 1 punch per second, but every 10 seconds, he instantaneously speeds up by 1 punch per second until he plateaus at 4 punches per second. Starting at the the time when there are 60 seconds left in his workout, he instantaneously slows down by 1 punch per second every 30 seconds, until the workout ends. How many punches does he land in total during his training session?

25. Andy kept track of his sparring matches at a neo arena and found he won $53\frac{1}{3}\%$ of the matches. If he wins the next one, his win percentage will increase to $56\frac{1}{4}\%$. How many matches has Andy done so far?

26. In every calendar year, May kth and October $2k$th fall on the same day of the week. Find the greatest possible value of k, where k is a positive whole number.

27. Jessica and Rebecca are playing a mini game where Jessica stands on square A and Rebecca stands on square B in the diagram below. On each turn, Jessica and Rebecca jump to a square chosen at random that shares a side with their respective squares at the same time, then return to their previous squares. What is the probability that after two turns, there will be at least one turn where Jessica and Rebecca jumped to the same square? Express your answer as a common fraction.

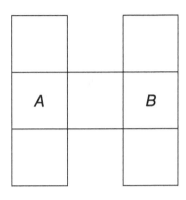

28. Quadrilateral $ABCD$ has side lengths $AB = 4$, $BC = 6$, $CD = 9$, and $DA = 9$, and diagonal length $AC = 6$. Diagonals AC and BD intersect at point E. What is $\frac{BD}{BE}$? Express your answer as a common fraction.

29. Kendra wants to arrange and divide the letters in her name to create 3 strings, each of which must contain at least one letter. In how many ways can she do so, assuming that the order in which she creates the strings is irrelevant, and she uses each letter exactly once?

30. Brandon is making a staircase out of blocks with at least one column where column 1 has 1 block, column 2 has 2 blocks, and so on. In general, column n should have n blocks. If Brandon has a collection of some number of blocks, he can use up all his blocks to make a staircase if there were either 1 more block or 8 fewer blocks. What is the sum of all possible number of blocks in Brandon's collection?

Target Round
12310

Place ID Sticker
Inside This Box

Name _____

Grade _____

School _____

Problems 1 & 2

1. Reagan is going on a road trip. She first travels 100 miles per day due north for seven days. Then she travels 30 miles per day due south for three days. At the end of the tenth day, how many miles due north is Reagan from her starting point?

1. [ ]

2. At the end of a soccer game, Ava's team and Grace's team line up in a line to shake hands. Ava and Grace are standing 10 meters apart and facing each other. Both Ava and Grace have 14 teammates from their respective teams standing behind them such that the teammates of each team are standing 2 meters apart. How many meters is the furthest distance from one player on Ava's team to one player on Grace's team?

2. [ ]

Target Round
12310

Place ID Sticker
Inside This Box

Name _____

Grade _____

School _____

Problems 3 & 4

3. Jimmy plans on buying every food item from another store. The store has 10 rows where each row has 80 food items. Jimmy notes that 1% of all the food items are canned beans and that the total cost of all the canned beans is $9.20. What is the average price of the canned beans in the store, in dollars? Express your answer as a decimal to the nearest hundredth.

3.

4. Let A be the intersection point of the graphs of $y = 2x^3 + 3x^2 - 4x$ and $x = -1.5$. Let B be the point $(0,0)$. What is the area of a right triangle whose legs are parallel to the coordinate axes and whose hypotenuse is AB? Express your answer as a common fraction.

4.

Target Round 12310 ©2022 mathleague.org

Place ID Sticker
Inside This Box

Name _____

Grade _____

School _____

Problems 5 & 6

5. On a mathleague.org high school test, the Sprint portion is worth 120 points and the Target portion is worth 80 points. The lowest percentage score that one can earn on the Sprint test and still get an overall score of 70 percent is n%. What is n?

5.

6. Emma is putting together a jigsaw puzzle where all the jigsaw pieces are equilateral triangles with side length 2 centimeters. Once all of the jigsaw pieces are correctly placed, the completed jigsaw puzzle is a regular hexagon with side length 12 centimeters. Emma creates a starting pile consisting of every "edge piece," which are jigsaw pieces that have at least one side that is not bordered by another jigsaw piece once the entire jigsaw puzzle is complete, and additional 60 "non-edge" pieces in the jigsaw puzzle. What fraction of all the pieces in the jigsaw puzzle are not in Emma's starting pile? Express your answer as a common fraction.

6.

Place ID Sticker
Inside This Box

Name _____

Grade _____

School _____

Problems 7 & 8

---

7. The 6×6 rectangle below can be split into four rectangles that each have dimensions 1×5 as well as another rectangle with whole number side lengths. What is the perimeter of the fifth rectangle?

7.

(grid image)

8. An amusement park opens at 9 AM and closes at 5 PM the same day. One day, Farmer John showcases his animals in two different sessions that each last one hour. The first session starts at 11 AM while the second session starts at 2 PM. What is the probability that some part of his sessions happens somewhere in between two randomly selected times that the park is open? Express your answer as a common fraction.

8.

Team Round
12310

School or Team

Name _____

Name _____

Name _____

Name _____

Place ID Sticker
Inside This Box

Place ID Sticker
Inside This Box

Place ID Sticker
Inside This Box

Place ID Sticker
Inside This Box

1.

2.

3.

4.

5.

6.

7.

8.

9.

10.

1. A lecture hall has 10 rows where each row has 10 seats, and each person who attends a lecture sits in a seat such that each seat has at most one student. Ellen keeps track of the number of students who attend lecture each day in the below table. In how many lectures do there remain an odd number of empty seats at that time?

Lecture Number	1st	2nd	3rd	4th	5th
Students Attending	96	79	68	53	41

2. Ethan pays for a ride with the transportation service Speedy, which comes at a base fee of $15, plus $1.50 for each mile traveled. He would have had to pay three times the amount if he had traveled four times as far as he did. How many miles did Ethan travel?

3. Thomas turned in his final exam at 2:30 PM on June 10. He learned from his TA that the probability that the final is graded within 24 hours after the exam is turned in is $\frac{1}{2}$, the probability that the final is graded from 24 to 48 hours after the exam is turned in is $\frac{1}{3}$, and the probability that the final takes longer than 48 hours to be graded is $\frac{1}{6}$. What is the probability that Thomas's final is graded by 2:30 PM on June 12? Express your answer as a common fraction.

4. As shown in the below diagram, $\angle AOC = 118\frac{3}{4}^{\circ}$ and $\angle BOC = 47\frac{1}{8}^{\circ}$. How many degrees are in the measure of the angle supplementary to $\angle AOB$? Express your answer as a mixed number.

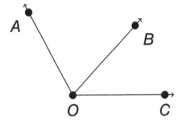

5. Tania is giving a presentation in which she speaks at 100 words per minute. Each slide of her presentation consists of anywhere between 40 and 125 words. If her presentation is between 10 and 12 minutes long, what is the positive difference between the minimum and maximum number of slides that she has?

6. Lucas has 15 acorns, 10 metal fragments, and 20 smooth stones available to make capsules. The below table lists the number of resources needed to make each capsule. What is the greatest number of capsules that Lucas could make?

Capsule	Acorns Needed	Metal Fragments Needed	Smooth Stones Needed
Standard	1	1	1
Light	1	1	0
Heavy	1	0	2

7. Garrett found a way to fix his leak and drain the water such that the water exits the bathtub at a constant rate. At 6:00 PM, the bathtub has 33 gallons of water, and at 6:03 PM on the same day, the bathtub has 16 gallons and 8 cups of water. How many *seconds* past 6:03 PM will it take for the bathtub to be completely empty? Note that 1 gallon equals 16 cups.

8. Chloe encounters a plane with four engines, but all but one engine has two broken parts. Chloe fixes one part every day, but for every day after the first, there is a $\frac{1}{2}$ probability that a friend joins Chloe and fixes one part every day. What is the probability that all the broken parts are fixed within four days? Express your answer as a common fraction.

9. Four equilateral triangles in a plane, each with side length 4, all share one common vertex. The eight unshared vertices form an equiangular octagon. The closest distance between any two unshared vertices can be expressed as $m\sqrt{n} - p\sqrt{q}$, where m, n, p, and q are positive whole numbers, and n and q are not divisible by the square of any prime. What is $m + n + p + q$?

10. Professor Christopher devises a method to encrypt a secret positive whole number n. He creates the sequence $a_0, a_1, a_2, \ldots$ such that $a_0 = n$ and a_{k+1} is the result when dividing a_k by 2 then rounding down to the nearest whole number for $k > 0$. His encrypted number would then be the sum of all non-zero numbers in the sequence. For example, if his secret number is 5, then the encrypted number is $5 + 2 + 1 = 8$. How many positive whole numbers have encrypted numbers that are less than or equal to 50?

1. Bella's bubble soccer team has 9 players, including Drake. She has to pick 5 players to be on the field, but she wants one of the players picked to be Drake. How many ways can Bella pick the rest of the players?

2. How many seconds are in a third of a day?

3. Matt is in a hall of mirrors that has 100 mirrors, each in a shape of a parallelogram. He observes that 56 mirrors are not rectangles, 42 mirrors are not rhombuses, and 14 mirrors are squares. How many mirrors are rectangles but not squares?

4. Point A has coordinates (24, 18) and the midpoint of AB is (3, -9). What is the product of the coordinates of B?

5. Daniel has a collection of trading cards about legendary dragons that are either fire, electric, or ice. He has 8 fewer fire cards compared to electric cards and ice cards combined, 12 fewer electric cards compared to fire cards and ice cards combined, and 4 fewer ice cards compared to fire cards and electric cards combined. If Daniel stores half of the total number of cards in the black case, how many cards are in the black case?

6. Evaluate: $38 + 16 \cdot 7 - 29$.

7. Calculate: $19 \cdot 301 \cdot 1001$.

8. The bullseye of one target is a circular area with area 30 square inches. The below table lists the distances from two arrows of each player to the center of that bullseye. How many arrows landed in the bullseye?

Player	1st Arrow Distance	2nd Arrow Distance
Andrea	2 inches	4 inches
Belinda	3 inches	3 inches
Chelina	3.5 inches	2.5 inches
Diana	1.5 inches	4 inches
Evelyn	3 inches	2 inches

9. Find the GCD of 8099 and 7800.

10. Rebecca's fan is a sector of a circle with radius 7.2 centimeters and a central angle of 140°. How many square centimeters is the area of Rebecca's fan when rounded to the nearest whole number?

11. An unfair coin lands heads $\frac{6}{7}$ of the time. If the coin is flipped 3 times, what is the probability that at most two of the flips land heads? Express your answer as a common fraction.

12. How many times does $\frac{18}{35}$ go into $\frac{1}{14}$? Express your answer as a common fraction.

13. Andy divides a rectangular field with area 240 square feet into smaller plots that are squares that each have area 16 square feet. The tomato plots do not share an edge with the edge of the entire rectangular field, and the total area of the tomato plots is 48 square feet. What is the perimeter of Andy's rectangular field?

14. Find the largest prime divisor of 7198.

15. Express $\frac{8}{21} + \frac{7}{18}$ as a common fraction.

16. Becca needs to obtain the books shown in the below table. Fortunately, a friend gave her used copies of the two most expensive books on the list, so Becca only needs to buy the rest of the books. If Becca has $3.28 left after buying the books, how many dollars does she have before buying the books? Express your answer as a decimal to the nearest hundredth.

Book	Cost
Blazing World	$12.99
Fahrenheit 451	$15.99
Frankenstein	$8.99
Secret Life of Bees	$11.99
The Odyssey	$10.99

17. The area of a 12-sided regular polygon inscribed in a circle with radius r is given by $A = 3r^2$. If a circle has a circumference of 28π, what is the area of a 12-sided regular polygon inscribed in it?

18. How many digits are in one of the numbers 24750 and 128053 but not both?

19. A circle is divided into a number of pieces by 6 straight lines, where each pair of lines is either parallel or perpendicular. What is the maximum number of pieces the circle is divided into?

20. Eugene and Marian are working on a jigsaw puzzle, where the puzzle once completed has 20 rows with each row having 25 pieces. So far, Marian completed the space ranger part, which used up 20% of the total pieces. Then Eugene completes the tricky green slime monster part, which uses 37.5% of the pieces not used for the space ranger part. How many remaining pieces are left?

21. If $f(x) = 303x + 33$, then find $f(33)$.

22. Below are five whole numbers. What is the sum of all the numbers that are not divisible by 7?
   - 109
   - 110
   - 111
   - 112
   - 113

23. A basketball game is 48 minutes long and has four quarters with each quarter lasting the same time. At the end of the third quarter, the Tunes have 73 points while the Monsters have 81 points. The Tunes average 3 points per minute in the fourth quarter, while the Monsters average 2 points per minute in the fourth quarter. At the end of the fourth quarter, what is the score of the team with the most points?

24. Find the distance between the point $(0, 0)$ and the line $5x + 12y = 60$. Express your answer as a decimal to the nearest tenth.

25. Maia kept track of how many pictures she took at national parks this year as well as the state of the national park in the below table. Last year, Maia took 20 pictures in Yosemite, but this year, she took 25% more pictures at Yosemite compared to last year. What percent of the national park pictures that Maia took this year were in California?

National Park	State	Pictures Taken
Crater Lake	Oregon	15
Grand Canyon	Arizona	18
Sequoia	California	12
Yosemite	California	
Yellowstone	Idaho, Montana, Wyoming	30

26. What is the sum of the three smallest integers n that satisfy the inequality $|n - 7| < 12$?

27. Find the 101st number in the arithmetic sequence: $275, 371, 467, 563 \ldots$.

28. Andrew needs four wheels for his gravity vehicle. The diagram below is a cross-section of one cylindrical wheel that is parallel to one of the faces, where the shaded sections are part of the wheel. The hole is a cylinder with radius 0.5 inch that runs through the entire larger cylinder, which has radius 5 inches. The height of the cylinder is 1 inch. How many cubic inches is the total volume he needs? Express your answer in terms of π.

29. If $x = 15$, what is the value of $2x^2 + (-2x)^2$?

30. A large square is divided into 100 unit squares, as shown below. What percent of the area of the large square is shaded?

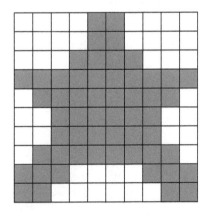

31. What is the second largest possible integer value of $30 - x^2$?

32. Cate is selling corsages for $12 and boutonnieres for $8. If John has $76 and buys two corsages, what is the greatest amount of boutonnieres that John can buy with the remaining cash?

33. Find the shortest distance between the graphs of the equations $(x+4)^2+(y-2)^2=64$ and $(x-8)^2+(y+3)^2=4$.

34. What is the surface area, in square inches, of a rectangular prism with side lengths 21 in, 19 in, and 10 in?

35. How many ways are there to draw a rectangle from a 9×2 grid of squares if the sides of the rectangle are on the lines of the grid?

36. Olivia needs 2 boxes of spinach and 1 onion to make 4 servings of spinach salad. She currently has 36 onions and 25 boxes of spinach, but a sailor who loves spinach gave her 45 boxes of spinach. After getting the extra boxes of spinach, what is the greatest number of servings of spinach salad that Olivia can make?

37. How many diagonals are there in a regular pentagon?

38. What is the least common multiple of the first five even positive integers?

39. Evaluate: $193 + 359$.

40. At a carnival, blue tickets are worth 2 points while gold tickets are worth 5 points. In one activity, the reward for scoring less than 5 points is a gold ticket, while scoring otherwise would reward a blue ticket. Jake earned 5 points in his first time, 4 points in his second time, and 6 points in his third time. Ashley earned 4 points in her first time, 4 points in her second time, and 5 points in her third time. How many points did the two get after all their games?

41. What is the degree measure of the supplement of an angle whose complement has a measure of 86.555 degrees? Express your answer as a decimal without trailing zeroes.

42. Evan went to sleep at 10:20 PM and woke up at 6:30 AM the next day. He spent 20% of the time sleeping in deep sleep. How many minutes did Evan spend in deep sleep?

43. Simplify: $\frac{\frac{18}{35}}{\frac{7}{2}}$. Express your answer as a common fraction

44. How many distinct positive integers n are there such that $n > 6$ and the remainder when 153 is divided by n is 6?

45. A garden has 4 white sage plants, 1 elderberry plant, and 8 coyote brush plants. Chloe selects one plant at random. What is the probability that the plant is a coyote brush plant? Express your answer as a common fraction.

46. Two fair six-sided dice are thrown. What is the probability that at least one of them lands on a 2 or a 5? Express your answer as a common fraction.

47. Solve for a if $5a + 4b = 535$ and $-8a + 2b = -520$.

48. What is the smallest integer value of y such that the equation $x^2 = 58 - 2y$ has no real solutions?

49. Calculate: $16^3 - 15^3$.

50. Dillon is watching one pair of twins doing three laps for an exercise drill in PE. He recorded the results in the below table. How many seconds is the average time of the twin with the faster average time?

Lap	Time for Twin 1	Time for Twin 2
1	5 minutes 3 seconds	5 minutes 10 seconds
2	4 minutes 45 seconds	4 minutes 55 seconds
3	4 minutes 57 seconds	4 minutes 48 seconds

51. In $\triangle ABC$, $\angle A = 28\frac{9}{10}^\circ$ and $\angle B = 59\frac{1}{5}^\circ$. What is the degree measure of the exterior angle to $\angle C$? Express your answer as a mixed number

52. What is the value of $939 + 949 + 959 + 961 + 971 + 981$?

53. Jacob draws the lines with equations $y = 3x + 8$ and $y = -3x + 8$ and $y = 3x + 2$, and Desi draws the lines with equations $y = 2x + 3$ and $y = 3x - 8$ and $y = 2x + 5$. How many intersection points are there between one of Jacob's lines and one of Desi's lines?

54. A cube has a surface area of 13.5 square inches. What is the number of cubic inches in the volume of the cube? Expres your answer as a common fraction.

55. The ratio between two consecutive positive multiples of 5 is $\frac{11}{12}$. Find the sum of the integers.

56. When the figure shown below is folded into a cube such that the squares shown become faces of the cube, what is the sum of all the numbers on all the faces that share an edge with the face marked with a star?

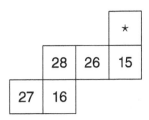

57. Ann is putting up flyers in 5 different non-overlapping square city boroughs that each have side length 15 kilometers for an resilience festival. The city has an area of 3750 square kilometers and a population of 25000, and she expects that the population density, with the units of people per square kilometer, will be the same within each borough as the entire city. Based on the given information, how many people would Ann expect to live in the square city borough with the petitions?

58. What is the least integer greater than $5\sqrt{13}$?

59. Find the number such that the sum of its double, triple, and quadruple is 711.

60. Lani measured how much storage four programs take up and recorded the results in the below table, where 1 terabyte (TB) equals 1024 gigabytes (GB). How many gigabytes is the median storage?

Program	Storage
rock.exe	3000 GB
roll.exe	0.25 TB
blues.exe	512 GB
forte.exe	1 TB

61. Evaluate: 6.2×0.22. Express your answer as a decimal without trailing zeroes.

62. What is the slope of the line $140x + 142y = 144$? Express your answer as a common fraction.

63. There are 61 points on a circle. How many ways are there to draw a triangle with vertices chosen from the 61 points?

64. Ellie has 5760 crystal beads and 4608 pieces of ribbon string. She plans on putting the supplies into as many boxes as she could such that the crystal beads are divided evenly among the boxes and the ribbon strings are divided evenly among the boxes. She then plans to place as many boxes as she could into a big-rig that could carry at most 1000 boxes. How many boxes would not be in the big-rig?

65. Given that $a^b = 729$ and a and b are both integers, what is the smallest possible value of a?

66. Find n if $2^{10} + 2^{10} + 2^{10} + 2^{10} = 4^n$.

67. Joeli observes some laths, which are rectangular pieces of wood, while surveying houses. She records the length and width of each lath in the below table. How many square centimeters is the range of the areas of the laths with the three biggest perimeters?

Lath	Length (centimeters)	Width (centimeters)
A	29	37
B	17	28
C	6	85
D	23	56
E	62	83

68. This morning, Melcka answered 27 customer care emails. Then April answered some emails. Afterwards, Roselle answered twice as many emails as April did. Finally, Yuna answered 32 emails so that the total number of emails answered today was 110. How many emails were answered by Roselle?

69. It takes three mathleague.org staff members 40 minutes to produce a sonnet. One staff member assembles the words, one edits for style and grammar, and one performs it in front of a focus group of would-be suitors. How many sonnets can fourteen mathleague.org staff members produce in a summer's day? Remember, like all days, a summer's day contains 24 hours, but it just happens to be more lovely and more temperate.

70. 20% of what number is 50% of 286?

71. What is the volume of a cube with side length 19?

72. How many two-digit prime numbers have no prime digits?

73. At a robot colosseum, each attendee roots for either the buzz-saw hammer robot or the wild cutter robot. Kyle keeps track of how many attendees rooted for each robot over six rounds in the below table. On which round number is the probability that a random attendee of that round rooted for the buzz-saw hammer robot the greatest?

Round Number	Buzz-Saw Hammer	Wild Cutter
1	1769236	1856354
2	1856295	1856385
3	1856425	1254853
4	1859476	1649265
5	1967262	1967251
6	1866251	1856254

74. Compute: $\frac{24}{3} + 4 \cdot 7$.

75. In how many ways can the letters in the word NATIONAL be arranged?

76. What is the maximum number of acute angles that can be formed from four lines that intersect in a single point?

77. Andersen is designing one of the walls of a seat for a roller coaster. On the blueprint, he made sketch of that wall, where a semicircle of diameter 6 centimeters is taken out of the top of the rectangle with length 8 centimeters and height 4 centimeters, as shown in the below diagram. The scale indicates that 1 centimeter on the blueprint equals 0.5 meters in real life. To the nearest tenth of a square meter, what is the area of the real life wall?

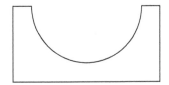

78. How many proper subsets does the set $\{1, 2, 4, 5, 6, 7\}$ have?

79. The average of three numbers is 60. If the largest number is 68, then what is the average of the two smallest numbers?

80. Nathan and Grace are running along the same path starting from the same point. Nathan runs at 10 km/h and Grace runs at 15 km/h. If Nathan has a 500 meter head start, how many minutes must Grace run before catching up to Nathan?

Sprint Round

1. 1
2. 4
3. $\frac{1}{2}$
4. 11
5. 10
6. 2
7. 135
8. 12
9. 1121
10. $\frac{2}{3}$
11. 5
12. 6
13. 16
14. 600
15. 105
16. 24
17. 42
18. $\frac{2}{5}$
19. 25
20. 110
21. 8
22. 12
23. 45
24. 330
25. 15
26. 15
27. $\frac{17}{81}$
28. $\frac{13}{4}$
29. 1200
30. 67

Target Round

1. 610
2. 66
3. 1.15
4. $\frac{9}{2}$
5. 50
6. $\frac{5}{9}$
7. 16
8. $\frac{13}{16}$

Team Round

1. 3
2. 20
3. $\frac{5}{6}$
4. $108\frac{3}{8}$
5. 22
6. 15
7. 180
8. $\frac{3}{4}$
9. 12
10. 27

Countdown

1. 70
2. 28800
3. 30
4. 648
5. 12
6. 121
7. 5724719
8. 7
9. 13
10. 63
11. $\frac{127}{343}$
12. $\frac{245}{9}$
13. 64
14. 61
15. $\frac{97}{126}$
16. ($)35.25
17. 588
18. 5
19. 16
20. 250
21. 10032
22. 443
23. 109
24. 4.6
25. 37(%)
26. −9
27. 9875
28. 99π
29. 1350
30. 56(%)
31. 29
32. 6
33. 3
34. 1598
35. 135
36. 35
37. 5
38. 120
39. 552
40. 21
41. 176.555
42. 98
43. $\frac{36}{245}$
44. 4
45. $\frac{8}{13}$
46. $\frac{5}{9}$
47. 75
48. 30
49. 721
50. 295
51. $88\frac{1}{10}$(°)
52. 5760
53. 7
54. $\frac{27}{8}$
55. 115
56. 96
57. 7500
58. 19
59. 79
60. 768
61. 1.364
62. $-\frac{70}{71}$
63. 35990
64. 152
65. −81
66. 6
67. 4906
68. 34
69. 168
70. 715
71. 6859
72. 6
73. 3
74. 36
75. 10080
76. 12
77. 4
78. 63
79. 56
80. 6

Sprint Round Solutions

1. We can easily draw a triangle that has one right angle. However, if a triangle has two or more right angles, then the sum of the angles would be greater than $180°$. Therefore, a triangle cannot have two or more right interior angles, so the greatest number of right interior angles must be $\boxed{1}$.

2. Patrick currently has $22. We could skip count by twos to get the answer, or we can write an equation where x is the number of weeks elapsed, which yields $22 + 2x = 30$. Either way, we find that it will take $\boxed{4}$ weeks.

3. A fair coin has two sides that come up with equal probability – heads or tails. Of the two possibilities, only tails results in Natalie going first. Therefore, the probability that Natalie goes first is $\boxed{\frac{1}{2}}$.

4. We can reasonably expect the answer to be less than 12 as $16 \cdot \frac{3}{4} = 12$. In fact, $\frac{11}{15}$ equals 0.733 to three decimal places, so Chase completed $\boxed{11}$ passes.

5. The perimeter of the square is $4 \cdot 6 = 24$. Thus, the perimeter of the triangle is also 24, and the length of the third side is $24 - 6 - 10 = 8$. Thus, the sides of the triangle are 6, 8, and 10, and the longest length is $\boxed{10}$.

6. Recall that the mode is the data value that appears the most often. When combining the data from the two dot plots, we can observe that the mode would be $\boxed{2}$.

7. For the first 450 trees, one drone would take 90 minutes. For the next 450 trees, two drones would be working. The combined rate is 10 trees per minute, and so it would take 45 minutes. Therefore, the total amount of time elapsed in minutes is $90 + 45 = \boxed{135}$.

8. The longest measurement will be the diagonal of the rectangle, and the other two measurements will be the side lengths of the rectangle. By the Pythagorean theorem, the sum of the squares of the two side lengths is equal to the square of the diagonal, so $5^2 + a^2 = 13^2$ where a is the remaining measurement. Solving gives $a = \boxed{12}$ inches.

9. If no borrowing occurs, then in the three-digit number the hundreds digit must be less than 6, the tens digit must be less than 2, and the ones digit must be less than 4. Since 1 is already used, the tens digit must be 0. Then the ones digit must be 3 and the hundreds digit must be 5. The answer to the subtraction problem is $1624 - 503 = \boxed{1121}$.

10. The elements in the set that are odd or multiples of 3 are 1, 3, 5, 7, 9, and 6, for a probability of $\boxed{\dfrac{2}{3}}$.

11. One way is to make a list where we keep track of the number of times Brian's power level doubles until the power level is greater than 8000. Alternatively, we can write an equation where x is the number of hours, and the equation is $300 \cdot 2^x > 8000$. Either way, we find that the minimum positive whole number x must be $\boxed{5}$.

12. We could consider the time during the gear technique as well as the cool down time right before that as one block of time. The first block is 5 seconds, but the next block is 15 seconds, then 25 seconds, and so on. Thus, we want to find the point where the sum $5 + 15 + 25 + \cdots$ grows larger than 180. By adding our way up, we find that $5 + 15 + \cdots + 55 = 180$ exactly. This means that immediately after the robot uses the gear technique for the sixth time, the three minutes has elapsed. In total, the robot can use the gear technique for $\boxed{6}$ times in 3 minutes.

13. There are $\binom{8-2}{2} = 15$ handshakes among the 6 people who are not in the last pair, and 1 handshake among the best friends pair, giving $\boxed{16}$ handshakes in total.

14. Every $\operatorname{lcm}(40, 30) = 120$ days, the RC toy uses 16 batteries while the RC controller uses 6 batteries, so 22 batteries in total are used every cycle. This means 110 batteries are used up after five cycles of 120 days, which is $\boxed{600}$ days.

15. First we need to determine what the two points are. We could calculate the slope, but a faster way is to do a rough sketch of the points on the graph and notice that the two points are B and D. The sum of the coordinates of points B and D is $40 + 4 + 66 - 5 = \boxed{105}$.

16. By subtracting the first equation from the second, we obtain $x^3 + 2y^3 = 0$. Thus, $y^3 = -12$ since $x^3 + y^3 = 12$; therefore, $x^3 = \boxed{24}$.

17. A multiple of 6 must contain at least one factor of both 2 and 3. Thus, the powers of 2 and 3 in the prime factorization must be either 1 or 2. We can count manually to get that the 6th smallest whole number with this property is $7 \cdot 6 = \boxed{42}$, as 24 is divisible by 2^3.

18. Being a multiple of 6 and 9 is the same as being a multiple of 18. $324 = 2^2 \cdot 3^4$ is small enough that we can count the factors which are multiples of 18 by hand: of the $(2+1)(4+1) = 15$ factors of 324, the factors 18, 36, 54, 108, 162, and 324 are divisible by 18. There are 6 such factors, giving a probability of $\frac{6}{15} = \boxed{\dfrac{2}{5}}$. (An alternative way of finding the factors that are multiples of 18 is to factor $18 = 2 \cdot 3^2$, and observe that there are $(1+1)(2+1) = 6$ multiples of 18 that go into 324.)

19. The arch bridge is essentially a large semicircle with radius 5 cm with a smaller semicircle with radius 3 cm taken out. Its area is then $\frac{1}{2}\pi(5^2 - 3^2) = 8\pi$. By using either 3.14 or $\frac{22}{7}$ for π as an approximation, we find that the area of the arch bridge is approximately $\boxed{25}$ square centimeters.

20. Let a be the entrance fee per passenger for Sakura Mountain and let b be the entrance fee per vehicle for Heaven's Park. A group of three needs one vehicle, so we get the equation $3a + b = 60$. A group of eight needs two vehicles, so we get the equation $8a + 2b = 140$. Then we have a system of equations that we can solve. One possible approach is elimination where subtracting $2(3a + b) = 2 \cdot 60$ from $8a + 2b = 140$ results in $2a = 20$, resulting in $a = 10$ then $b = 30$. Now if Audrey, Melody, Lily, Jaedyn, and Madison all travel as a group, they need two vehicles, so the cost would be $5 \cdot 10 + 2 \cdot 30 = \$\boxed{110}$.

21. We begin solving this problem by determining the prime factors of 90. The prime factors of 90 are 2, 3, and 5. Then we find that $2 \cdot 45 = 90$ and $3 \cdot 30 = 90$ but $5 \cdot 18 = 90$. This means that there are only 2 ways to pick the numbers. However, there are no restrictions on color, so there are $2 \cdot 2^2 = \boxed{8}$ possible harm card configurations.

22. There are two possibilities: the equation that results from expanding and simplifying either results in a linear equation or a quadratic with a double root. In the first case, the coefficient of x^2 must be 0; this can be attained when $3 \cdot 4 = a \cdot 1$, or when $a = 12$. In the second case, simplifying results in $(12 - a)x^2 + (26 - 5a)x - 1 = 0$. The discriminant should be zero, so $(26 - 5a)^2 + 4(12 - a) = 0$. However, that quadratic does not have any real solutions. Therefore, the only way there can be only one solution to the equation is when $a = \boxed{12}$.

23. Let the altitude from B to $\overline{AC}$ intersect $\overline{AC}$ at D. We have $AC \cdot BD = 18$, with $BD > 2$, so $AC < 9$. Then since ABC is a right triangle, $AB \cdot BC = 18$. By the Pythagorean Theorem, $AB^2 + BC^2 = AC^2 < 9^2$. Therefore, AB and BC must be 3 and 6 since $2^2 + 9^2 = 85$ and $1^2 + 18^2 = 325$ are greater than 81, meaning that the only possible value of AC^2 is $3^2 + 6^2 = \boxed{45}$.

24. In the first 30 seconds, Luke hits the bag $10 + 20 + 30 = 60$ times. Then in the next 30 seconds, Luke hits $40 + 40 + 40 = 120$ times. Finally, in the last minute, Luke hits $30(3 + 2) = 150$ times. Hence, his total is $60 + 120 + 150 = \boxed{330}$ punches.

25. First, note that $53\frac{1}{3}\% = \frac{8}{15}$ and that $56\frac{1}{4}\% = \frac{9}{16}$. We could set up an equation, but a quicker way is observing how the difference between the numerators and the difference between the denominators are both 1. This means that Andy has done $\boxed{15}$ matches.

26. From May kth to May 31st, there are $31 - k$ days. Between May 31st and September 30th, there are $30 + 31 + 31 + 30 = 122$ days. Finally, there are $2k$ more days until October $2k$th. Thus, the total number of days that pass is $(31 - k) + 122 + 2k = 153 + k$, which should be a multiple of 7. This implies that k leaves a remainder of 1 when divided by 7. Additionally, since there are 31 days in October, $2k$ is at most 31, so $k \leq 15$. The greatest whole number up to 15 that leaves a remainder of 1 when divided by 7 is $\boxed{15}$, which is the greatest possible value of k.

27. The only time where where Jessica and Rebecca can choose the same square is when Jessica and Rebecca chose the square right between square A and square B, and they each have a $\frac{1}{3}$ probability of choosing that square. This means that the probability that Jessica and Rebecca choose the same square at a turn is $\frac{1}{9}$. Since the probability that the two turns result in them picking different squares is $(\frac{8}{9})^2 = \frac{64}{81}$, the probability that there is at least one turn where the same square is chosen is $1 - \frac{64}{81} = \boxed{\frac{17}{81}}$.

28. By SSS similarity, triangles ABC and ACD are similar, so $\angle BAC = \angle CAD$. Therefore, AE bisects $\angle BAD$, and by the Angle Bisector Theorem, $\frac{DE}{BE} = \frac{DA}{BA} = \frac{9}{4}$. Then $\frac{BD}{BE} = \frac{DE}{BE} + \frac{BE}{BE} = \boxed{\frac{13}{4}}$.

29. There are $\binom{6}{3} = 20$ ways to choose the starting letters of the strings. Then, there are $3! = 6$ ways to order the remaining three letters, and there are $\binom{5}{2} = 10$ ways to split the letters using dividers into three strings to attach to the starting letters. Therefore, the number of sets of strings is $20 \cdot 6 \cdot 10 = \boxed{1200}$.

30. Let B be the number of blocks in Brandon's collection. Then $B+1 = \frac{m(m+1)}{2}$ and $B-8 = \frac{n(n+1)}{2}$ for some positive whole numbers $m > n$. Taking the difference of these equations gives $9 = \frac{m(m+1)}{2} - \frac{n(n+1)}{2}$, which could be simplified to $18 = m^2 - n^2 + m - n$. Note that by difference of squares, $m^2 - n^2 = (m+n)(m-n)$, so the right hand side factors as $18 = (m+n+1)(m-n)$. Since $m+n+1$ and $m-n$ have to be positive whole numbers, and $m+n+1 > m-n$, we consider the factors of 18 as cases.
   - If $m+n+1 = 18$ and $m-n = 1$, then $2m+1 = 19$, so $m = 9$ and $n = 8$. This corresponds to $\frac{9 \cdot 10}{2} - 1 = 44$ blocks.
   - If $m+n+1 = 9$ and $m-n = 2$, then $2m+1 = 11$, so $m = 5$ and $n = 3$. This corresponds to $\frac{5 \cdot 6}{2} - 1 = 14$ blocks.
   - If $m+n+1 = 6$ and $m-n = 3$, then $2m+1 = 9$, so $m = 4$ and $n = 1$. This corresponds to $\frac{4 \cdot 5}{2} - 1 = 9$ blocks.

Thus, the sum of the possible values of B is $44 + 14 + 9 = \boxed{67}$.

Target Round Solutions

1. We can skip count or multiply to find out Reagan's position. Reagan travels $100 \cdot 7 = 700$ miles due north for the first seven days and $30 \cdot 3 = 90$ miles due south for the next three days. Thus, Reagan is $700 - 90 = \boxed{610}$ miles due north from her starting point.

2. We want the distance from Ava's teammate that is furthest from Ava to Grace's teammate that is furthest from Grace. When 15 teammates are standing 2 meters apart, there are 14 spaces of 2 meters and so the distance from the person in front to the person in the back is $14 \cdot 2 = 28$ meters. Since Ava and Grace are standing 10 meters apart, the distance would be $28 \cdot 2 + 10 = \boxed{66}$ meters.

3. The total number of food items in the store is $80 \cdot 10 = 800$. Since 1% of the food items in the store are canned beans, the store has a total of 8 canned beans. Thus, the average price of the canned beans (in dollars) is $\frac{\$9.2}{8} = \$\boxed{1.15}$.

4. First, find point A by substituting $x = -1.5$ into the equation $y = 2x^3 + 3x^2 - 4x$. This gives $y = 6$, so $A = (-1.5, 6)$. This indicates that the triangle has base 1.5 and height 6, so its area is $\boxed{\dfrac{9}{2}}$.

5. Assume a perfect Target score. 70 percent of 200 is 140, so 60 points can be missed in total. If all of these points are on Sprint, the resulting score is 60/120, which is $\boxed{50}$ percent. (Another way is to recognize that Sprint is worth 60% and Target is worth 40%.)

6. A regular hexagon with side length 12 centimeters is made up of six equilateral triangles with side length 12 centimeters. Since the jigsaw pieces are equilateral triangles with side length 2 centimeters, it takes $1 + 3 = 4$ jigsaw pieces to make an equilateral triangle with side length 4 centimeters, $1 + 3 + 5 = 9$ jigsaw pieces to make an equilateral triangle with side length 6 centimeters, and $1+3+5+7 = 16$ jigsaw pieces to make an equilateral triangle with side length 8 centimeters. Following this pattern, it takes 36 jigsaw pieces to make an equilateral triangle with side length 12 centimeters. The completed puzzle is composed of 6 equilateral triangles of side length 12 centimeters, which equates to $36 \cdot 6 = 216$ jigsaw pieces. The edge pieces form the perimeter of the completed puzzle, and since each side of the hexagon is 12 centimeters long, the total number of edge pieces is $\frac{12}{2} \cdot 6 = 36$ pieces. Thus, Emma's starting pile has $36 + 60 = 96$ pieces, which means $216 - 96 = 120$ jigsaw pieces are not in Emma's starting pile, so $\frac{120}{216} = \boxed{\dfrac{5}{9}}$ of all the pieces in the jigsaw puzzle are not in Emma's starting pile.

Solutions 12310 ©2022 mathleague.org

7. We could try experimentation but another way to approach this problem is by area. The area of the 6×6 rectangle is 36, and the area of each 1×5 rectangle is 5. This means that the area of the fifth rectangle is $36 - 4 \cdot 5 = 16$. Since the lengths of the fifth rectangle are whole numbers, we can consider pairs of factors that multiply to 16. Furthermore, by observing that the rectangle must actually fit in the 6×6 rectangle, we can conclude that the remaining rectangle must be a 4×4 rectangle, which has a perimeter of $\boxed{16}$, which indeed works as shown in the setup below.

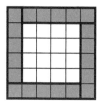

8. There are a lot of cases if we approach directly, so a good approach is by complementary counting. The two sessions split the times where there isn't a session into three parts. Now observe that the first session ends at 12 PM and the second session ends at 3 PM. This means that each of the parts are 2 hours long each, and the total time the amusement park is open is 8 hours. A part of a session does not happen between the times if and only if both times are in the same part without a session, so the probability that there is no part of the session between the times is $3 \cdot (\frac{1}{4})^2 = \frac{3}{16}$. With the complement found, we find that our desired probability and answer is $1 - \frac{3}{16} = \boxed{\dfrac{13}{16}}$.

Team Round Solutions

1. There are a total of $10 \cdot 10 = 100$ seats. We could do subtraction and count the number of even and odd numbers, but a faster way is to use parity. In particular, an even number minus an even number is an even number, and an even number minus an odd number is an odd number, so we just want to count the number of days where there are an odd number of students attending. Based on the table, we find that there are $\boxed{3}$ lectures with an odd number of empty seats.

2. Let m be the distance Ethan traveled. The cost for traveling $4m$ miles is $15 + 4m \cdot 1.50 = 15 + 6m$, while the cost for m miles is $15 + 1.50m$. Then $15 + 6m = 45 + 4.5m$, or $1.5m = 30$. Solving for m yields $m = \boxed{20}$.

3. If the final is graded by 2:30 PM on June 12, then the final must be graded within 48 hours. All the probabilities listed in the problem statement are mutually exclusive, so the probability that Thomas's final is graded by then is $\frac{1}{2} + \frac{1}{3} = \boxed{\dfrac{5}{6}}$.

4. By the Angle Addition Postulate, $\angle AOC = \angle AOB + \angle BOC$, so $\angle DBE = 118\frac{3}{4}^\circ - 47\frac{1}{8}^\circ = 71\frac{5}{8}^\circ$. Since supplementary angles add up to 180°, the measure of the angle supplementary to $71\frac{5}{8}^\circ$ is $180^\circ - 71\frac{5}{8}^\circ = \boxed{108\dfrac{3}{8}}^\circ$.

5. The length of the presentation multiplied by the number of words per minute, divided by the number of words per slide, equals the number of slides. The minimum number of slides is then $\frac{10 \cdot 100}{125} = 8$, and the maximum is $\frac{12 \cdot 100}{40} = 30$. Thus, the difference is $\boxed{22}$.

6. Each capsule requires an acorn, so the upper bound is at most 15. To show that 15 capsules are attainable, we can observe that Lucas can make 10 light capsules with 10 acorns and 10 metal fragments, then 5 heavy capsules with 5 acorns and 10 smooth stones. This means that Lucas can make up to $\boxed{15}$ capsules.

7. First we observe that 16 gallons and 8 cups of water equals 16.5 gallons of water. Then we find that water flows out at a rate of 5.5 gallons per minute. Now $16.5 = 5.5 \cdot 3$ meaning the remaining amount of water will drain in 3 minutes, and so $3 \cdot 60 = \boxed{180}$ seconds would have elapsed.

8. A total of $3 \cdot 2 = 6$ parts need to be fixed. The only cases where Chloe needs to take longer than four days is when she either works all by herself or only one friend joins for the fourth day. Both of these scenarios happen when no one joined for the second and third day, which has a $\frac{1}{2} \cdot \frac{1}{2} = \frac{1}{4}$ chance of happening. Thus, the probability that the plane gets fixed within four days is $1 - \frac{1}{4} = \boxed{\frac{3}{4}}$.

9. The shortest distance between any two unshared vertices is the shorter of the side lengths of the octagon. To find its length, we can draw a 45-45-90 triangle with that side as the hypotenuse. Then the distance between two opposite longer sides of the octagon, which is just two equilateral triangle heights or $4\sqrt{3}$, is two leg lengths plus a longer length of the octagon; if we let a be the length of a leg, then we get the equation $4\sqrt{3} = 2a + 2$, and solving gives $a = 2\sqrt{3} - 2$. Then the length of the hypotenuse is $\sqrt{2}(2\sqrt{3} - 2) = 2\sqrt{6} - 2\sqrt{2}$, so $m + n + p + q = 2 + 6 + 2 + 2 = \boxed{12}$.

10. For convenience, let $f(n)$ be the encrypted number. Now, $f(n) = \lfloor n \rfloor + \lfloor \frac{n}{2} \rfloor + \lfloor \frac{n}{4} \rfloor + \lfloor \frac{n}{8} \rfloor + \cdots$. Based on the effect as n increases, we can conclude that $f(n)$ is a strictly increasing function over the positive whole numbers. This tells us that we can find the greatest possible n such that $f(n) \leq 50$ and all possible numbers whole numbers would just be the positive whole numbers less than or equal to n. At this point, we approach by estimation and trial-by-error, though a good first guess can be 25 as $f(n)$ is similar to a geometric series with common difference $\frac{1}{2}$. As it turns out, $f(27) = 27 + 13 + 6 + 3 + 1 = 50$, and the number of positive whole numbers satisfying the property is $\boxed{27}$.

Sprint Round
12311

Place ID Sticker
Inside This Box

Name _____

Grade _____

School _____

1.

2.

3.

4.

5.

6.

7.

8.

9.

10.

11.

12.

13.

14.

15.

16.

17.

18.

19.

20.

21.

22.

23.

24.

25.

26.

27.

28.

29.

30.

1. At El Green's Supermarket, each banana costs $1. However, the banana lounge that is only half a mile away has free bananas. How many dollars would David save by getting 10 bananas from the banana lounge instead of buying them at El Green's Supermarket?

2. Maria is playing a kingdom battle video game as a rabbit avatar that started with 200 health points. In the first battle, Maria's rabbit avatar was injured and lost 75 health points. After the second battle, Maria's rabbit avatar only has 60 health points remaining. How many health points did Maria's rabbit avatar lose during the second battle?

3. A regular polygon has a perimeter of 420. What is the greatest possible length of one side of the polygon?

4. Reagan made the below table to find availability for her bracelet-weaving club, where an X indicates that a person is available on that date. If Reagan picks a day of the week from the chart at random, what is the probability that more than half of the club members of the table are available on that day? Express your answer as a common fraction.

	Monday	Tuesday	Wednesday	Thursday	Friday
Becca	X	X		X	X
Jessica		X		X	X
Kara	X		X		
Nicole	X	X	X		
Rebecca	X			X	X
Sophie		X	X		X

5. Ian took part in a march that had fewer than 150 students. He observes that the front row has 3 students and the rest of the rows have 4 students each. What is the greatest possible number of rows in the march?

6. Jeremy's teacher shared three jellyfish videos that had on average 50 jellyfish. After that, his teacher shared a video with 86 jellyfish and a video with 64 jellyfish. What is the average number of jellyfish per video that Jeremy's teacher shared over the five videos?

7. Right triangle ABC has a right angle at A, and right triangle BCD lies outside of triangle ABC with a right angle at C. If $AB = 3$, $AC = 4$, and $CD = 12$, what is BD?

8. The distances between every two different places in Dracula's Castle are shown below. Charlotte has to go from the dungeon to the clock tower, then back to the dungeon before exiting through the gates within 2.5 minutes. She travels at 5 meters per second from the dungeon to the clock tower. How many meters per second should her average speed be at minimum for the rest of the way?

	Dungeon	Clock Tower	Gates
Dungeon		250 meters	150 meters
Clock Tower	250 meters		350 meters
Gates	150 meters	350 meters	

9. Suppose a, b, c, and k are real numbers such that $a + 2b + 3c = k$ and $2a + 4b + 12c = 3k$. What is the value of $\frac{k}{c}$?

10. Triangle ABC has $AB = 80$, $BC = 80$, and $\angle BAC = 75°$. Triangle $A'B'C'$ is formed by translating triangle ABC such that B' is the midpoint of $\overline{AC}$. If lines BC and $A'B'$ intersect at X, how many degrees are in the measure of $\angle A'XC$?

11. A deck of cards has 52 standard cards and 2 additional cards that are jokers. Morgan pulls two cards out of the deck at random. What is the probability that she gets both jokers? Express your answer as a common fraction.

12. In the geometric sequence $2, x, 4, y$, what is the value of y^2?

13. Sam is wearing a power suit that can morph into a sphere with volume $\frac{9}{2}\pi$ and travel at a rate of 2 feet per second. Once in spherical form, Sam's power suit traveled through a cylindrical tube with volume 225π cubic feet. If the radius of the cylindrical tube is equal to the radius of the power suit in spherical form, how many seconds elapsed from the time the center of the spherical power suit entered the tube to the time the center of the spherical power suit exited the tube?

14. A positive whole number n has the property that both $n^{\frac{1}{12}}$ and $n^{\frac{1}{15}}$ are whole numbers. In the prime factorization of n, the exponents of each prime must be a multiple of k. What is the greatest possible value of k?

15. Let x and y be real numbers. If $x = y + 4$ and $x = 20y + 19$, what is the value of $\frac{x}{y}$? Express your answer as a common fraction.

16. Eliza starts at point B of right triangle ABC with $\angle ABC = 90°$, and she wants to walk to point C. If she walks the shorter leg $\overline{AB}$ and then the hypotenuse $\overline{AC}$, then her trip will be twice as long as it would be if she only walked the longer leg $\overline{BC}$. What is $\frac{BC}{AB}$? Express your answer as a common fraction.

17. During an *at-bat*, a baseball player will either hit the ball or miss the ball but not both. A baseball player's *hit-miss ratio* is defined as the number of at-bats in which they have hit the ball, divided by the number of at-bats in which they have missed the ball (provided that the number of misses is strictly positive). What is the hit-miss ratio r for which if the corresponding percentage of hits out of all at-bats is written as $a\%$, then a is exactly 22 times r? Express your answer as a common fraction.

18. Harrison is at an archery range with a red target and purple target. If Harrison aims an arrow at a target and fires, he has a $\frac{3}{4}$ probability of hitting one of the targets, regardless of which target he was aiming at. In this situation, if the arrow does hit one of the targets, there is a $\frac{1}{3}$ probability that the arrow hit the target Harrison was not aiming at. If Harrison aims one arrow at the red target and another at the purple target, what is the probability that he hits the purple target at least once? Express your answer as a common fraction.

19. Let a and b be positive whole numbers with $(a+b)^2 - (a-b)^2 = 120$. What is the sum of all possible values of $a+b$?

20. A well-known fighting game has 12 playable characters, and Jack likes 10 of these characters. Jack randomly selects a character from the entire roster three times, with each selection independent from that of the previous selection. What is the probability that Jack gets at least one character he likes? Express your answer as a common fraction.

21. What is the greatest whole number n such that there exists an octagon with positive area and side lengths $n+1, n+2, \ldots, n+7$ and $8n+8$ in some order?

22. What is the smallest whole number n such that all whole numbers greater than or equal to n can be written as the sum of positive multiples of 20 and 21?

23. Zakariah is playing a game of cat-and-mouse with his younger sister Liyana in their living room, which is a 7×7 square grid. Zakariah starts at the top-left corner of the grid, while Liyana starts at the bottom-right corner. Each move involves going to a square that shares an edge with the square they were previously on. Zakariah and Lilyana take their turns simultaneously, where Zakariah takes one move per turn, while Liyana, being more energetic, takes two moves per turn. How many move sequences of four turns each can Zakariah and Liyana have such that they end up in the same square immediately after all their turns?

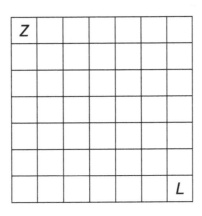

24. The projection of a point T onto a line is the intersection point of the line and the line perpendicular to it passing through T. Let $P = (m, n)$, and let P' be the projection of P onto the line $5x + 3y = 15$. If $PP'^2 = 34$ and $m + n = -3$, what is the least possible value of mn?

25. Adam got a total of three hugs from some of thirty possible lightning bugs, where each possible set of hugs is equally likely. For example, two hugs from lightning bug A and one hug from lightning bug B in any order is one possible set. What is the probability that more than half of the hugs came from one specific lightning bug? Express your answer as a common fraction.

26. What is the sum of the digits of 5^{35}, given that the answer is between 90 and 100?

27. What is $102 \cdot 100 + 105 \cdot 99 + 108 \cdot 98 + \cdots + (102 + 3k)(100 - k) + \cdots + 399 \cdot 1$?

28. How many positive whole numbers less than 1000 have digits summing to a perfect square?

29. Right $\triangle ABC$ has $\angle BAC = 90°$, $AB = 28$, and $AC = 21$. A semicircle is inscribed inside $\triangle ABC$ such that its diameter $\overline{PQ}$ lies on side $\overline{BC}$, with B, P, Q, and C lying in that order. What is $BP - CQ$?

30. In the year 2022, which begins and ends on a Saturday and has 365 days, Umar vows to go out to as many places as he can! He plans out his travels as follows.
- On each day, he may visit either the grocery store, the library, or the local restaurant.
- The library is closed on weekends (Saturday and Sunday).
- Umar can only go to one location each day, and he cannot go out on two consecutive days of the year.

Let N be the number of ways in which he can schedule outings during the year 2022 such that he maximizes the number of times he goes out. What is the remainder when N is divided by 1000?

Place ID Sticker
Inside This Box

Name _____

Grade _____

School _____

Problems 1 & 2

1. A regular hexagon has a perimeter of 72. Six squares that have the same side length as that of a side of the hexagon are attached to the hexagon, forming the below polygon. What is the perimeter of the polygon?

1.

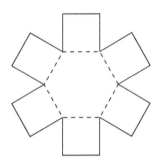

2. Dillon participates in a rafting competition where the course is 300 meters long and has the following rules.

2.

- There is a checkpoint a third of the way through and two-thirds of the way through. Falling off while rafting partway through the course requires one to restart at the last checkpoint passed or the beginning if no checkpoints are passed.

- The *scoring time* is measured by the total time rafting.

Dillon initially rafts for 70 seconds before falling for the first time, but after restarting, he manages to finish rafting without falling a second time. Dillon rafts at a rate of 2.5 meters per second. How many seconds is Dillon's scoring time?

Place ID Sticker
Inside This Box

Name _____

Grade _____

School _____

Problems 3 & 4

3. A *yojijukugo* is a type of Japanese idiom that consists of four kanji characters, each of which requires a certain number of strokes to write. Haruka reads a yojijukugo and remarks, "There are exactly 31 total strokes in this yojijukugo." What is the fewest possible number of strokes in the kanji character with the most strokes in this yojijukugo?

3. _____

4. A rental store allows customers to either buy a movie for $15, or rent the movie for seven days at a time at a cost of n^2 cents on the nth day of that seven-day period. If a rental cannot be cancelled at any point during the seven-day period, what is the greatest possible number of times that a customer can rent a movie and save money over buying the movie?

4. _____

Place ID Sticker
Inside This Box

Name _____

Grade _____

School _____

Problems 5 & 6

5. How many positive whole numbers are common divisors of any two positive whole numbers that have a greatest common divisor of 1860?

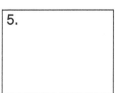

5.

6. In the diagram below, a shaded unit square travels along the diagonals of the unit squares of an 8×6 rectangle such that the center of the shaded square only makes right-angled turns when an edge of the shaded square touches an edge of the 8×6 rectangle, and the shaded square itself never rotates upon its center. The shaded square continues moving until the next time one of its corners touches a corner of the 8×6 rectangle. The first part of the path is shown below. What is the square of the total distance that the center of the shaded square travelled once it stops moving?

6.

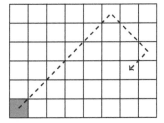

Place ID Sticker
Inside This Box

Name _____

Grade _____

School _____

Problems 7 & 8

7. Let $f(x) = \frac{x^2}{x+1}$. Let $k > 0$ be a positive real number such that the slope of the line passing through the points $(1, f(1))$ and $(1+k, f(1+k))$ is $\frac{99}{100}$. What is the value of k?

7. ☐

8. How many distinct arrangements of nine of the letters in *ABRACADABRA* are there such that not all of the *A*'s appear in the arrangement?

8. ☐

Team Round
12311

School or Team

Name _____

Name _____

Name _____

Name _____

Place ID Sticker
Inside This Box

Place ID Sticker
Inside This Box

Place ID Sticker
Inside This Box

Place ID Sticker
Inside This Box

1.	2.	3.	4.	5.

6.	7.	8.	9.	10.

1. Aidan and Carson are playing a game in which they throw three darts at a dartboard and add up their number of points depending on where the darts landed according to the below table. In round 1, Aidan's darts landed in the white area once and the blue area twice. In round 2, Aidan's darts landed in each colored area once. In round 3, all of Aidan's darts landed in the red area. What is the average number of points Aidan scored in the three rounds?

Region Color	White	Blue	Red
Points Per Dart	1	5	10

2. Let A, E, and T be distinct digits such that $\overline{ATE} + \overline{EAT} + \overline{TEA} = 1554$. What is the value of $A + E + T$?

3. A trick-or-treat candy bag contains six of candy A, four of candy B, twice as many of candy C as candy B, and ten percent candy D. What is the probability that, if one of the candies is selected uniformly at random, it will be anything but candy C? Express your answer as a common fraction.

4. Rick starts a mobile game that begins at Level 0. The leveling system of the mobile game involves leveling up by one after playing 10 minutes, then leveling up by one after playing another 20 minutes, then leveling up by one after playing another 10 minutes, and so on, alternating between leveling up by one after playing another 10 minutes and leveling up by one after playing another 20 minutes. Rick plays the game from 7:00 PM to 8:20 PM every day, and the game saves his progress after each day. If Rick reaches Level 1 at 7:10 PM on Monday, what level number is Rick on at the end of the first Sunday following that Monday?

5. How many right triangles with whole number side lengths each less than or equal to 100 units have the property that their hypotenuse is 2 units longer than their longer leg?

6. How many positive whole numbers less than or equal to 2022 can be written as the product of two perfect squares in at least two different ways, where the order in which the perfect squares are written does not matter (e.g. $4 \cdot 49$ and $49 \cdot 4$ are considered identical)?

7. For some positive integer $k \geq 2$, let $\{a_n\}$ be an arithmetic sequence such that $a_0 = 1$ and $a_k = k^2$. Then, let $\{b_n\}$ be a geometric sequence such that $b_0 = 1$ and $b_1 = \frac{1}{a_1}$. Given that $\{b_n\}$ has a finite sum of at least $1 + \frac{1}{10^4}$, what is the sum of all possible values of k?

8. Ivanova is making a cloak for a medieval costume. The design of the cloak calls for a semicircle with a radius of 60 inches, but at the fabric store, she can only find fabric that is 48 inches wide. To work around this, she decides to cut the semicircle into four congruent sectors and arrange them on a rectangular piece of fabric, as shown below. In the diagram, $\overline{AB}$ has a length of 48 inches, $\overline{AD}$ and $\overline{CD}$ each have a length of 60 inches, and the arcs of two of the sectors are tangent at a point F. At least how many whole inches must AE be in order for the four sectors to completely fit on the fabric in this manner?

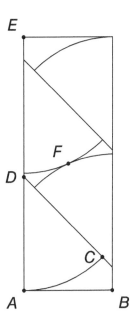

9. Three positive whole numbers less than or equal to 10 are chosen uniformly at random without replacement. What is the expected value of their product? Express your answer as a common fraction.

10. Jerry is standing at 0 on the number line, between two walls at -10 and $+5$. Each move, he flips a fair coin, and then he takes a step one unit in the positive direction if he flips heads and a step one unit in the negative direction if he flips tails. He repeatedly moves in this manner until he reaches either wall, at which point he stops. What is the probability that he stops at the $+5$ wall? Express your answer as a common fraction.

1. Three years ago, the age of the castle in years was 22 times the age of the Ferris wheel. In two years, the age of the castle in years will be 15 times the age of the Ferris wheel. How many years old is the castle right now?

2. What is the distance between $(21, 12)$ and $(15, 10)$? Express your answer in simplest radical form.

3. An arcade game character can do a sequence of moves, which are either jumps or dashes. In the sequence, the character can do at most two jumps. How many possible sequences of four moves are there?

4. How many ways can each of the faces of a regular octahedron be colored either red or blue?

5. A certain animated-picture studio has made 26 films. Michael has already watched 18 films, and over the course of four months, he wants to watch the same number of films each month such that after the four months, Michael has watched all the films of that studio. How many films should Michael watch each month in order to meet his goal?

6. What is the greatest prime factor of $2^{2023} - 2^{2019}$?

7. Three balls, labeled 4, 8, and 12, are placed in a bag. Two balls are removed at random. What is the expected value of the sum of the labels of the balls removed?

8. A fair wheel is divided into some number of equally-sized sectors and lands on a sector chosen at random when the wheel is spun. The degree measure of each sector is $30°$, and two of the sectors are painted black. What is the probability that when the wheel is spun, it lands at one of the sectors painted black? Express your answer as a common fraction.

9. Solve for a if $4^{23} - 4^{21} = a \cdot 4^{21}$.

10. Samantha listened to four songs, one of each genre. The table below lists the time of each of the four songs. How many seconds is the median time of the four songs?

Song Genre	Time
Rock	3 minutes 20 seconds
Jazz	5 minutes 15 seconds
Country	4 minutes 52 seconds
Pop	3 minutes 58 seconds

11. How many positive whole number factors does the number 1599 have?

12. Suppose that $f(n)$ is the number of ways to climb a staircase of n steps, 1, 2, or 3 steps at a time. If $f(n) \geq 123$, what is the smallest possible value of n?

13. The time displayed in Sacramento is three hours earlier compared to the time displayed in Boston. For example, if it is 3 PM in Sacramento, it is 6 PM in Boston. Evan attended a school dance at 7 PM in Sacramento time, and the dance lasted three hours. In the middle of the dance, Evan shared a photo with a friend in Boston who received the photo at 11:25 PM in Boston time. How many minutes are there between the time the friend received the photo and the end of the dance?

14. If $\sqrt[x]{3} = ((((27)^{\frac{1}{2}})^{\frac{1}{3}})^{\frac{1}{4}})^{\frac{1}{5}}$, then what is the value of x?

15. One of the angles in a triangle measures $50°$. How many degrees is the average of the measures of the other two angles?

16. Compute the sum of the median and the range of the following set: $\{31, 52, 17, 4, -9, 29, 68\}$.

17. As shown in the diagram below, a square of side length 27 is divided into 9 equally-sized squares, and four of the squares are further divided into 9 equally-sized squares. What is the area of the region that is not shaded?

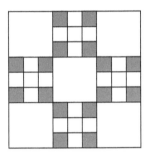

18. Evaluate: $\binom{15}{3}$.

19. Below are three statements about a two-digit number.
    - The number is not prime.
    - The number has distinct digits.
    - The number has at least one digit that is even.
    What is the largest two-digit number that satisfies *exactly* two of the statements?

20. What is the sum of all the odd whole numbers between 0 and 50?

21. What is the probability of getting exactly one head when flipping five fair coins? Express your answer as a common fraction.

22. What is the value of $(\sqrt{3} + \sqrt{48})(\sqrt{27} + \sqrt{12})$?

23. What is the volume of a cube with side length 2?

24. What number is 80% of 135?

25. A triangle with whole number side lengths has two sides of length 20 and 23. What is the sum of the greatest possible value for the length of the third side and the least possible value for the length of the third side?

26. Let x and y be real numbers such that $x + \frac{1}{y} = 7$ and $y + \frac{1}{x} = 8$. What is $xy + \frac{1}{xy}$?

27. In the diagram below representing a board game, a player starts at circle A and must follow the arrows to get from one circle to another circle. How many paths can the player take to travel from circle A to circle B that pass through the black circle?

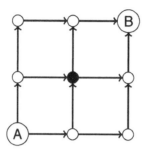

28. What is the sum of all values of x such that $\frac{484}{x^2+22x-2022} + \frac{529}{x^2+23x-2023}$ is undefined?

29. At 7:40 AM, how many degrees are in the acute angle formed by the minute and hour hand of a clock?

30. Two positive whole numbers have a GCD of 2 and an LCM of 2022. What is the product of the two whole numbers?

31. Let points A, B, C, D, and E lie on a plane such that A, B, and C are collinear in some order, and C, D, and E are collinear in some order. If $AB = 5$, $BC = 6$, $CD = 7$, $DE = 8$, and $EA = 9$, what is $AC + CE$?

32. Diana has 6 comic books in her drawer: 2 comic books about a bat, 2 comic books about a wonderful woman, and 2 comic books about a flashy speedster. Diana randomly grabs three comic books from the drawer. What is the probability that she has two comic books about the same character? Express your answer as a common fraction.

33. If $f(x)$ and $g(x)$ are polynomials such that the degree of f is 8 and the degree of g is 9, what is the degree of $f(x) + g(x)$?

34. Olivia is gathering square album covers to make a giant mosaic that has 12 rows with each row having 12 album covers. So far, she has $55\frac{5}{9}\%$ of the album covers that she needs. How many album covers does Olivia still need to get to complete the mosaic?

35. Evaluate: $22^2 - 48 \div 4$.

36. What is the area of a circle with radius π^2? Express your answer in terms of π.

37. Jill has an alpaca that plans to walk across a pumpkin patch that is 1 kilometer long. Jill thought that the alpaca travels at a rate of 5 meters per second and wrote down the time it takes for the alpaca to walk across that pumpkin patch at that rate. However, Jill later learned that the alpaca is actually 3 meters per second slower. How many seconds is the difference between actual time the alpaca takes to walk across the pumpkin patch and Jill's written time?

38. A party of three heroes can battle two monsters in 15 minutes. Assuming all heroes within the party battle monsters at the same rate, how many monsters can a party of six heroes battle in an hour?

39. Let $P(x)$ be a quadratic. If the sum of its coefficients is -4, the sum of the coefficients of $P(-x)$ is 44, and the sum of the roots of $P(x)$ is 6, what is the product of the roots of $P(x)$?

40. An elevator in a high-rise building serves the 1st through 100th floors. Assume that the floors are equally spaced, and each floor is the same height. If it is going up, what fraction of the way is it from its starting point to its ending point when it reaches the 40th floor? Express your answer as a common fraction.

41. Evaluate: $-\left|4\frac{5}{11}\right| + \left|-5\frac{7}{11}\right|$. Express your answer as a mixed number.

42. In the decimal representation of $\frac{4}{21}$, how many of the first 300 digits to the right of the decimal point are even?

43. A basketball game is 48 minutes long and has four quarters with each quarter lasting the same amount of time. At the end of the third quarter, Scott's team has 68 points while his opponent's team has 78 points. Scott's team averages 3 points per minute in the fourth quarter, while his opponent's team averages 2 points per minute in the fourth quarter. At the end of the fourth quarter, how many points does the team with the most points have?

44. Two interior angles of a quadrilateral measure 40°, and one of the remaining two interior angles has a measure 44° greater than the measure of the other. How many degrees are in the measure of the largest interior angle of the quadrilateral?

45. Emma wants to build a cube by attaching poles to blocks. Each block would be a vertex of the cube, and each pole would be an edge of the cube. At the bazaar, each block costs $4 and each pole costs $5. How many dollars does Emma need to buy enough supplies to build the cube?

46. If a whole number between 1 and 50, inclusive, is chosen at random, what is the probability that it is a prime number? Express your answer as a common fraction.

47. A right triangle has side lengths that are positive whole numbers. The shortest side of the triangle has length 21. What is the smallest possible area of the triangle?

48. Cole is watching a football game where the home team has 12 points and the away team has 22 points. If the away team does not score any more points and the home team can only score 3 points at a time or 7 points at a time, what is the fewest possible number of points that the home team can gain in order for the home team to have more points than the away team?

49. How many positive whole numbers less than 500 do not contain the digit 1?

50. The smallest composite number is 4. The second smallest composite number is 6. What is the 23rd smallest composite number?

51. What number n should be placed between 9×360 and 64×160 so that the three numbers form a geometric sequence, in that order?

52. What is the sum of the reciprocals of 2, 3, and 12? Express your answer as a common fraction.

53. The digits in the number 12345 are rearranged such that the number is a multiple of 4, the tens digit is even, the thousands digit is greater than the hundreds digit, and the number is greater than 40000. What is this new number?

54. What is the area of a regular hexagon with side length 6? Express your answer in simplest radical form.

55. What is the area of a triangle with side lengths 11, 60, and 61?

56. How many seconds are in a third of a day?

57. What is the value of $14 \cdot 22 + 16$?

58. Evaluate: 82×23.

59. Evaluate: $125^{-1/3}$. Express your answer as a common fraction.

60. Ava kept track of the number of students performing on each of the four floats. For each float after the first, she counted five more students compared to the previous float. If Ava counted a total of 86 students, how many students are on the float with the greatest number of students?

61. How many diagonals are there in a regular nonagon?

62. What is the sum of the distinct prime factors of 2023?

63. October 1, 2022 is a Saturday. A homecoming parade took place on October 27, 2017. What day of the week was that homecoming parade?

64. Find the number such that the sum of its double, triple, and quadruple is 342.

65. If $\frac{a}{b^2} = 19$ and $b = 4$, then what is a?

66. Ruben is setting up a bonfire, where the bonfire circle has an area of 400π square meters. How many meters is the circumference of the bonfire circle? Express your answer in terms of π.

67. Two prime numbers have a sum of 124. What is the largest possible value of their difference?

68. Four fair six-sided dice are rolled. What is the probability that none of the dice show a composite number? Express your answer as a common fraction.

69. Ben is planning an itinerary where he wants to visit Athens, Barcelona, Milan, London, and Oslo in some order. How many ways can Ben order the places he plans on visiting?

70. What is the units digit of 2023^{2023}?

71. Fourteen consecutive whole numbers sum to 2023. What is the greatest of the fourteen numbers?

72. A large rectangle is divided into 48 unit squares, as shown below. What fraction of the area of the large rectangle is shaded? Express your answer as a common fraction.

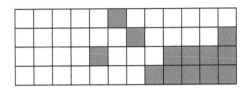

73. What is the total surface area of a cylinder with volume 484π and radius 11? Express your answer in terms of π.

74. Two numbers sum to 2023. The value of the greater number minus the lesser number is 223. What is the lesser number?

75. The number $\sqrt{2022}$ lies between two consecutive whole numbers. What is the sum of these whole numbers?

76. Steve is tallying the votes for the six candidates nominated to be prince or princess and found the average number of votes cast for each candidate is 83. If the average number of votes cast for the two winning candidates is 95, then what is the average number of votes cast for the other four candidates?

77. What is the value of $\frac{23!-22!}{21!}$?

78. How many milligrams are in 3.62 grams?

79. Evaluate: 404 · 59.

80. The ID number of the last clone is 20001, which has exactly two prime factors greater than 10 and is not divisible by the square of a prime number greater than 10. How many factors of 20001 are there?

Answers
12311

Sprint Round

1. 10	11. $\frac{1}{1431}$	21. 19
2. 65	12. 32	22. 421
3. 140	13. 50	23. 924
4. $\frac{3}{5}$	14. 60	24. -928
5. 37	15. $-\frac{61}{15}$	25. $\frac{45}{248}$
6. 60	16. $\frac{4}{3}$	26. 92
7. 13	17. $\frac{39}{11}$	27. 1015050
8. 4	18. $\frac{5}{8}$	28. 148
9. 6	19. 72	29. 5
10. 30	20. $\frac{215}{216}$	30. 808

Target Round

1. 216
2. 150
3. 8
4. 10
5. 24
6. 2450
7. 48
8. 37800

Team Round

1. 19
2. 14
3. $\frac{3}{5}$
4. 37
5. 7
6. 29
7. 50004999
8. 134
9. $\frac{605}{4}$
10. $\frac{2}{3}$

Countdown

1. 223	21. $\frac{5}{32}$	41. $1\frac{2}{11}$	61. 27
2. $2\sqrt{10}$	22. 75	42. 150	62. 24
3. 11	23. 8	43. 104	63. Friday
4. 256	24. 108	44. 162	64. 38
5. 2	25. 46	45. 92	65. 304
6. 5	26. 54	46. $\frac{3}{10}$	66. 40π
7. 16	27. 4	47. 294	67. 102
8. $\frac{1}{6}$	28. -45	48. 12	68. $\frac{16}{81}$
9. 15	29. 10	49. 323	69. 120
10. 265	30. 4044	50. 35	70. 7
11. 8	31. 26	51. 5760	71. 151
12. 9	32. $\frac{3}{5}$	52. $\frac{11}{12}$	72. $\frac{1}{4}$
13. 95	33. 9	53. 53124	73. 330π
14. 40	34. 64	54. $54\sqrt{3}$	74. 900
15. 65	35. 472	55. 330	75. 89
16. 106	36. π^5	56. 28800	76. 77
17. 585	37. 300	57. 324	77. 484
18. 455	38. 16	58. 1886	78. 3620
19. 95	39. 4	59. $\frac{1}{5}$	79. 23836
20. 625	40. $\frac{13}{33}$	60. 29	80. 8

Sprint Round Solutions

1. At the banana lounge, David would get his 10 bananas for free, spending $0. He would pay $10 \cdot 1 = 10$ dollars for 10 bananas at El Green's Supermarket. Therefore, he would save $\boxed{10}$ dollars by getting his bananas from the banana lounge instead of El Green's Supermarket.

2. After the end of the first battle, the rabbit had $200 - 75 = 125$ health points. The rabbit has 60 health points after the end of the second battle, so the rabbit lost $125 - 60 = \boxed{65}$ health points during the second battle.

3. We want to have the fewest possible number of sides of the polygon. All polygons have at least 3 sides, which means that the greatest possible side length is $\frac{420}{3} = \boxed{140}$.

4. We are looking for days where 4 or more club members are available. These days are Monday, Tuesday, and Friday, so the probability that more than half of the club members of the table are available on a random day is $\boxed{\dfrac{3}{5}}$.

5. We need to determine the greatest number less than 150 that leaves a remainder of 3 when divided by 4. The remainder when 150 is divided by 4 is 2, so we find that the greatest number less than 150 that leaves a remainder of 3 when divided by 4 is 147. Then, we find that $147 = 4 \cdot 36 + 3$, and so the number of rows of students at the march is $36 + 1 = \boxed{37}$.

6. In the first three videos, there was a total of $3 \cdot 50 = 150$ jellyfish. Now, note that Jeremy's teacher showed two additional videos that had a total of $86 + 64 = 150$ jellyfish. This means that there were $150 + 150 = 300$ jellyfish over the five videos, for an average of $\boxed{60}$ jellyfish per video.

7. By the Pythagorean Theorem, $BC = \sqrt{AB^2 + AC^2}$ which is $\sqrt{3^2 + 4^2} = 5$. By the Pythagorean Theorem again, $BD = \sqrt{BC^2 + CD^2}$ which is $\sqrt{5^2 + 12^2} = \boxed{13}$.

8. Let r be the average speed in meters per second for the rest of the way. The total time is $2.5 \cdot 60 = 150$ seconds. So far, Charlotte takes $\frac{250}{5} = 50$ seconds, and she still has $250 + 150 = 400$ meters to go. We can then set up the equation $50 + \frac{400}{r} \leq 150$. Solving for r yields $r \geq \boxed{4}$.

9. Doubling the first equation yields $2a + 4b + 6c = 2k$, so $6c = k$, and $\frac{k}{c} = \boxed{6}$.

10. Since we are working with translations, $\triangle A'B'C'$ is congruent to triangle $\triangle ABC$. This means that $\angle ABC = \angle A'B'C'$, and since B' is on $\overline{AC}$, we find that $AB \parallel A'B'$. This means that $\angle A'XC = \angle ABC$. Finally, by the Base Angle Theorem, $\angle ABC = 180° - (75° \cdot 2)$, so $\angle A'XC = \boxed{30}^°$.

11. The deck has a total of 54 cards. We can consider Morgan pulling cards one at a time, where she needs to get a joker both times. The first time, there are 2 jokers out of 54 cards, so the probability is $\frac{1}{27}$. The second time, there is 1 joker out of 53 cards, so the probability is $\frac{1}{53}$. Since the events happen one after the other, the probability is $\frac{1}{27} \cdot \frac{1}{53} = \boxed{\dfrac{1}{1431}}$.

12. The common ratio r satisfies $r^2 = 2$, so $y = 4r$. Squaring both sides yields $y^2 = 16r^2$, or $y^2 = \boxed{32}$.

13. The radius of the power suit in spherical form is equal to $\frac{3}{2}$ feet, which is also the radius of the cylindrical tube. Therefore, the height of the cylindrical tube is $225\pi \div \frac{9}{4}\pi = 100$ feet, and it took Sam $\frac{100}{2} = \boxed{50}$ seconds to get the center of the ball form through the tube.

14. Consider numbers a and b such that $n^{\frac{1}{12}} = a$ and $n^{\frac{1}{15}} = b$. Then, $n = a^{12}$ and $n = b^{15}$, indicating that the exponents in the prime factorization of n must be a multiple of 12 and a multiple of 15. The least common multiple of 12 and 15 is 60, which means that every exponent in the prime factorization of n is a multiple of 60. This means that k is at least 60, but we need to determine whether k can be greater than 60. Since we can let $n = 2^{60}$, where 60 is the greatest factor of 60, we confirm that the greatest possible value of k is $\boxed{60}$.

15. Let $\frac{x}{y} = k$ for some constant k, which rearranges to $x = yk$. Then, $yk = y + 4$, or $4 = (k - 1)y$, and $yk = 20y + 19$, or $19 = (k - 20)y$. It follows that $\frac{19}{4} = \frac{k-20}{k-1}$, or $4k - 80 = 19k - 19$. Solving yields $k = \boxed{-\dfrac{61}{15}}$.

16. Let the shorter leg length be x and the longer leg length be ax, where $a \neq 0$. Then, the hypotenuse length is $x\sqrt{1 + a^2}$, so $1 + \sqrt{1 + a^2} = 2a$, so $\sqrt{1 + a^2} = 2a - 1$, or $1 + a^2 = 4a^2 - 4a + 1$. This becomes $3a^2 - 4a = 0$, where we find that $a = \boxed{\dfrac{4}{3}}$.

17. If r is the hit-miss ratio, then $\frac{r}{r+1}$ is the ratio of hits to all at-bats, and so $\frac{100r}{r+1}\%$ is the corresponding percentage. Thus, $\frac{100r}{r+1} = 22r$, and so $\frac{50}{11} = r + 1$, or $r = \boxed{\dfrac{39}{11}}$.

18. We will find the complementary probability, or the probability that Harrison does not hit the purple target. Harrison could either miss both targets entirely, or he could hit the red target, which may or may not match which target Harrison aimed at and intended to hit. If Harrison aims at the red target, his probability of not hitting the purple target is $\frac{1}{4} + \frac{3}{4} \cdot \frac{2}{3} = \frac{3}{4}$. If Harrison aims at the purple target, his probability of not hitting the purple target is $\frac{1}{4} + \frac{3}{4} \cdot \frac{1}{3} = \frac{1}{2}$. Both actions are independent, so Harrison has a probability of $\frac{3}{4} \cdot \frac{1}{2} = \frac{3}{8}$ of not hitting the purple target. Therefore, the probability that Harrison hits the purple target at least once is the complement of that, which is $1 - \frac{3}{8} = \boxed{\dfrac{5}{8}}$.

19. We have $(a^2 + 2ab + b^2) - (a^2 - 2ab + b^2) = 4ab = 120$, so $ab = 30$. Then $(a, b) = (1, 30), (2, 15), (3, 10)$, or $(5, 6)$, up to permutations, so $a + b = 31, 17, 13, 11$, which sum to $\boxed{72}$.

20. Note that if A is the probability that Jack gets at least one character he prefers after three selctions and B is the probability that Jack does not get any character he prefers after three selections, then $A + B = 1$. Computing B is easier, and since character selection is independent, $B = \left(\frac{2}{12}\right)^3 = \frac{1}{216}$. Therefore, $A = \boxed{\dfrac{215}{216}}$.

21. Clearly, $8n + 8$ is the greatest side length. Then, by the Triangle Inequality, we require $(n + 1) + (n + 2) + \cdots + (n + 7) > 8n + 8$, which becomes $7n + 28 > 8n + 8$, or $n < 20$. The greatest whole number n which satisfies this inequality is $\boxed{19}$.

22. By the Chicken McNugget Theorem, since 20 and 21 are relatively prime, the largest n for which we *cannot* express n as the sum of non-negative whole number multiples of 20 and 21 is $20 \cdot 21 - 20 - 21$. However, for strictly *positive* multiples of 20 and 21, $n + 20 + 21 = 20 \cdot 21 = 420$ is actually the largest non-achievable value, so 421 and above are all attainable (421, in particular, can be expressed as $20 \cdot 20 + 1 \cdot 21$). Thus, the answer is $\boxed{421}$.

23. Let Zakariah's starting point be $(1, 7)$ and Liyana's starting point be $(7, 1)$. Then, note that there is a bijection between the number of ways that Zakariah and Liyana can take their four turns and end up at the same point afterwards and the number of sequences of 12 moves going from $(1, 7)$ to $(7, 1)$ by only moving one unit down or to the right, since we can merely split any path into thirds, where the first four moves are Zakariah's moves, and the last eight moves are Liyana's moves. Note that if Zakariah or Liyana move away from their point of meeting, then this adds more wasteful moves, and the two will not be able to meet after four turns. Thus, the answer is $\binom{12}{6} = \boxed{924}$.

24. The line $5x + 3y = 15$ has slope $-\frac{5}{3}$, so its perpendicular has slope $\frac{3}{5}$. Now, note that $PP'^2 = 34 = 3^2 + 5^2$. There are two possible locations for point P'.
    - If $(m + 5, n + 3)$ lies on $5x + 3y = 15$, then $5(m + 5) + 3(n + 3) = 15$, so $5m + 3n = -19$. Then, we can use $m + n = -3$ to set up a system of equations to solve for m and n. Doing so results in $(m, n) = (-5, 2)$, which gives $mn = -10$.
    - If $(m - 5, n - 3)$ lies on $5x + 3y = 15$, then $5(m - 5) + 3(n - 3) = 15$, so $5m + 3n = 49$. Then, we can use $m + n = -3$ to set up a system of equations to solve for m and n. Doing so results in $(m, n) = (29, -32)$, which gives $mn = -928$.

    Of the two locations, we find that the least possible value of mn is $\boxed{-928}$.

25. Either all 3 hugs come from a single lightning bug (which can happen in 30 ways) or 2 come from one bug and 1 from a second bug (which can happen in $30 \cdot 29 = 870$ ways). Using sticks-and-stones, we find that the bugs can give a total of 3 hugs in $\binom{30+3-1}{3} = 4960$ ways. Thus, the probability that more than half of the hugs came from one specific lightning bug is $\frac{30+870}{4960} = \boxed{\frac{45}{248}}$.

26. The divisibility rule for 9 gives that the remainder when 5^{35} is divided by 9 is the same as the remainder when the sum of its digits is divided by 9. We can find this remainder by finding a pattern with the first few powers of 5, which leave remainders of $5, 7, 8, 4, 2, 1, 5, \ldots$. We can see that the pattern $5, 7, 8, 4, 2, 1$ repeats, so the remainder when 5^{35} is divided by 9 is the same as if $5^{35-6\cdot5} = 5^5$ were divided by 9, or 2. So, the sum of the digits divided by 9 leaves a remainder of 2, and the only whole number between 90 and 100 that leaves a remainder of 2 when divided by 9 is $\boxed{92}$.

27. This is the sum $(101^2 - 1^2) + (102^2 - 3^2) + (103^2 - 5^2) + \cdots + (200^2 - 199^2)$, which reduces to $(101^2 + 102^2 + 103^2 + \cdots + 200^2) - (1^2 + 3^2 + 5^2 + \cdots + 199^2)$. The first sum is $\frac{200 \cdot 201 \cdot 401}{6} - \frac{100 \cdot 101 \cdot 201}{6} = \frac{201 \cdot 100 \cdot 701}{6}$, or $67 \cdot 35050$, while the second sum is $\frac{199 \cdot 200 \cdot 399}{6} - 2^2 \cdot \frac{99 \cdot 100 \cdot 199}{6} = \frac{199 \cdot 200 \cdot 201}{6}$, or $199 \cdot 100 \cdot 67$, or $67 \cdot 19900$. The difference is then $67 \cdot 15150 = \boxed{1015050}$.

28. Since we are looking for numbers less than 1000, the largest possible sum of the digits of such a number would be $9 + 9 + 9 = 27$. Thus, we look for perfect squares less than 27. The number of positive whole numbers with digits summing to 25 is 6 (the permutations of 799 and 889). The number of numbers with digits summing to 16 is $3 + 66 = 69$ (3 among the two-digit numbers, namely 79, 88, and 97, and $4 + 5 + 6 + \cdots + 10 + 9 + 8 = 66$ among the three-digit numbers, by casework on the hundreds digit). The numbers of numbers with digit sums of 9, 4, and 1 are $\binom{11}{2} = 55$, $\binom{6}{2} = 15$, and $\binom{3}{2} = 3$, respectively, by sticks-and-stones. Summing these together, we obtain $6 + 69 + 55 + 15 + 3 = \boxed{148}$ numbers.

29. Our first step is finding the radius r of the semicircle. Let O be the center of the semicircle, and let X and Y be the points where the semicircle touches sides $\overline{AB}$ and $\overline{AC}$, respectively. We can see that, since $\angle BAC$ is a right angle, $\triangle BXO \sim \triangle OYC$. Thus, $BX \cdot CY = OX \cdot OY$, or $BX \cdot CY = r^2$. Since $AC = 21$, we have that $CY = 21 - r$. Thus, $BX = \frac{r^2}{21-r}$. We also have that $AB = 28$, so $r + \frac{r^2}{21-r} = 28$, which yields $r = 12$. This means that $BX = 16$ and $CY = 9$. Next, by Pythagorean Theorem, we have that $CO = 15$, and $BO = 20$. This means that $BP = 8$, and $CQ = 3$. Thus, $BP - CQ = 8 - 3 = \boxed{5}$.

30. If Umar wants to maximize his number of outings, he can go out on 183 days of the year, of which 130 are weekdays and 53 are weekends. Thus, $N = 3^{130} \cdot 2^{53}$, which equals $2 \cdot 972^{26} \equiv 2 \cdot (-28)^{26}$ mod 1000. The negative cancels out, leaving us with $2 \cdot 28^{26}$ mod 1000. By the Chinese Remainder Theorem, it suffices to compute 28^{26} mod 125 and 28^{26} mod 8. Clearly, we see that $28^{26} \equiv 0$ mod 8. For 28^{26} mod 125, we can write 28^{26} as $(25+3)^{26} = 25^{26} + \binom{26}{1} \cdot 25^{25} \cdot 3 + \cdots + \binom{26}{25} \cdot 25 \cdot 3^{25} + 3^{26}$. All of the terms except for $\binom{26}{25} \cdot 25 \cdot 3^{25}$ and 3^{26} are equivalent to 0 modulo 125 since they contain at least three powers of 5. We then calculate $26 \cdot 25 \cdot 3^{25}$ mod 125. We get $25 \cdot 3^{25} \equiv 75$ mod 125 (as $3^{25} \equiv 3$ mod 5 by Fermat's Little Theorem) and $3^{26} \equiv 79$ mod 125 (from $3^5 = 243$, which is -7 mod 125, and hence, $3^{25} \equiv (-7)^5$ mod 125, which is 68 mod 125, making $3^{26} \equiv 79$ mod 25). It follows that $28^{26} \equiv 29$ mod 125, and therefore, that $28^{26} \equiv 904$ mod 1000. Finally, we conclude that $N \equiv \boxed{808}$ mod 1000.

Target Round Solutions

1. The side length of the hexagon is $\frac{72}{6} = 12$. Based on the diagram, we find that the perimeter of the polygon involves summing eighteen of those side lengths, and so the perimeter is $12 \cdot 18 = \boxed{216}$.

2. In the first 70 seconds, Dillon travels for $2.5 \cdot 70 = 175$ meters. Thus, when Dillon falls for the first time, he has passed the first checkpoint but not the second checkpoint. This means that Dillon has 200 meters to go, and that would take $\frac{200}{2.5} = 80$ seconds. Altogether, Dillon's scoring time is $70 + 80 = \boxed{150}$ seconds.

3. By the Pigeonhole Principle, if there are 31 total strokes and four kanji characters, at least one of the kanji characters must contain at least $\frac{31}{4}$ raised to the nearest whole number greater than it, or 8, strokes. We can see that 8 strokes in the kanji character with the most strokes is achievable by having 7, 8, 8, and 8 strokes in the four kanji characters, in some order. Thus, the answer is $\boxed{8}$.

4. In each week, the total cost is $1^2 + 2^2 + \cdots + 7^2 = 140$ cents. Thus, after 10 rentals, the cost will be 1400 cents. After another rental, the cost will become 1540 cents, which is greater than \$15 for the first time. Thus, the answer is $\boxed{10}$.

5. We must have that the positive whole number is a divisor of 1860. Consider positive whole numbers a and b such that $\gcd(a, b) = 1860$. This means that $\frac{a}{1860}$ and $\frac{b}{1860}$ are whole numbers, so dividing a and b by a divisor of 1860 would still result in a whole number. On the contrary, if a whole number c does not divide 1860, then $\text{lcm}(c, 1860)$ must also divide both a and b (from considering the prime factorization of a and b), but that would contradict 1860 being the GCD of a and b. Therefore, we need to count the divisors of $1860 = 2^2 \cdot 3 \cdot 5 \cdot 31$, and by either manually writing divisors or using the counting divisor formula, we get a total of $\boxed{24}$ positive whole numbers.

6. Since the center of the shaded square is always at least 0.5 units away from the perimeter of the 8×6 rectangle, we may "shave off" the region inside the 8×6 rectangle that the center of the shaded square cannot cover; i.e., the outer "rim" of the 8×6 rectangle with width 0.5. Then, we are left with a 7×5 rectangle with a point moving from one corner of the rectangle to another corner of the rectangle. We notice that if we divide this 7×5 grid into 35 unit squares, all of the unit squares in the grid will have a diagonal traced by this point's path. The length of one of these diagonals is $\sqrt{2}$, so the distance that the center of the shaded square travelled is $35\sqrt{2}$, the square of which is $\boxed{2450}$.

7. The slope of the line is equal to $\frac{f(1+k) - f(1)}{(1+k) - 1} = \frac{\frac{(k+1)^2}{k+2} - \frac{1}{2}}{k}$. This becomes $\frac{2(k+1)^2 - (k+2)}{(2k+4)k}$. This simplifies to $\frac{2k^2 + 3k}{(2k+4)k} = \frac{2k+3}{2k+4}$, so $\frac{2k+3}{2k+4} = \frac{99}{100}$, which gives us $k = \boxed{48}$.

8. Since there are five A's and six non-A letters, we can pick either three or four A's. If we pick three A's, then there are no letters to discard. The resulting arrangements are those of $AAABRCDBR$, of which there are $\frac{9!}{3! \cdot 2! \cdot 2!} = 15120$. If we pick four A's, then of the two B's, one C, one D, and two R's, we can choose one letter to discard. Picking the B or R to discard yields $\frac{9!}{4!2!} = 7560$ arrangements each (we do not multiply by 2 for each B or each R since the arrangements from them are identical), and picking the C or D yields $\frac{9!}{4!2!2!} = 3780$ arrangements each. Hence, the total for the four-A's case is $2 \cdot (7560 + 3780) = 22680$. In total, we have $22680 + 15120 = \boxed{37800}$ nine-letter arrangements that can be formed from the letters in ABRACADABRA without all five A's.

Team Round Solutions

1. Aidan scored $1 + (2 \cdot 5) = 11$ points in round 1, $1 + (1 \cdot 5) + (1 \cdot 10) = 16$ points in round 2, and $3 \cdot 10 = 30$ points in round 3. Thus, the average number of points Aidan scored in the three rounds is $\frac{11+16+30}{3} = \boxed{19}$.

2. We have $(100A + 10T + E) + (100E + 10A + T) + (100T + 10E + A) = 1554$; combining terms, $111A + 111E + 111T = 1554$. Dividing both sides by 111 gives $A + E + T = \boxed{14}$. (There are multiple solutions for A, E, and T; one solution replaces these letters with their digit analogues: $A = 4$, $E = 3$, and $T = 7$.)

3. There are $4 \cdot 2 = 8$ of candy C (and so $6 + 4 + 8 = 18$ of candies A, B, and C). Then, if there are x of candy D, then we have $\frac{x}{18+x} = \frac{1}{10}$, which gives us $x = 2$. Then, there are $6 + 4 + 2 = 12$ of candies A, B, and D, so the probability of drawing anything but candy C is $\frac{12}{20} = \boxed{\dfrac{3}{5}}$.

4. Rick plays for 80 minutes every day. We should note that on some times like Monday at 8:10 PM, Rick needs to play another 20 minutes to level up, but he only plays for 10 more minutes on Monday. However, because the game saves Rick's progress after each day, he can play for 10 more minutes to level up on Tuesday at 7:10 PM, then he levels up again after playing for 10 more minutes because of the alternating requirements to level up. This means that we only need to consider the total amount of time played. Rick played for $80 \cdot 7 = 560$ minutes, and he levels up twice every 30 minutes up to 540 minutes. Then he levels up once more after playing for 10 minutes. This means that at the end of the first Sunday, Rick's level number is $2 \cdot \frac{540}{30} + 1 = \boxed{37}$.

5. Let the longer leg length be x, so that the shorter leg has length $\sqrt{4x + 4} = 2\sqrt{x + 1}$. Then, since x and $2\sqrt{x+1}$ are whole numbers, $x + 1$ must be a perfect square. We have $x + 2 \leq 100$, so $x \leq 98$. This gives $x = 3, 8, 15, 24, 35, 48, 63, 80$ as possibilities. However, if $x = 3$, then $2\sqrt{x+1} = 4$, so 3 cannot be a length of the longer leg. Thus, we have $8 - 1 = \boxed{7}$ possible triangles.

6. We are considering all perfect squares whose square roots are composite and are less than or equal to 44. There are 14 prime numbers less than or equal to 44, and the number 1 is also not composite, so there are $44 - 14 - 1 = 29$ composite numbers less than or equal to 44. Thus, our answer is $\boxed{29}$.

7. The common difference of $\{a_n\}$ is $\frac{k^2-1}{k}$; adding 1 to this to obtain a_1 gives $a_1 = \frac{k^2+k-1}{k}$, or $b_1 = \frac{k}{k^2+k-1}$. Then, b_1 is the common ratio of $\{b_n\}$, so the sum of the series is $\frac{1}{1-b_1} = \frac{k^2+k-1}{k^2-1} = 1 + \frac{k}{k^2-1}$. From here, we want $\frac{k}{k^2-1} \geq \frac{1}{10^4}$, so $k \leq 10000$. The requested sum is thus $2+3+\cdots+10000 = 10001 \cdot 5000 - 1$, or $\boxed{50004999}$.

8. Let's begin by placing reference points G and H (as shown on the diagram) as well as point I such that $GI \perp AE$. The four congruent sectors can be put together to form a semicircle with a radius of 60 inches, so the sector angle of each sector is $\frac{180}{4} = 45$ degrees. Now, observe that $\triangle DIG$ is a 45-45-90 triangle and $AIGB$ is a rectangle, so $DI = IG = AB = 48$ inches, and $AI = AD - DI = 60 - 48 = 12$ inches. With similar steps, we can find that $EH = 12$ inches.

To find length HI, we draw imaginary line segment $\overline{GH}$. We now have right triangle HIG. Since the radius of each wedge is 60 inches, $HF + FG = 60 + 60 = 120$ inches. Now that we know two sides of $\triangle HIG$, we can use the Pythagorean Theorem to solve for HI, which comes to $\sqrt{120^2 - 48^2} \approx 109.98$ inches. Then, with the Segment Addition Postulate, we find that $AE = AI + IH + HE$, which is approximately $12 + 109.98 + 12 = 133.98$ inches. Finally, since 134 is the smallest whole number greater than 133.98, the answer is $\boxed{134}$.

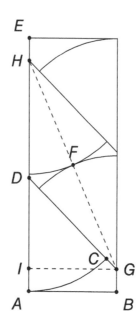

9. This is equal to $\frac{1 \cdot 2 \cdot 3 + 1 \cdot 2 \cdot 4 + 1 \cdot 2 \cdot 5 + \cdots + 1 \cdot 2 \cdot 10 + \cdots + 1 \cdot 9 \cdot 10 + \cdots + 8 \cdot 9 \cdot 10}{\binom{10}{3}}$. Let the numerator be equal to S. Then, note that $(1 + 2 + \cdots + 10)^3 = 6S + 3(1 \cdot 2^2 + 1 \cdot 3^2 + \cdots + 1 \cdot 10^2 + \cdots + 10 \cdot 8^2 + 10 \cdot 9^2) + 1^3 + 2^3 + \cdots + 10^3$. Note that $1 \cdot 2^2 + 1 \cdot 3^2 + \cdots + 1 \cdot 10^2 + \cdots + 10 \cdot 8^2 + 10 \cdot 9^2 = (1^2 + 2^2 + \cdots + 10^2)(1 + 2 + \cdots + 10) - 1^3 - 2^3 - \cdots - 10^3$. We know that $1 + 2 + \cdots + 10 = 55$, $1^2 + 2^2 + \cdots + 10^2 = 385$, and $1^3 + 2^3 + \cdots + 10^3 = 3025$, so we get that $1 \cdot 2^2 + 1 \cdot 3^2 + \cdots + 1 \cdot 10^2 + \cdots + 10 \cdot 8^2 + 10 \cdot 9^2 = 21175 - 3025$, or 18150. Then, we have that $55^3 = 6S + 54450 + 3025$. Solving for S gives us $S = 18150$. The denominator is $\binom{10}{3} = 120$, so the expected value is $\frac{18150}{120} = \boxed{\frac{605}{4}}$.

10. Let i be Jerry's distance from the -10 wall. Then, his starting position is $i = 10$. Let p_i be the probability of Jerry stopping at the $+5$ wall, for a fixed value of i. Then, we have that $p_0 = 0$ and $p_{15} = 1$. In between, we have that there is a $\frac{1}{2}$ chance of moving to either $i - 1$ or $i + 1$, so $p_i = \frac{1}{2}(p_{i-1} + p_{i+1})$. Then, solving for p_i explicitly gives us $p_i = \frac{i}{15}$. We want $i = 10$, since the distance from the -10 wall to 0 is 10. Finally, we arrive at $p_{10} = \boxed{\frac{2}{3}}$.

Sprint Round
12312

Place ID Sticker
Inside This Box

Name _____

Grade _____

School _____

1.	2.	3.	4.	5.
6.	7.	8.	9.	10.
11.	12.	13.	14.	15.
16.	17.	18.	19.	20.
21.	22.	23.	24.	25.
26.	27.	28.	29.	30.

1. A candle game involves 10 candles numbered from 1 to 10 and is scored by the lowest candle number that did not get blown out. For example, if the candles numbered 1 and 2 get blown out but not the candle numbered 3, then the score would be 3. Below are the results of one candle game. What is the sum of the scores of the three players?

Player	List of Candles Blown Out
Nick	1,2,3,4,5,8
Preston	1,2,3,7,8,10
Ryan	2,3,4,5,6,7,8,9,10

2. A diagonal of a regular pentagon can split the pentagon into two different polygons. Of those two smaller polygons, how many sides does the polygon with the greater area have?

3. Curtis wants to make 25 free throws in a minute. In the first half of the minute, Curtis makes free throws at a constant rate of one free throw every three seconds. How many free throws does Curtis need to make in the second half of the minute?

4. Ayaka multiplies her favorite number by 6, then divides the result by 2, and finally, subtracts 4 from the result, after which she once again obtains her favorite number. What is Ayaka's favorite number?

5. If two fair six-sided dice are rolled, what is the probability that the square of the value of one of the dice is greater than the square of the other? Express your answer as a common fraction.

6. In rectangle $ABCD$, AD is three times as long as AB. Mark points E and F on $\overline{AD}$ and $\overline{BC}$ respectively such that $AE = AB$ and $CF = CD$. What is the ratio of the area of $EBFD$ to the area of a square with side length AD? Express your answer as a common fraction.

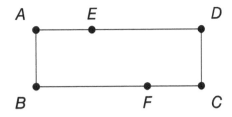

7. Tomomi has at least three students and must give away some tokens to the students. She notices that if she had two more students or two fewer students, then she could give away her tokens so that each student gets an equal number of tokens. What is the sum of all possible numbers of tokens less than 10 that Tomomi could have?

8. Ian did three trials to see how fast his hedgehog can travel 150 meters. The hedgehog took 100 seconds for the first trial, 125 seconds for the second trial, and 100 seconds for the third trial. Ian then calculated the average speed and used that speed to calculate how long his hedgehog would take to travel 7 kilometers. How many seconds was Ian's result? Express your answer as a common fraction.

9. Given that $4^{1.25} + 4^{1.25} + 4^{1.25} + 4^{1.25} = a^b$, where a is a positive whole number that is as small as possible, and b is a real number, what is the value of $a + b$? Express your answer as a common fraction.

10. To make a spiky cloth turtle shell, Jack puts together some number of cloth pieces that are regular hexagons as shown below and glues a cone of radius 2 centimeters and height 6 centimeters on top of each piece. If the volume of all of Jack's cones is $a\pi$ cubic centimeters, what is the value of a?

11. If $x = \sqrt{2}$, then what is the square of the value of $x^5 - (2 + \sqrt{2})x^3 + 2x^2 + 3x - \sqrt{2}$?

12. Integers a, b, and c are chosen at random such that the absolute values of each of a, b, and c are at most 5. What is the probability that the graph of $y = ax^2 + bx + c$ is a line? Express your answer as a common fraction.

13. Let r be a positive common fraction. If the denominator of r is increased by 1, then the resulting number will be 10% less than r. What is the denominator of r?

14. Rectangle $ABCD$ has $AB = 5$ and $BC = 4$. Point P lies on $\overline{CD}$ such that $CP = 3$. Let M be the midpoint of $\overline{AP}$. What is BM^2?

15. How many positive whole numbers less than 100 have the property that their remainder upon being divided by 9 is one of their digits? For example, 20 has this property because 20 leaves a remainder of 2 when divided by 9, but 25 does not.

16. The table below lists how many students and teachers prefer putting pineapple on pizza. Amee wants to select two students and two teachers but wants at least one of the four people to like pineapple on pizza. If the order in which the people are selected does not matter, how many ways can Amee select the four people?

	Pineapple on Pizza	No Pineapple on Pizza
Students	4	6
Teachers	2	5

17. Given that $a + b = 5$ and $a^2 + b^2 = 21$, what is $a^6 + b^6$?

18. What is the remainder when the product of the even positive whole numbers up to and including 18 is divided by 900?

19. Black Friday is on the day immediately after Thanksgiving, which is on the fourth Thursday of November. Given that November 1, 2022, is a Tuesday, in how many calendar years from 2022 to 2099, inclusive, is Black Friday *not* on the fourth Friday of November?

20. In $\triangle ABC$ with $AB = 7$ and $AC = 11$, let D be on side $\overline{AB}$ such that $BD = 2$, and let E be on side $\overline{AC}$ such that $CE = 3$. If $DE = 5$, what is CD^2?

21. In how many ways can we arrange the letters of the word *RESERVE* such that no two identical letters are adjacent?

22. Square $ABCD$ has side length 4. Points E and F are on sides $\overline{BC}$ and $\overline{CD}$, respectively, such that the lengths BE, CE, CF, and DF are all positive whole numbers. What is the sum of the two smallest possible areas of $\triangle AEF$? Express your answer as a common fraction.

23. What is the sum of all whole numbers $0 \le x \le 125$ for which x^3 is 1 more than a multiple of 126?

24. Triangle ABC has side lengths $AB = 13$, $BC = 14$, and $CA = 15$. Point P lies on line $\overline{BC}$ between B and C so that the circle with radius $\overline{AP}$ and center at A has a point Q lying on its circumference whose distance from line BC is 25, and this circle's radius is minimized. What is BP?

25. What is the sum of all real values of x for which $36(x + 6)^4 = 16(x + 8)^4$?

26. Becker has ten marbles and two jars, each of which can hold up to five marbles. Marbles of the same color, and the two jars, are indistinguishable from one another, and the order in which the marbles are placed in each jar does not matter. If Becker has two each of five different colors of marbles, how many visually distinguishable arrangements of all ten of the marbles in the jars are there?

27. What is the remainder when the sum of the first 2026 positive perfect squares is divided by 2022?

28. Let triangle ABC with positive area have $\angle ABC = 22°$. Let D be the point on side $\overline{BC}$ such that $\overline{AD}$ bisects $\angle BAC$. What is the greatest possible whole number of degrees in the measure of $\angle ADC$?

29. Fabian is planning a trip itinerary for one day where he travels for 8 hours and passes by a rest stop after every half hour of travel. He plans to stop at at least three rest stops along the way, and each rest stop must be at least an hour apart from any other rest stop. In how many ways can Fabian plan the rest stops on his day trip?

30. Let x, y, and z be real numbers such that $y(x - z + 1) = -1$, $x(y - z - 1) = -1$, and $xyz = 1$. What is the sum of all possible values of z^2?

 Place ID Sticker
Inside This Box

Name _____

Grade _____

School _____

Problems 1 & 2

1. Brendan is travelling through eight different regions. In each region, he chooses one of three possible starting creatures. How many ways can Brendan pick a creature from each of the eight regions?

1.

2. Haruka has three similar octagons. She knows that the perimeters of the octagons are 12, 24, and 48. If the area of the largest octagon is 160, what is the sum of the areas of the other two octagons?

2.

Place ID Sticker
Inside This Box

Name _____

Grade _____

School _____

Problems 3 & 4

3. In a $3 \times 3 \times 3$ cube, a corner $2 \times 2 \times 2$ cubical section is removed. Then, a $1 \times 1 \times 1$ cube is glued to where the center $1 \times 1 \times 1$ cube of the $3 \times 3 \times 3$ cube used to be. What is the surface area of the resulting figure?

3.

4. Daniel is doing karate. He has an ample supply of boards, each of which is either three or four inches thick, that he must chop. Daniel chops until the sum of the thicknesses of all the boards he has chopped reaches at least 78 inches. At least how many four inch boards must Daniel chop so that he ends up chopping fewer than 24 boards?

4.

Place ID Sticker
Inside This Box

Name _____

Grade _____

School _____

Problems 5 & 6

---

5. At their local convenience store, Lance only buys packs of small drinks while his friend Suranne only buys packs of large drinks, with the volume and pricing for the packs of drinks listed in the table below. If Lance receives a 20% discount off every pack he buys, and the two friends always buy the same total number of drinks in whole packs, how many cents per fluid ounce, on average, does Suranne save over Lance? Express your answer as a common fraction.

5.

Pack	Volume per Drink	Cost per Pack
2 Small Drinks	12 fluid ounces	$ 1.90
3 Large Drinks	16 fluid ounces	$ 2.90

6. How many ordered tuples of positive whole numbers (a, b, c, d, e, f) are there such that $a + b + c + d = 20$, $c + d + e + f = 22$, and both $|a - e|$ and $|b - f|$ are at most 2?

6.

Place ID Sticker
Inside This Box

Name _____

Grade _____

School _____

Problems 7 & 8

7. The price of strawberries from a very generous vendor starts off at 50 cents per strawberry and decreases by 1 cent after every 10 strawberries the customer buys. That is, strawberries 1 to 10 each cost 50 cents, strawberries 11 to 20 each cost 49 cents, and so on. After the 500th strawberry, all strawberries are free. Orion wants to buy enough strawberries so that the average cost of the strawberries he buys is 15 cents or less. At least how many strawberries does he need to buy?

7.

8. For how many non-negative integers n is $\frac{1296}{2^n}$ a perfect pth power of some rational number that is at least $\frac{1}{1000}$, for some whole number $p \geq 2$?

8.

School or Team

Name _____

Name _____

Name _____

Name _____

Place ID Sticker
Inside This Box

Place ID Sticker
Inside This Box

Place ID Sticker
Inside This Box

Place ID Sticker
Inside This Box

1.	2.	3.	4.	5.
6.	7.	8.	9.	10.

1. The table below lists the height of 4 teams' towers halfway through a tower-building competition. Afterward, the team with the shortest tower moves 5 blocks from the tallest tower onto their own tower. How many blocks is the range of tower heights once the competition ends?

Team Name	Height (in Blocks)
The Smartest Team on Earth	7
Life Pact Again	8
We Are Okay	4
Team10s	1

2. The "cube rule" is a food classification that models starched foods with a cube and counts shaded faces that represent the starch location to classify the food. Below are some of the classifications from the cube rule.
   - If a food is a sandwich, then the corresponding cube has only 2 opposite faces shaded.
   - If a food is a taco, then the corresponding cube has only 3 faces shaded.

   Jared wants to shade some parts of a cube with side length 5 centimeters to model a hot dog, which he considers to be a taco. How many square centimeters should he shade in his cube model of a hot dog?

3. In the year 2022 in California, daylight savings time begins on March 13, where clocks are set one hour forward once the time reaches 2 AM, and it ends on November 6, where clocks are set one hour backward once the time reaches 2 AM. How many days in the year 2022 are there such that daylight savings time is in effect at noon on that day in California?

4. How many positive whole number divisors of 2160 are there such that at least one of its prime divisors is raised to an odd exponent in its prime factorization?

5. Jake mixes a 2.5% salt solution and a 12.5% salt solution to produce a 5% salt solution. He wants to mix 10% and 25% salt solutions in the same ratio as the 2.5% and 12.5% salt solutions respectively, in order to produce a new solution. What fraction of this new solution consists of salt? Express your answer as a common fraction.

6. Triangle ABC has side lengths $AB = 7$, $BC = 8$, and $CA = 9$. Points D and E lie on the extension of $\overline{BC}$ such that $\triangle ADE$ is equilateral. What is DE^2?

7. In the Mathleaguian language, each character is composed of several strokes, which are meant to be written in a specific order. In Mathleaguian, there are five different 6-stroke characters, three different 5-stroke characters, and two different 4-stroke characters. Suppose Maxwell wants to encode a message in Mathleaguian using a string of not necessarily distinct characters with a total of 15 strokes. How many possible strings of characters can Maxwell encode in his message?

8. Two even positive whole numbers have 8 and 12 positive whole number divisors. What is the largest possible number of divisors of their product?

9. Anabia and Andrei are working on a group project together at the same constant rate, starting at 12:00 PM. After every hour of work, Anabia takes a 15 minute break, and after every 75 minutes of work, Andrei takes a 30 minute break. The two of them eventually finish at 8:24 PM. In how many minutes could Andrei have finished the entire group project by himself without taking breaks?

10. Rectangle $ABCD$ has $AB = 8$. Let M be the midpoint of side $\overline{AB}$. Suppose there is a point P on side $\overline{AD}$ such that $\overline{CM} \perp \overline{BP}$. If $\overline{CP}$ bisects $\angle BPD$, the length of $\overline{CM}$ can be expressed as $m\sqrt{n} + p$, where m, n, and p are positive whole numbers, and n is not divisible by the square of any prime. What is $m + n + p$?

1. If $4^a = 7$ and $7^b = 256$, what is ab?

2. How many two-digit prime numbers have two composite digits?

3. Scott and 5 friends ate at a Thai restaurant, but Scott offered to pay for all of his friends' food. As a result, Scott paid an extra $85 compared to if they all shared the bill equally. If everyone only ordered one pad thai serving, how many dollars did the pad thai serving cost per person?

4. A cube with side length 2 is cut into 8 cubes with side length 1. How much does the total surface area increase?

5. Evaluate: $-\left|2\frac{3}{9}\right| + \left|4\frac{4}{9}\right|$. Express your answer as a mixed number.

6. Victoria ordered a pizza that has a diameter of 12 inches. The pizza has 10 pieces of pepperoni that each have a radius of half an inch, and none of the pepperoni are stacked on top of each other. What fraction of the pizza is covered by pepperoni? Express your answer as a common fraction.

7. How many ways can each of the faces of a regular octahedron be colored either red or blue? Assume that rotations are considered distinct.

8. If $a\#b = a^b + b^a$, what is $3\#6$?

9. Ethan has 20 dollars to spend on durians, which cost 2 dollars, and dragonfruits, which cost 3 dollars. How many combinations of durians and dragonfruits can Ethan buy, if he must spend all of his money?

10. The number 2520 can be expressed as the product of five consecutive whole numbers. What is the sum of those whole numbers?

11. Andrew ordered sandwiches for 100 children from Simplex Subs for lunch, but some children cannot have gluten bread and some children do not want meat. He served 64 sandwiches with gluten bread and 75 sandwiches with meat. If 49 children got sandwiches with meat and gluten bread, how many children got sandwiches with no meat and no gluten bread?

12. If the side lengths of an equilateral triangle and regular hexagon are in the ratio 1 : 2, what is the ratio of the area of the triangle to that of the hexagon? Express your answer as a common fraction.

13. Chloe oversees four plots in the garden and picks a plot at random. The length in meters of the tallest bean plant, tallest corn plant, and tallest squash plant in each plot is shown in the below table. What is the probability that the tallest plant in the plot is a corn plant? Express your answer as a common fraction.

	Plot 1	Plot 2	Plot 3	Plot 4
Bean Plant	3.56	3.32	3.25	3.05
Corn Plant	3.65	3.43	3.24	3.55
Squash Plant	0.92	0.91	1.01	0.99

14. An angle of a regular polygon measures 135°. How many sides does the polygon have?

15. Evaluate $123.4 + 12.34 + 1.234 + 0.1234 + 0.01234 + 0.001234$. Express your answer as a decimal to the nearest thousandth.

16. Amy lives in a hamlet where the closest market with fresh food to her home is 8 kilometers. However, the hamlet turned an empty lot into a garden with fresh food that Amy can get to by walking 1500 meters east from her home then 2000 meters north. How many meters shorter is the shortest distance from Amy's home to the garden compared to the distance from Amy's home to the market?

17. Points A, B, C, D lie on a line in that order. If $AC = 20$, $BD = 22$, and $AD = 33$, what is BC?

18. What value of a satisfies $4^a = 4^{1/2} + 4^{1/2} + 4^{1/2} + 4^{1/2}$? Express your answer as a common fraction.

19. Stephanie is cooking some pho noodle soup in a cylindrical pot. The pot has a radius of 10 inches and a height of 8 inches. If 80% of the pot is filled with soup, how many cubic inches does the soup take up? Express your answer in terms of π.

20. The sum of six consecutive whole numbers is 63. What is the largest of those whole numbers?

21. How many noncongruent rectangles are there with whole number side lengths and area 64?

22. What integer value of p satisfies the equation $p^3 + 3p^2 + 3p = -28$?

23. Recall that when reading a book, the reader can see two pages at a time, with the smaller page number on the left and the larger page number on the right. The barbecue section in the recipe book starts on page 125 on the left and ends on 142 on the right. If Audrey starts at the very beginning of the barbecue section, how many times does she need to turn the page to read all the pages of the barbecue section?

24. A rectangular prism has faces with areas 20, 24, and 30. Find the sum of the edge lengths of the prism.

Countdown Round 12312 ©2020 mathleague.org

25. The graph of a line passes through the two points shown on the coordinate plane below. What is the *x*-coordinate of the *x*-intercept of this line? Express your answer as a common fraction.

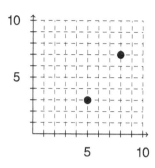

26. In square *ABCD*, points *E* and *F* are drawn outside of the square such that $\triangle AEB$ and $\triangle CDF$ are equilateral. Find the number of lines of symmetry of hexagon *AEBCFD*.

27. What is the minimum value of $x^2 - 6x + 16$?

28. Rachel has two identical pieces of chicken and three identical pieces of onion. She plans on putting the pieces in a kebab stick, and two arrangements of the pieces are identical if the stick can be flipped to get pieces in that arrangement. How many arrangements can Rachel make on her kebab stick?

29. Find the number of positive divisors of 117.

30. Suppose *x* and *y* are positive numbers such that $xy = x + 1$ and $x = y - 1$. Find *x*.

31. Kay's Cafe can house 100 customers, but it's the middle of the lunch rush! The resturant currently has 5 customers at 12:30 PM. At 12:31 PM, 11 customers enter. At 12:32 PM, 4 customers leave. The pattern of 11 customers entering at every odd minute and 4 customers leaving at every even minute continues until the cafe is full. How many minutes past 12:30 PM would Kay's Cafe be full?

32. If 2 adjacent sides of a parallelogram have lengths of 8 and 13 and the angle between them is 30 degrees, what is the area of the parallelogram?

33. What is the greatest common divisor of 264 and 336?

34. If $a \triangle b = a + 7b - ab$, what is $11 \triangle 17$?

35. Ruben operates Ruben's Types Tacos, a taco restaurant that offers 8 different types of tacos. He wants to showcase some positive whole number of tacos on a promotional flyer that can show at most three types of tacos. How many ways can Ruben select types of tacos for the flyer?

36. What is the sum of all values of *x* such that $\frac{49}{x^2+3x-1000} + \frac{64}{x^2+10x-2000}$ is undefined?

37. How many three-digit whole numbers have their units digit less than their hundreds digit and their tens digit less than their units digit?

38. What is the sum of the first 50 positive even whole numbers?

39. The relationship between temperatures in Fahrenheit and Celsius is $F = \frac{9}{5}C + 32$, where F is the temperature in degrees Fahrenheit and C is the temperature in degrees Celsius. Andy found that the temperature of his food compost pile is $149°F$. How many degrees Celsius is the temperature of Andy's food compost pile?

40. Let f and g be functions such that $f(x) = x + \frac{1}{x}$ and $g(x) = x - \frac{1}{x}$. What is $f(g(2)) + g(f(2))$? Express your answer as a mixed number.

41. Jacob plans on buying boxes of chicken nuggets, where each box either has 6 nuggets or 8 nuggets. What is the maximum even number of nuggets that Jacob cannot get in exact amount from buying some number of boxes that can be either size?

42. Liya plans to order ten kosharies, which have rice and lentils, and hopes to get the food ready in 45 minutes. She knows that three chefs can prepare two kosharies in 15 minutes. How many chefs will it take to have Liya's food on time?

43. A fair coin is flipped six times. What is the expected number of coins showing heads?

44. What is the greatest possible perimeter of a rectangle with whole number side lengths and area 24?

45. Kou did a survey to see which type of rice people like the most. He listed the five most popular types of rice in the following table and filled out the results. If 5000 people did a survey and the vote results of the top three choices are in the ratio 7:4:2, how many votes were for Jasmine rice?

Popularity	Rice	Votes
1st	Basmati	
2nd	Jasmine	
3rd	Jollof	
4th	Spanish	50
5th	Wild	36

46. Two circles with radii of length 5 and 6 are inscribed in a circle with a radius of length 11 and do not overlap. What is the area of the region inside the largest circle but outside the two smaller circles? Express your answer in terms of π.

47. The number $\frac{12}{13}$ can be expressed as a repeating decimal $0.\overline{abcdef}$. Find d.

48. One day, Kana bought 8 pieces of sushi and 4 pieces of sashimi for $17. On another day, she bought 4 pieces of sushi and 8 pieces of sashimi for $16. If the price per piece of sushi and price per piece of sashimi remain the same, how many dollars would Kana pay to buy 4 pieces of sushi and 4 pieces of sashimi?

49. What is the value of $\frac{6^6}{3^6}$?

50. Find the greatest prime factor of $\frac{100!}{50!}$.

51. A circle is divided into a number of pieces by 4 straight lines, where each pair of lines is either parallel or perpendicular. What is the maximum number of pieces the circle is divided into?

52. The area of a rectangular paper towel is 144 square inches. The length of the paper towel is 7 inches longer than the width. How many inches is the perimeter of the paper towel?

53. When the figure shown below is folded into a cube such that the squares shown become faces of the cube, what is the sum of all the numbers on all the faces that share an edge with the face marked with a star?

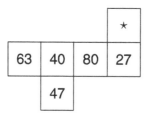

54. Express as a common fraction: $\frac{1}{2} - \frac{2}{3} + \frac{3}{4}$.

55. Calculate: $19 \cdot 501$.

56. An isosceles right triangle has a leg of length 20. The altitude to the hypotenuse of this right triangle partitions the triangle into two smaller triangles. What is the area of one of these smaller triangles?

57. Evaluate: $891 + 29$.

58. Deven kept track of the number of calories of six breakfast foods for one serving and recorded the results in the table below. He then wrote down the number of calories for two servings of each breakfast food somewhere else and calculated the median of those numbers. What would be that median number of calories?

Program	Calories for One Serving
Cereal	200
Egg Sandwich	230
Oatmeal	160
Pancake	90
Toast	75
Waffle	85

59. 28 is what percent of 70?

60. Find the smallest prime divisor of 1615.

61. This morning, Rohan delivered 39 meals to people in need. Then Nadia came and delivered 11 meals. Afterward, Kaylee delivered even more meals. At the end of the day, Isabel delivered 11 meals. If the four delivered a total of 100 meals, how many meals did Kaylee deliver?

62. How many numbers x satisfy $x^2 = 121$?

63. Evaluate: $1 \cdot 14 + 2 \cdot 7 + 7 \cdot 2 + 14 \cdot 1$.

64. Find the arithmetic mean of the following set of numbers: 93, 77, 85, 82, 78.

65. Cole needs 1 piece of chicken, 2 cups of broth, and 2 cups of tomatoes to make 6 servings of curry. How many servings of curry can Cole make with 16 pieces of chicken, 18 cups of broth, and 20 cups of tomatoes?

66. How many square centimeters is the surface area of a rectangular prism with side lengths of 6 cm, 7 cm, and 2 cm?

67. How many ways are there to arrange the letters in the word *FOOD*?

68. The country of Peru has the currency of sol, where 1 sol equals 100 centimos. A ceviche, which is an appetizer with fish, originally costs 18 soles, but John bought it on sale where the price is 10% off. How many centimos did John pay for that ceviche?

69. Evaluate: 34×34.

70. If $x = 16$ and $y = 4$, what is $x\sqrt{y} + y\sqrt{x} + \sqrt{xy}$?

71. What is the remainder when 7162534 is divided by 9?

72. The poke restaurant serves poke that are classified as either aku poke or tako poke but not both. Christopher observes from the menu that the restaurant offers six types of aku poke and two types of tako poke. What fraction of the poke that is offered at the restaurant is aku poke? Express your answer in simplest form.

73. Two fair dice are rolled. What is the probability that the sum of the numbers facing up is 5? Express your answer as a common fraction.

74. Express as a decimal to the nearest tenth: $\frac{68.75}{12.5}$.

75. What is the value of $12 \cdot 18 + 9$?

76. Joeli observes that the latest reviews of the pasta from Restaurante de Excellente for the week are $\{5, 5, 5, 4, 5, 4, 5, 5, 1, 4\}$. What is the mean review score of the pasta that week? Express your answer as a decimal to the nearest tenth.

77. If $x = 9$ and $y = \frac{1}{3}$, what is the value of $\frac{xy}{3} + 3y$?

78. If a triangle has whole number side lengths 20, 22, and x, what is the difference between the maximum and minimum possible values of x?

79. Edward and Eric are operating food trucks. Edward serves 50 customers per hour while Eric serves 55 customers per hour. As of 3 PM, Eric had served 35 more customers than Edward. As of 5 PM, how many more customers had Eric served compared to Edward?

80. Christine's family goes to a food court with 10 restaurant options, and her family picks an option at random. In the last ten trips, Christine's family went to the salad restaurant. What is the probability that Christine's family goes to the salad restaurant the next time they visit the food court? Express your answer as a common fraction.

Answers
12312

Sprint Round

			Target Round	Team Round
1. 11	11. 8	21. 96	1. 6561	1. 4
2. 4	12. $\frac{1}{11}$	22. $\frac{17}{2}$	2. 50	2. 75
3. 15	13. 9	23. 567	3. 54	3. 238
4. 2	14. 20	24. 10	4. 9	4. 34
5. $\frac{5}{6}$	15. 33	25. −4	5. $\frac{7}{24}$	5. $\frac{11}{80}$
6. $\frac{2}{9}$	16. 795	26. 26	6. 2907	6. 60
7. 19	17. 9009	27. 367	7. 850	7. 207
8. $\frac{45500}{9}$	18. 360	28. 100	8. 21	8. 72
9. $\frac{13}{2}$	19. 11	29. 1490		9. 789
10. 80	20. 58	30. 6		10. 10

Countdown

1. 4	21. 4	41. 10	61. 39
2. 1	22. −4	42. 5	62. 2
3. 17	23. 8	43. 3	63. 56
4. 24	24. 60	44. 50	64. 83
5. $2\frac{1}{9}$	25. $\frac{11}{4}$	45. 1512	65. 54
6. $\frac{5}{72}$	26. 2	46. 60π	66. 136
7. 256	27. 7	47. 0	67. 12
8. 945	28. 6	48. 11	68. 1620
9. 4	29. 6	49. 64	69. 1156
10. 25	30. 1	50. 97	70. 56
11. 10	31. 25	51. 9	71. 1
12. $\frac{1}{24}$	32. 52	52. 50	72. $\frac{3}{4}$
13. $\frac{3}{4}$	33. 24	53. 210	73. $\frac{1}{9}$
14. 8	34. −57	54. $\frac{7}{12}$	74. 5.5
15. 137.111	35. 92	55. 9519	75. 225
16. 5500	36. −13	56. 100	76. 4.3
17. 9	37. 120	57. 920	77. 2
18. $\frac{3}{2}$	38. 2550	58. 250	78. 38
19. 640π	39. 65	59. 40	79. 45
20. 13	40. $4\frac{4}{15}$	60. 5	80. $\frac{1}{10}$

Sprint Round Solutions

1. Based on the rules and the table, we find that Nick's score is 6, Preston's score is 4, and Ryan's score is 1. The sum of the scores is $6 + 4 + 1 = \boxed{11}$.

2. No matter what diagonal we use, we will always split that pentagon into a quadrilateral and a triangle. Then, we can see that the quadrilateral will have the greater area, and the quadrilateral has $\boxed{4}$ sides.

3. We know that half a minute is 30 seconds. By setting up a proportion, we can find that Curtis makes 10 free throws in the first half of the minute. Since his goal is 25 free throws, we find that Curtis still needs to do $25 - 10 = \boxed{15}$ free throws in the second half of the minute.

4. Let Ayaka's favorite number be x. Then, we get that Ayaka's final result is $\frac{6x}{2} - 4$, or $3x - 4$. Thus, we have that $x = 3x - 4$. Solving for x gives us $x = \boxed{2}$.

5. If the results of the two dice are not equal to each other, then we can note that the square of the larger result is greater than the square of the smaller result. If the results of the two dice are equal to each other, then the squares are equal to each other. The condition is satisfied when the dice are not equal. Five of the six outcomes for the second die are not equal to whatever the result of the first die is, so the probability is $\boxed{\dfrac{5}{6}}$.

6. First, note that $ABCD$ is a third of the area of a square with side length AD. Next, note that the square with side length AB is one-third of the area of $ABCD$. We find that the area of $EBFD$ is the area of $ABCD$ minus the sum of the areas of ABE and CDF. Then, the area of $EBFD$ is $\frac{2}{3}$ of the area of $ABCD$, and so the area of $EBFD$ is $\frac{2}{3} \cdot \frac{1}{3} = \boxed{\dfrac{2}{9}}$ of the area of a square with side length AD.

7. We start looking for positive whole numbers from 1 that have two factors that differ by four. Upon inspection, we see that 5 works because it has the factors 1 and 5, 6 works because it has the factors 2 and 6, and 8 works because it has the factors 4 and 8. Thus, our answer is $5 + 6 + 8 = \boxed{19}$.

8. We know that average speed can be calculated by dividing the total distance traveled by the total time, so we get the average speed to be $\frac{3 \cdot 150}{100+125+100} = \frac{18}{13}$ meters per second. Therefore, to travel 7 kilometers, or 7000 meters, the hedgehog would take $\frac{7000}{\frac{18}{13}} = \boxed{\frac{45500}{9}}$ seconds.

9. The left-hand side evaluates to $4 \cdot 4^{1.25} = 4^{2.25} = 2^{4.5}$, so $a = 2$ and $b = \frac{9}{2}$. Thus, $a + b = \boxed{\frac{13}{2}}$.

10. We count 10 pieces that are regular hexagons. The volume of each cone is $\frac{1}{3} \cdot 4\pi \cdot 6 = 8\pi$ cubic centimeters, so the volume of all of Jack's cones is $10 \cdot 8\pi = 80\pi$ cubic centimeters. Thus, we have that $a = \boxed{80}$.

11. The given expression simplifies to $x^5 - (x^2 + x)x^3 + x^2(x^2) + 3x - x$, which is $x^5 - x^5 - x^4 + x^4 + 2x = 2x$. We want to find $(2x)^2 = 4x^2$, which is $4 \times 2 = \boxed{8}$.

12. We are choosing a, b, c where $-5 \leq a, b, c \leq 5$, there are 11 options to choose for each of the variables. However, note that if $a = 0$, then the graph of $bx + c$ would be a line, and if $a \neq 0$, then the graph of $ax^2 + bx + c$ would not be a line but rather a parabola. In the end, the only value that would matter is a, and the probability that $a = 0$ is $\boxed{\frac{1}{11}}$.

13. Let $r = \frac{p}{q}$, for positive whole numbers p and q. Then, $\frac{p}{q+1} = \frac{9p}{10q}$, or $10pq = 9pq + 9p$, implying that $q = \boxed{9}$.

14. Note that $\triangle BCP$ is a 3-4-5 right triangle, so $\triangle ABP$ is isosceles with two legs of length 5. In addition, $AP = 2\sqrt{5}$, so $AM = \sqrt{5}$ and $MP = \sqrt{5}$, and so $BM^2 = \boxed{20}$.

15. The whole numbers with this property are the single-digit positive whole numbers excluding 9, then 10 and 19, 20 and 29, 30 and 39, and so forth, up until 80 and 89, and then 90 through 98, because $10x$ leaves the same remainder as x when divided by 9. Note that we do not include 9 and 99 because the remainder when these numbers are divided by 9 is 0, not 9. This gives a total of $\boxed{33}$ positive whole numbers.

16. There are 10 students and 7 teachers, so Amee has $\binom{10}{2}\binom{7}{2} = 45 \cdot 21$ ways to choose two students and two teachers. However, we do not want to include any of the ways to choose two students and two teachers who all do not like pineapple on pizza, and there are $\binom{6}{2}\binom{5}{2} = 15 \cdot 10$ ways of doing so. This means that there are $45 \cdot 21 - 15 \cdot 10 = \boxed{795}$ ways for Amee to select the four people.

17. We note that $a^6 + b^6$ is the sum of two perfect cubes and can be rewritten as $(a^2 + b^2)(a^4 + b^4 - a^2b^2)$ and further manipulated to be $(a^2 + b^2)((a^2 + b^2)^2 - 3a^2b^2)$. We have $a + b = 5$ and $a^2 + b^2 = 21$, so $ab = 2$ and $a^2b^2 = 4$. Plugging everything in, we get that $a^6 + b^6 = (a^2 + b^2)((a^2 + b^2)^2 - 3a^2b^2) = (21)(441 - 12) = \boxed{9009}$.

18. Note that this product is equal to $2^9 \cdot 9!$, and that $900 = (2 \cdot 3 \cdot 5)^2$. We see that the product is divisible by 2^2 and 3^2. Then, note that $2^7 \equiv 3 \bmod 25$, so $2^9 \equiv 12 \bmod 25$, and $9! = 362880$, which is congruent to $5 \bmod 25$. Thus, we have that the product is equivalent to $12 \cdot 5 \equiv 10 \bmod 25$. Thus, by the Chinese Remainder Theorem, the product leaves a remainder of $\boxed{360}$ when divided by 900.

19. This occurs if and only if November begins on a Friday, which it does in 2024. As the day on which November 1 falls advances by 5 days along the 7-day cycle every 4 years, it becomes Friday again every 28 years. Thus, November 1 is a Friday in 2024, 2030, 2041, 2047, and 2052, after which the cycle repeats. There are 4 such years in every 28-year cycle, hence 8 of them (including 2024, but not 2080) in the cycles up to 2079. Also, November 1 is on a Friday in 2080, 2086, and 2097, so there are $\boxed{11}$ such years in total from 2022 to 2099, inclusive.

20. We see that $AD = 5$, so $\triangle ADE$ is isosceles with $AD = DE$. Thus, if M is the midpoint of $\overline{AE}$, then $\overline{DM} \perp \overline{AE}$. Then, $CM = 7$ and $DM = 3$, so by the Pythagorean Theorem, $CD^2 = 3^2 + 7^2$, or $\boxed{58}$.

21. Consider the three Es. If we allow the two Rs to be adjacent, there are $\frac{4!}{2} = 12$ ways to order the remaining 4 letters and $\binom{5}{3} = 10$ ways to pick the positions of the Es, for 120 possibilities. We now need to subtract the cases where the Rs are adjacent. If we put the 2 Rs together and consider them as a single letter, there are $3! = 6$ orderings for the RR, S, and V, and $\binom{4}{3} = 4$ ways to pick the positions of the Es, for 24 possibilities. Subtracting, we get $120 - 24 = \boxed{96}$.

22. Let $BE = x$ and $DF = y$. Then, we have that $CE = 4 - x$ and $CF = 4 - y$. The sum of the areas of $\triangle ABE$, $\triangle ADF$, and $\triangle CEF$ is $\frac{1}{2} \cdot 4 \cdot x + \frac{1}{2} \cdot 4 \cdot y + \frac{1}{2} \cdot (4-x) \cdot (4-y) = \frac{xy}{2} + 8$. Then, the area of $\triangle AEF$ is equal to $8 - \frac{xy}{2}$. Since x, y, $4 - x$, and $4 - y$ are all positive whole numbers, we must have that x and y are between 1 and 3, inclusive. In order to minimize the area of $\triangle AEF$, we want to maximize $\frac{xy}{2}$. To do so, we choose $(x, y) = (2, 3)$ (or $(3, 2)$) and $(x, y) = (3, 3)$, giving us $\frac{xy}{2} = 3$ and $\frac{xy}{2} = \frac{9}{2}$, respectively. Then, $8 - \frac{xy}{2} = 5$ and $8 - \frac{xy}{2} = \frac{7}{2}$, respectively, so our answer is $\frac{7}{2} + 5 = \boxed{\dfrac{17}{2}}$.

23. By the Chinese Remainder Theorem, $x^3 \equiv 1 \bmod 2$, $x^3 \equiv 1 \bmod 7$, and $x^3 \equiv 1 \bmod 9$. This translates to $x \equiv 1 \bmod 2$, $x \equiv 1, 2, 4 \bmod 7$, and $x \equiv 1 \bmod 3$, or $x \equiv 1, 25, 37 \bmod 42$. The desired sum is then $(1 + 25 + 37) + (43 + 67 + 79) + (85 + 109 + 121) = \boxed{567}$.

24. As the altitude length from A to $\overline{BC}$ is 12 (from Heron's formula, which gives the area of $\triangle ABC$ as 84), the radius of the circle must be at least 13. This is because if the circle is minimized, there should be only one point Q whose distance from line BC is 25, and this would be the point such that $\overline{AQ} \perp \overline{BC}$. Thus, the radius must be $25 - 12 = 13$. Then, if F denotes the foot of the perpendicular from A to $\overline{BC}$, we obtain $FP = 5$. As $BF = 5$, we get $BP = \boxed{10}$.

25. Note that $\sqrt{36(x+6)^4} = 6(x+6)^2$ while $\sqrt{16(x+8)^4} = 4(x+8)^2$. Because $x + 6$ and $x + 8$ cannot both be 0, and square numbers are nonnegative, we cannot have one side be negative while the other side is positive so we must have $6(x+6)^2 = 4(x+8)^2$ which simplifies to $2x^2 + 8x - 40 = 0$. By Vieta's theorem, the sum of the roots is $\boxed{-4}$.

26. If one jar contains two pairs of identically-colored marbles and one marble of one of the other three colors, we have $\binom{5}{2} = 10$ ways to choose the pair colors for one jar and 3 ways to choose the individual marble's color, but we have to divide by 2 since the jars are indistingushable. This gives us $\frac{10 \cdot 3}{2} = 15$ arrangements. If there is one pair of identically-colored marbles and three marbles that are of different colors, we have $\binom{5}{3} = 10$ ways to choose the three different colors, and the remaining marbles are fixed. There is also the possibility that all five marbles in a jar are of different colors in which the two jars are identical, giving $15 + 10 + 1 = \boxed{26}$ arrangements in total.

27. We can consider the remainders when dividing by 2, 3, and 337, by the Chinese Remainder Theorem. We have that $1^2 + 2^2 + 3^2 + \cdots + 2026^2 = \frac{2026 \cdot 2027 \cdot 4053}{6}$, or $1013 \cdot 2027 \cdot 1351$, so the remainder upon division by 2 is 1, and the remainder upon division by 3 is 1. It remains to compute this value modulo 337, which is $2 \cdot 5 \cdot 3 = 30$, so the remainder upon division by 2022 is $\boxed{367}$.

28. Let the measures of equal angles $\angle BAD$ and $\angle CAD$ be x. Then, $\angle ADB = 158° - x$, and $\angle ADC = 22° + x$. Next, note that if $\angle BAC \geq 158°$, then $\angle ACB \leq 0°$, which is not allowed. Thus, we want $\angle BAC < 158°$. This means that $2x < 158°$, or $x < 79°$. This means that $22° + x < 101°$, so the largest possible whole number of degrees is $\boxed{100}$.

29. There are 15 possible locations (in half-hour increments) for the rest stops, and they must be spaced out at least 2 half-hour increments away from each other. Thus, there may be at most 8 rest stops along Fabian's trip. With 3 rest stops, there are $\binom{15-3+1}{3} = \binom{13}{3} = 286$ choices for their positions, by sticks-and-stones. With 4 rest stops, there are similarly $\binom{15-4+1}{4} = \binom{12}{4} = 495$ choices. With 5, 6, 7, and 8 rest stops, there are $\binom{11}{5} = 462$, $\binom{10}{6} = 210$, $\binom{9}{7} = 36$, and $\binom{8}{8} = 1$ choices, respectively. These sum to $\boxed{1490}$.

30. Expand the first and second equations to get $xy + 1 = yz - y$ and $xy + 1 = xz + x$. Dividing by y and x, respectively, and simplifying, we have $x + \frac{1}{y} = z - 1$ and $y + \frac{1}{x} = z + 1$. We can multiply the resulting equations to get $xy + \frac{1}{xy} + 2 = z^2 - 1$. Using the third equation, this implies $\frac{1}{z} + z = z^2 - 3$, so $z^3 - z^2 - 3z - 1 = 0$. Immediately, we can see that $z = -1$ is a root, so we have $(z+1)(z^2 - 2z - 1) = 0$, which implies the possible values of z are -1, $1 - \sqrt{2}$, and $1 + \sqrt{2}$. However, notice that plugging in $z = -1$ to all the equations yields $xy + 1 = -2y$, $xy + 1 = 0$, and $xy = -1$. This implies $y = 0$, so $xy = 0$, a contradiction. The other two values of z can be verified to both work, so the requested answer is $(1 - \sqrt{2})^2 + (1 + \sqrt{2})^2 = \boxed{6}$.

Target Round Solutions

1. Each choice per region is independent, so we multiply the number of possibilities for each region. Since there are 8 regions, Brendan has a total of $3^8 = \boxed{6561}$ ways to pick a creature from each of the eight regions.

2. The perimeters of the octagons are in a $1:2:4$ ratio. Thus, since the octagons are similar, the areas of the octagons are in a $1^2 : 2^2 : 4^2 = 1:4:16$ ratio. Since the largest octagon has an area of 160, the smallest octagon has an area of $\frac{1}{16} \cdot 160 = 10$, and the other octagon has an area of $\frac{4}{16} \cdot 160 = 40$. Thus, the sum of the areas of the other two octagons is $10 + 40 = \boxed{50}$.

3. The original surface area of the $3 \times 3 \times 3$ cube is $6 \cdot 3^2 = 54$. Removing a corner $2 \times 2 \times 2$ cubical section removes $3 \cdot 2^2 = 12$ from the surface area, but it also adds 12 to the surface area, granting a net change of 0. Similarly, by adding the center $1 \times 1 \times 1$ cube back, 3 faces get covered, but 3 new faces are added to the surface area, yielding another net change of 0. Therefore, the surface area has not changed, so it is still $\boxed{54}$.

4. In the worst case scenario, Daniel will have to chop 23 boards and chop a total of 78 inches of thickness. Thus, we set up a system of equations: $x + y = 23$, $3x + 4y = 78$, where x and y denote the number of three inch boards and four inch boards, respectively. Solving gives us $x = 14$ and $y = 9$, so our answer is at most 9 four inch boards. We show that 8 four inch boards is not sufficient. Note that $4 \cdot 8 = 32$, so Daniel needs to cut at least $78 - 32 = 46$ more inches, which requires at least 16 three inch boards since $15 < \frac{46}{3} < 16$. However, $8 + 16 = 24$, which means that Daniel will chop 24 boards. Thus, the answer is $\boxed{9}$ four inch boards.

5. For Lance and Suranne to buy the same number of drinks, Lance must buy 3 packs of small drinks for every 2 packs of small drinks that Suranne buys since the least common multiple of 2 and 3 is 6. Using this information, we find that, per quantity of 6 drinks, Lance pays $3 \cdot \$1.90 \cdot 0.80 = \$4.56$ after his discount, or 456 cents, while Suranne pays $2 \cdot \$2.90 = \$5.80$, or 580 cents. Since the volume of 6 small drinks is $6 \cdot 12 = 72$ fluid ounces, and the volume of 6 large drinks is $6 \cdot 16 = 96$ fluid ounces, we have that Suranne saves $\frac{456}{72} - \frac{580}{96}$ cents per fluid ounce over Lance. Finally, simplifying both fractions gives us $\frac{19}{3} - \frac{145}{24} = \frac{152-145}{24}$, or $\boxed{\dfrac{7}{24}}$ as our final value.

6. Let $a' = a-1$, $b' = b-1$, $c' = c-1$, and $d' = d-1$. Then, we require that $a'+b'+c'+d' = 16$. By sticks-and-stones, there are $\binom{16+4-1}{4-1} = 969$ ways to choose a, b, c, and d. Then, note that $(e+f)-(a+b) = 2$. If either $e - a$ or $f - b$ were negative, then the other difference would have to be greater than 2 in order for the sum to be equal to 3, which we do not want. Thus, we must have that $e - a$ and $f - b$ are both non-negative. Thus, if $e = a + m$ and $f = b + n$, where m and n are whole numbers, we have that $(m, n) = (0, 2), (1, 1), (2, 0)$, for three choices. Thus, the answer is $969 \cdot 3 = \boxed{2907}$.

7. In total, the first 500 strawberries cost $10(50 + 49 + 48 + \cdots + 1) = 12750$ cents. If Orion buys n strawberries, we then want $\frac{12750}{n} \le 15$, or $n \ge \frac{12750}{15}$, which gives us $n \ge \boxed{850}$.

8. Note that $1296 = 36^2$, which is equal to $(2^2 \cdot 3^2)^2 = 2^4 \cdot 3^4$. Since $\frac{1296}{2^n}$ will always have 3^4 in the prime factorization, we need p to divide 4, so $p = 2$ or $p = 4$.

- If $p = 2$, we have $\frac{1296}{2^n} = x^2$ where x is a rational number that is at least $\frac{1}{1000}$. This means $x^2 = 2^{4-n} \cdot 3^4$ so we need $n = 2k$ for some whole number k. In other words, $x = 2^{2-k} \cdot 3^2$, and since $x \geq \frac{1}{1000}$, it follows that $2^{-k} \geq \frac{1}{2^2 \cdot 3^2 \cdot 1000}$ or $2^k \leq 36000$. This means $k \leq 15$ so there are 16 solutions in this case. In particular, our solutions here are $n =$ 0, 2, 4, 6, 8, 10, 12, 14, 16, 18, 20, 22, 24, 26, 28, or 30.

- If $p = 4$, we have $\frac{1296}{2^n} = x^4$ and by a similar logic, we have $n = 4k$ for some whole number k. This gives us $x = 2^{1-k} \cdot 3$, which needs to be at least $\frac{1}{1000}$, so $2^k \leq 6000$, or $k \leq 12$. This gives us $n =$ 0, 4, 8, 12, 16, 20, 24, 28, 32, 36, 40, 44, or 48. The only 5 values of n here that were not counted in the previous case are 32, 36, 40, 44, and 48.

In total, this gives us $16 + 5 = \boxed{21}$ possible values of n.

Team Round Solutions

1. Halfway through the competition, the team with the shortest height is Team10s, while the team with the tallest height is Life Pact Again. At the end of the competition, Team10s has 6 blocks, while Life Pact Again has 3. Life Pact Again now has the shortest height, and The Smartest Team on Earth now has the tallest height at 7 blocks. Thus, the range in height at the end of the competition is $\boxed{4}$ blocks.

2. Jared considers a hot dog to be a taco, and the corresponding cube of a taco has only 3 faces shaded. Therefore, Jared's cube model of a hot dog should have only 3 faces shaded. The area of each face of a cube with 5 centimeters is 25 square centimeters, so the area that Jared should shade is $\boxed{75}$ square centimeters.

3. Daylight savings time is in effect at noon each day from March 13 to March 31, all days in all months from April to October, inclusive, and from November 1 to November 5. Therefore, there are $(31 - 13 + 1) + 30 + 31 + 30 + 31 + 31 + 30 + 31 + 5 = \boxed{238}$ days in 2022 where daylight savings time is in effect at noon on that day in California.

4. The prime factorization of 2160 is $2^4 \cdot 3^3 \cdot 5^1$. We will first count the number of divisors where none of its prime divisors is raised to an odd exponent and subtract it from the total number of divisors. To do so, we require the exponent of 2 to be 0, 2, or 4, the exponent of 3 to be 0 or 2, and the exponent of 5 to be 0. Hence, there are $3 \cdot 2 \cdot 1 = 6$ divisors of 2160 that do not have any prime divisors raised to an odd exponent, or $(4 + 1)(3 + 1)(1 + 1) - 6 = 40 - 6 = \boxed{34}$ divisors that do.

5. The 2.5% and 12.5% mixtures should be mixed in the ratio $3 : 1$, as $(3 \cdot 2.5) + (1 \cdot 12.5) = (3 + 1) \cdot 5$ (that is, 5 is $\frac{1}{4} = \frac{1}{3+1}$ of the way from 2.5 to 12.5). Thus, we seek the number $\frac{1}{4}$ of the way from 10% to 25%, which is $\frac{1}{100} \cdot (10 + \frac{25-10}{4}) = \boxed{\dfrac{11}{80}}$.

6. Let P be the foot of the altitude from A to $\overline{BC}$. Let $BP = x$ so that $CP = 8 - x$. Then, we have that $49 - x^2 = 81 - (8 - x)^2$. Solving for x gives us $x = 2$. Then, the length of the altitude from A to $\overline{BC}$ is $\sqrt{7^2 - 2^2} = 3\sqrt{5}$. Then, if the side length of $\triangle ADE$ is s, then s satisfies $\left(\frac{s}{2}\right)^2 + (3\sqrt{5})^2 = s^2$, so $s^2 = \boxed{60}$.

7. The only ways to use exactly 15 strokes are to use one 6-stroke character, one 5-stroke character, and one 4-stroke character, or to use three 5-stroke characters. For the first option, there are $3! = 6$ ways to choose which order the 6-stroke character, the 5-stroke character, and the 4-stroke character go in, and there are $5 \cdot 3 \cdot 2 = 30$ choices for the three characters, for a total of $6 \cdot 30 = 180$ strings. For the second option, there are $3^3 = 27$ choices for the first, second, and third 5-stroke character in the string. Thus, there are $180 + 27 = \boxed{207}$ distinct strings.

8. The whole number with 8 divisors can either be of the form $2pq$ for odd primes p and q, $2^3 \cdot p$ for an odd prime p, $2p^3$ for an odd prime p, or 2^7. Now, in order to maximize the number of divisors of the product, we want the whole number with 12 divisors to contain as many factors not involving the prime factor 2 as possible. This is because as the exponent e of 2 increases, the ratio $\frac{e+1}{e}$ decreases, which means that there will be fewer divisors in the product. Thus, we want the whole number with 12 divisors to include one power of 2 and either have the rest of the prime factorization be of the form p^2q for odd primes p and q or p^5 for an odd prime p. The preferred forms of the whole number with 8 divisors are $2pq$ and $2p^3$, since adding 1 to the exponent of 2 has the greatest effect (in that it multiplies the number of divisors by $\frac{1+1}{1} = 2$ rather than $\frac{3+1}{3} = \frac{4}{3}$). Then, we have an example such as $(2 \cdot 3 \cdot 5) \cdot (2 \cdot 7^2 \cdot 11)$, which will have $\boxed{72}$ divisors.

9. Anabia's and Andrei's "work cycles" are 75 and 105 minutes long, respectively. Since $\text{lcm}(75, 105) = 525$, Anabia will complete 420 minutes of total work and Andrei 375 minutes of work every time their cycles coincide. Their total amount of work is 795 minutes' worth in 525 minutes. Since it took them 504 minutes to finish working together, and the last 15 minutes of the 525 minute period were spent by both of them in a break, the last 6 minutes in Anabia's work cycle is "excess" time, so only $795 - 6 = \boxed{789}$ minutes' worth of work were actually necessary to complete the project.

10. Since $\overline{CP}$ bisects $\angle BPD$, we have that $\angle DPC = \angle BPC$. Then, by transversals, $\angle DPC = \angle BCP$, so $\angle BPC = \angle BCP$, making $\triangle BCP$ isosceles with $BC = BP$. Next, let Q be the intersection of $\overline{CM}$ and $\overline{BP}$, and let R be the foot of the perpendicular from P to side $\overline{BC}$. Note that $\overline{CQ}$ and $\overline{PR}$ are both altitudes of $\triangle BCP$ from sides of equal length. Thus, since $PR = 8$ because of the fact that $AB = 8$, we have that $CQ = 8$. We also see that $BQ = BR$. Let $MQ = x$. By the Pythagorean Theorem on $\triangle BMQ$, we have that $BQ = BR$, both with length $\sqrt{16 - x^2}$. Then, by the Pythagorean Theorem on $\triangle ABP$, $AR = \sqrt{80 - x^2}$, where $AR = BP$ and $BP = BC$. Then, by the Pythagorean Theorem on $\triangle BCM$, $16 + (80 - x^2) = (x + 8)^2$. By the Quadratic Formula, we get $x = -4 \pm 4\sqrt{2}$. Since x must be positive, we get that $x = 4\sqrt{2} - 4$, so $CM = 4\sqrt{2} + 4$, so $m + n + p = \boxed{10}$.

Sprint Round
12313

Place ID Sticker
Inside This Box

Name _____

Grade _____

School _____

1.

2.

3.

4.

5.

6.

7.

8.

9.

10.

11.

12.

13.

14.

15.

16.

17.

18.

19.

20.

21.

22.

23.

24.

25.

26.

27.

28.

29.

30.

1. Eric got a pack of water bottles for his soccer team, which has 11 players. The pack has 4 rows of 5 water bottles each, and each player takes exactly one water bottle from the pack. How many water bottles remain in the water bottle pack?

2. One day, Carter travelled 2.4 kilometers to get from the apartment to the park. He then travelled 3.9 kilometers to get from the park to the museum. Finally, Carter took the same route back to his apartment. How many kilometers did Carter walk? Express your answer as a decimal without trailing zeroes.

3. A cube has a face with area 45. What is the surface area of the cube?

4. Juliet needs $1\frac{1}{2}$ cups of flour to make 8 servings of pancakes. Of the ten people at a banquet, eight people want one serving of pancakes, but the rest want two. How many cups of flour does Juliet need? Express your answer as a mixed number.

5. Each of the letters of the word *MATH* are to be placed in one of the squares of a grid of squares with 2 rows and 2 columns. If the letter *M* must be placed in the square in the first row and first column, in how many ways can the other three letters be placed?

6. A circle has an area of 100π. When the length of its diameter decreases by 4, the area of the circle will be *a*π. What is the value of *a*?

7. Sarah is operating a merry-go-round that can seat at most 15 people per session. There are a total of 80 people in line for Sarah's ride, but everyone in line is paired with a friend with whom they must ride the merry-go-round. For each ride session, Sarah will seat as many people as possible. Assuming that Sarah operates as few ride sessions as possible to save money, how many total empty seats will Sarah have had after everyone in line has ridden the merry-go-round?

8. In a list of eight positive whole numbers, each number is either a 1, 2, 3, or 4. This list has the following properties: the number 4 appears more times than the number 3, the number 2 appears more times than the number 1, and the number 3 appears exactly twice. What is the smallest possible sum of the the numbers in the list?

9. A bag contains only red and blue marbles, 60% of which are red. What fraction of the red marbles must be removed so that there are an equal number of red and blue marbles left in the bag? Express your answer as a common fraction.

10. A 7-day blizzard hits the city of Snowmound! Thankfully, the tireless snow-shovellers can model the snowfall as a linear function of the day of the blizzard as shown in the table below. If the snow-shovellers manage to remove 1 centimeter of snow from the ground every day, how many days after the blizzard begins will all of the snow be gone for the first time?

Day of the Blizzard	1	2	3
Additional Centimeters of Snow	2	3	4

11. In India, 1-rupee coins, 2-rupee coins, 5-rupee coins, 10-rupee coins, and 10-rupee banknotes are commonly used currency denominations. Megan plans on buying a drink that costs 10 rupees. How many distinct ways can she get that exact amount using any number of these coins and banknotes?

12. In 2017, Tamsin was 95 percent as tall as Joanie. By 2022, Joanie had grown 15 inches taller, and Tamsin had grown 20 inches taller, so Joanie was now 95 percent as tall as Tamsin. How many inches tall was Tamsin in 2017? Express your answer as a common fraction.

13. Point A is at $(25,80)$, point B is at $(30,70)$, and point C is at $(82,0)$. Triangle $A'B'C'$ is formed by rotating triangle ABC about the origin $60°$ clockwise. What is the square of the maximum distance from a vertex of triangle $A'B'C'$ to the origin?

14. A certain arithmetic sequence satisfies the property that the sum of the first three terms is four times the sum of the next three terms. What is the value of the sixth term?

15. Suppose that x and y are real numbers such that $\frac{x}{y} + \frac{y}{x} = 2$ and $x + y = 20$. What is $|x - y|$?

16. Jet was having a hard time beating the ice level of his video game. He first tried the ice level on the first Tuesday of June and continued to try it daily until he finally beat the level on the fourth Thursday of that same June. Including the days when he first tried and finally beat the level, Jet spent n days on the ice level. What is the sum of all possible values of n?

17. The number 35 is the product of two prime numbers that differ by exactly 2. How many positive whole numbers less than or equal to 1000 have this property?

18. How many whole numbers between 512 and 1023, inclusive, can be written as a sum of five distinct powers of 2 that are at least 4?

19. International time zones are often defined relative to Greenwich Mean Time, which is used in countries such as Portugal and Ghana. The Baker Islands run on the world's earliest time zone at 12 hours behind Greenwich Mean Time, and Kiribati runs on the world's latest time zone at 14 hours ahead of Greenwich Mean Time. For a randomly chosen time in a given day, what is the expected number of distinct dates simultaneously displayed around the world? Express your answer as a common fraction.

20. What is the greatest number of triangles with side lengths $2\sqrt{3}$, $2\sqrt{3}$, and 6 that can fit entirely inside a regular hexagon with side length 12 without overlapping?

21. How many ways are there to arrange the letters in *EVEREST* such that the arrangement contains the word *EVER* but no consecutive *E*'s? Note that the word *EVEREST* is one possible arrangement.

22. Excluding trailing zeros, how many digits does the number $0.4^{20} \cdot 0.375^{22}$ have to the right of the decimal point?

23. In right triangle $\triangle ABC$ with $\angle BAC = 90°$ and $AB = 3$, points P and Q trisect side $\overline{BC}$ such that B, P, Q and C lie in that order. If the circle with center P and diameter $\overline{BQ}$ is tangent to side $\overline{AC}$, what is AP^2?

24. If the difference of the cubes of two positive real numbers a and b is equal to 2022, and their positive difference is a whole number, what is the number of distinct values of $a + b$?

25. Tina is playing a game in which she starts with 0 points, and each turn, she can either earn one or two points with equal probability. What is the probability that, immediately after the turn in which she first ends up with a total of at least 4 points, she has an odd number of total points? Express your answer as a common fraction.

26. Let A, B, and C be the midpoints of the sides of an equilateral triangle. A circle is drawn inside the triangle, not tangent to any of its sides. Then, every line tangent to the circle and passing through at least one of A, B, and C is drawn, partitioning the triangle into n distinct regions. If fewer than five distinct lines are drawn, what is the sum of all possible values of n?

27. How many ways are there to split the set of positive divisors of 144 greater than 1 into two non-overlapping subsets such that it is *not* true that the greatest common divisor of the numbers in one subset is a multiple of the greatest common divisor of the numbers in the other subset?

28. A four-sided die has faces labeled with 1, 2, 3, and 4 dots, each equally likely to be rolled. Each time a face is rolled, one of its dots is removed, unless it has no dots, in which case it remains without dots. What is the expected number of total dots remaining on the die after it has been rolled three times? Express your answer as a common fraction.

29. For what whole number n is the sum of the real solutions to $x + \sqrt{5 - x^2} = n$ equal to n?

30. In a group of 10 students, each student has exactly three favorite colors. A meeting is held where every pair of students with at least one common favorite color shakes hands. If there are 24 different colors that are at least one student's favorite color, what is the greatest possible number of handshakes in the meeting?

Place ID Sticker
Inside This Box

Name _____

Grade _____

School _____

Problems 1 & 2

1. Jack is searching for a hidden diamond island in the sea. On his map, which is shown below, he knows that the hidden diamond island is located at the same distance from four other islands marked as points with whole number coordinates. What is the sum of the x-coordinate and the y-coordinate of the hidden diamond island on Jack's map?

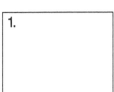

1. ⬚

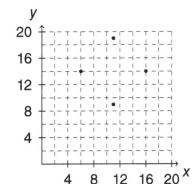

2. Two common fractions, each less than 1, have denominators of 6 and 10. What is the smallest possible denominator of the product of these two fractions when the product is written as a common fraction?

2. ⬚

Place ID Sticker
Inside This Box

Name _____

Grade _____

School _____

Problems 3 & 4

3. Given that $(5x^4 + 4x^2)(3x + 2)$ can be expressed as $Fx^5 + Ox^4 + Ix^3 + Lx^2$, where F, O, I, and L are constants, what is the value of $F - O + I - L$?

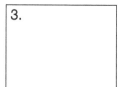

3.

4. A rectangular grid of squares consists of 20 rows and 22 columns. Anna writes exactly one number in each square such that the squares in the mth row from the top have the whole numbers from $22(m-1)+1$ to $22m$ from left to right. Then, Beth writes exactly one more number in each square such that the squares in the nth column from the left have the whole numbers from $20(n - 1) + 1$ to $20n$ from top to bottom. Suppose that Anna writes the number 380 in a certain square. What is the number that Beth writes in that square?

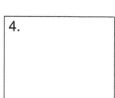

4.

Place ID Sticker
Inside This Box

Name _____

Grade _____

School _____

Problems 5 & 6

5. A concave quadrilateral *ABCD* has a reflex angle of 270° at *D* and side lengths $AB = 12$, $BC = 13$, $CD = 4$, and $AD = 3$. What is the area of *ABCD*?

5.

6. The number 2021 has the property that all digits that are zero are immediately adjacent to two non-zero digits. The number 438 also has this property because there are no digits that are zero. How many five-digit positive whole numbers have this property?

6.

 Place ID Sticker
Inside This Box

Name _____

Grade _____

School _____

Problems 7 & 8

7. Stephen has a collection of crystal gems that consists of one ruby, one sapphire, one amethyst, and one pearl. He plans on arranging the gems into the six square spaces of a 2×3 rectangular box that has a distinct front side such that each space has at most one gem and two spaces are empty. Further, the space the ruby is in shares a side with the space the sapphire is in. How many ways can Stephen put the crystal gems in the box?

7.

8. Let m and n be positive whole numbers such that $\sqrt{m} - \sqrt{n} = \sqrt{mn} - 5$. What is the sum of all possible values of $3m + 2n$?

8.

School or Team

Name _____

Name _____

Name _____

Name _____

Place ID Sticker
Inside This Box

Place ID Sticker
Inside This Box

Place ID Sticker
Inside This Box

Place ID Sticker
Inside This Box

1.

2.

3.

4.

5.

6.

7.

8.

9.

10.

1. Nathan looked at the three fastest luge times from a sprint race shown in the table below and found that the fourth place finisher took 0.137 seconds longer to finish than the third place finisher. How many seconds faster did the first place finisher finish than the fourth place finisher? Express your answer as a decimal without trailing zeroes.

Place	Time (Seconds)
1st	34.273
2nd	34.383
3rd	34.391

2. An airplane has 25 rows of seats, and each row has two groups of three seats. Each group of three seats has one seat known as the "middle seat." Tanya does not want to get a middle seat. What is the maximum number of passengers that could already be on the plane such that when Tanya boards the plane, she is guaranteed to not have to sit in a middle seat?

3. After a long day, Fatigued Finn is debating whether to take the elevator or the stairs up to his apartment. If he takes the elevator, he knows that it will take exactly 2 minutes to arrive at the lobby, then another 10 seconds per floor to actually deliver him to his apartment floor. However, if he takes the stairs, Finn can climb up a floor in exactly 15 seconds, but must rest for 15 seconds after every 5 floors he climbs and needs to finish resting before walking down the hall to his apartment. If Finn saves a non-zero amount of time by taking the elevator rather than the stairs, what is the minimum number of floors above the lobby that his apartment could be on?

4. In parallelogram $ABCD$, $AB = 3$, $BC = 13$, and $\angle ABD$ and $\angle CDB$ are both right angles. What is AC?

5. How many arrangements of the letters in the word *CHECK* contain a palindromic substring, meaning that the substring is the same regardless of whether it is read forwards or backwards, of more than one letter?

6. Let f be a function defined such that for negative real numbers x, $f(x^2 - 2x + 1) = x^4 - 2x^2 + 1$. What is the value of $\sqrt{f(f(36))}$?

7. The diagonal of an $m \times n$ rectangular grid of squares passes through the interiors of exactly 10 squares. How many ordered pairs (m, n) satisfy this condition?

8. Carawyn is leaving a class in Building A to go to her next class in Building E, which starts in 10 minutes. Her path is split into even $\frac{1}{8}$-mile marks by Buildings B, C, and D. Suppose that Carawyn is able to run at 8 miles per hour, and can choose to rest a non-negative whole number of minutes at each building. Furthermore, if she decides to get a coffee at Building C, which takes her 2 minutes, the coffee will slow her down by 1 minute in getting from Building C to Building E. In how many ways can she make her way to Building E to avoid being late to class? In case it's not clear, two ways are different if one contains a coffee stop and the other does not, or if any of the rest times at any of the buildings are different.

9. Given a circle with center O, points A and B lie outside of the circle such that $\overline{AB}$ is tangent to the circle. The angle bisector of $\angle AOB$ intersects $\overline{AB}$ at P. Given that $AO = 16$, $BO = 8$, and $OP = 8$, what is the square of the radius of the circle?

10. Kaori has a prime number p. She notices that exactly one of $2p + 1$ and $4p + 1$ is also prime, while the other is composite. What is the sum of the two largest possible values of this composite number that are at most 140?

1. A chess board is an 8×8 grid of squares where each square has at most one piece. One chess board has 15 black chess pieces and 16 white chess pieces. What fraction of the squares have a chess piece? Express your answer as a common fraction.

2. How many ways are there to arrange the letters in the word *SEEK*?

3. A convex pentagon and a unit square with the same area share exactly two sides and an axis of symmetry. If the pentagon is composed of a triangle and a rectangle, what is the ratio between the lengths of the short side and the long side of this rectangle? Express your answer as a common fraction.

4. In golf, "par" is the intended number of strokes taken to finish a hole. For example, scoring par in a hole that is Par 4 means taking 4 strokes to complete the hole. Scoring a "birdie" is scoring one less stroke than par, and scoring a "bogey" is scoring one more stroke than par. Connor played four holes in his round of golf and recorded the results in the table below. What is the mean number of strokes that Connor took in the four holes?

Hole Number	1	2	3	4
Par	3	4	4	6
Result	Par	Bogey	Birdie	Birdie

5. What is the surface area of a hemisphere with radius 5, including the bottom face? Express your answer in terms of π.

6. What is the value of $a + b^2 + c^3$ if $a = 4$, $b = 3$, and $c = 2$?

7. After the guest speaker's presentation, Ben hosts an animal show that had some number of cats and dogs as well as one rat. The ratio of cat to dog attendees is 4 : 3, and there are 30 more cats than dogs attending. How many animals attended the show?

8. What is the largest prime divisor of 2425?

9. What is 40% of 50% of 200?

10. In a revolutionary dancing game, Emily can step on an up arrow, a down arrow, a left arrow, or a right arrow. If Emily steps at one arrow at a time, how many ways can Emily step on four arrows such that she doesn't step on all four types of arrows?

11. Justin currently has 12 points, while his opponent has 18 points. A deck of cards has three cards worth 5 points, four cards worth 7 points, four cards worth 9 points, and thirteen cards worth 10 points. Justin draws a card from the deck at random and adds the number of points to his score. What is the probability that Justin has more points than his opponent and does not get over 21 points? Express your answer as a common fraction.

12. Let $P(x)$ be a quadratic. If the sum of the coefficients of $P(x)$ is 20, the sum of the coefficients of $P(-x)$ is 4, and the sum of the roots of $P(x)$ is 2, what is the product of the roots of $P(x)$?

13. Evaluate: $20 \div 22$. Express your answer as a decimal to the nearest hundredth.

14. Collin is getting a collection of stamps from Hawaii, where he can either get it in packs of 6 or packs of 8. What is the greatest even number of stamps that Collin cannot get by getting some number of each pack?

15. A cube has the volume of 216. What is its total surface area?

16. What is the slope of a line perpendicular to the line given by the equation $3x + 4y = 5$? Express your answer as a common fraction.

17. Cindy has a hamster wheel that is a circle with a diameter of one foot. Given that 1 foot equals 12 inches, how many inches is the circumference of Cindy's hamster wheel? Express your answer in terms of π.

18. What is the only real value that the function $f(x) = \frac{x^2+8x+12}{x+2}$ cannot attain?

19. In a geometric sequence of positive numbers, the sum of the first and third terms is 25% greater than the sum of the second and fourth terms. What is the common ratio of the sequence? Express your answer as a common fraction.

20. Compute: $\frac{1.2}{1.5} + \frac{4.8}{1.5}$.

21. Three positive whole numbers are in the ratio $2 : 3 : 8$. If the difference between the largest number and the smallest number is 2022, then what is the value of the middle number?

22. Recall that in Pascal's triangle, the value of a number is the sum of the number above it just to the left and the number above it just to the right. The first few rows of Pascal's triangle are shown below, and the top row is row 0. How many even numbers are in Row 7?

Row 0				1		
Row 1			1		1	
Row 2		1		2		1
Row 3	1		3		3		1
Row 4	1	4		6		4	1
Row 5	1	5	10		10	5	1

23. Calculate the volume of a right circular cylinder with base area 20π and height 22. Express your answer in terms of π.

24. Find the distance between $(13, 5)$ and $(-3, 10)$. Express your answer in simplest radical form.

25. Compute: $-475 - (-515)$.

26. Two fair six-sided dice are thrown. What is the probability that at least one of them lands on a 3 or a 4? Express your answer as a common fraction.

27. How many positive whole numbers less than 50 are divisible by 3?

28. If $\sqrt{9 + 4\sqrt{5}} = a + \sqrt{b}$, where a and b are whole numbers, what is $a + b$?

29. How many integers x satisfy $|2x + 5| \leq 25$?

30. A rectangle is cut by three vertical lines and four horizontal lines. How many rectangles can be formed so that all of their sides are on the lines or the sides of the rectangle (including the original rectangle)?

31. Emma travels to a dock this week wtih 20 flags, each in a shape of a polygon with at most four sides. She observes that 14 flags are triangles, 8 flags are not regular polygons, and 4 flags are squares. How many flags are equilateral triangles?

32. The figure below is made up of some number of regular hexagons. The perimeter of each regular hexagon is 24. What is the area of the figure? Express your answer in simplest radical form.

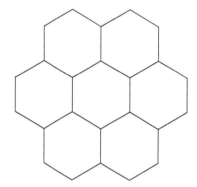

33. What is the sum of all positive whole numbers less than 22 that are divisible by either 2 or 3, but not both?

34. In how many ways can the numbers $1, 2, 3, 4, 5, 6$ be ordered such that the even numbers are increasing from left to right, and the odd numbers are decreasing from left to right?

35. At a bookstore, each magazine costs the same amount and each newspaper costs the same amount. Two magazines and a newspaper cost $51, while one magazine and two newspapers costs $30. Ashley has $30 and buys a magazine and a newspaper. How many dollars does Ashley have left?

36. One of the angles in a triangle measures $22°$. What is the average of the degree measures of the other two angles?

37. Each of the digits 1, 4, 2, and 7 are used exactly once to create an odd 4-digit number. What is the least possible value of this number?

38. What is the fifth positive triangular number?

39. The race track near the coconut mall is 720 meters per lap. Jonathan goes three laps around the course, where his go-kart travels at 10 meters per second in the first two laps and at 12 meters per second in the final lap. How many meters per second is Jonathan's average speed in all three laps? Express your answer as a common fraction.

40. In square $ABCD$, points E and F are drawn outside of the square such that $\triangle BCE$ and $\triangle ADF$ are equilateral. Find the number of lines of symmetry of hexagon $ABECDF$.

41. A hexagon is formed by placing two equilateral triangles with side length 6 on opposite sides of a square with side length 6. What is the area of this hexagon? Express your answer in simplest radical form.

42. Kaylee models the distance a watermelon falls with the formula $d = 4.9t^2$, where t is the number of seconds in free fall while d is the distance in meters the watermelon falls. Kaylee drops a watermelon at a height of 21 meters off the ground. At most how many whole number of seconds elapsed before the watermelon hits the ground?

43. Dawsen needs to correctly sort 16 words into 4 distinct groups with the same number of words. He has already correctly made 2 groups, and he finds 2 more words that could be in the third group. If Dawsen picks 2 of the remaining words at random, what is the probability that both these words are also in the third group? Express your answer as a common fraction.

44. What is the mean of the first n even numbers? Express your answer in terms of n.

45. How many trailing zeroes does 102! have?

46. For a legendary league, Elli needs to select his load, where he picks a master rune, two different spells, and a costume from 25 master runes, 12 spells, and 10 costumes. How many ways can Elli select his load?

47. A square has an area of 25. What is the smallest whole number greater than the length of the diagonal of that square?

48. A point lies within the unit circle. What is the probability that it is closer to the circumference of the circle than it is to the center of the circle? Express your answer as a common fraction.

49. Aidan and Brandon plan on swimming four laps where each lap is 75 feet. Aidan swims at 3 feet per second while Brandon swims at 2.5 feet per second. Brandon plans on getting a head start such that they both finish their four laps at the same time. How many seconds should Brandon's head start be?

50. What is the 100th smallest non-negative even whole number?

51. The radius of circle A is 30% of the radius of circle B. The area of circle A is what percent of the area of circle B?

52. What is the surface area in square centimeters of a rectangular prism with orthogonal side lengths of 4 centimeters, 4 centimeters, and 10 centimeters?

53. What is the remainder when 106312 is divided by 8?

54. What is the sum of the tens and units digits of $202 \times 303 \times 404$?

55. The side lengths of a rectangle are all whole numbers. If the perimeter of the rectangle is 14, what is the largest possible value of the area of the rectangle?

56. If $f(x) = 7x + 9$, then what is $f(11)$?

57. The number 22 is 8% of what number?

58. How many 2×2 inch tiles can completely fit inside of a 20×22 inch area, without cutting or overlapping any of the tiles?

59. Three times a number plus 7 is equal to seven times that number minus 9. What is that number?

60. Simplify: $\frac{3}{7} \times 16 - \frac{3}{7} \times 2$.

61. Joy subscribes to the Ether Salamander phone plan, which charges a \$26/month flat rate plus \$0.50 per phone call. Joy allocates \$50 for phone calls with friends this month. How many phone calls could Joy do at most to stay within budget?

62. Two interior angles of a convex quadrilateral measure $21°$, and one of the remaining two interior angles has a measure $12°$ greater than the measure of the other. How many degrees is the measure of the largest interior angle of the quadrilateral?

63. Evaluate: 44×46.

64. Express as a decimal: $4 \times 200 + 22 \times 1 + \frac{12}{20}$.

65. Find the area of a square with side length 17.

66. After cooking in the wild, Esther recorded the number of hearts restored after eating each of the three foods one time in the bar graph below. She found that if she eats the same food twice, the number of hearts restored is always a whole number. How many hearts would Esther restore after eating each food one time? Express your answer as a mixed number.

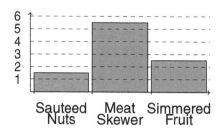

67. What is the range of the set $\{17, 29, 93, 49, 2, 48, 9, 47, 20, 18\}$?

68. Phoenix flies an RC plane away from him at a constant rate. The plane is 2.5 meters away from Phoenix after a total of 50 seconds of flying and 3 meters away from Phoenix after a total of 55 seconds of flying. How many meters away is the plane from Phoenix after a total of one minute of flying? Express your answer as a decimal without trailing zeroes.

69. Round to the nearest hundredth: 1913.271

70. What whole number is closest to the value of 4.51×8.02?

71. Riley plans to rotate a side of Rubik's cube repeatedly that currently has the top side of that part as blue such that in the rotations, the top side of that part cycles to red, then green, then orange, and then back to blue. How many times does Riley need to rotate that side such that the top side becomes orange for the 15th time?

72. Two fair coins are flipped. What is the probability that at least one coin shows tails? Express your answer as a decimal to the nearest hundredth.

73. A right triangle has side lengths that are positive whole numbers. The shortest side of the triangle has length 8. What is the area of the triangle?

74. Katelyn is painting a smaller rectangular painting on a rectangular canvas that is 18 inches by 24 inches. Her smaller painting is a rectangle with side length 5 inches by 6 inches. How many square inches of the canvas is not taken up by the smaller painting?

75. How many four-digit positive whole numbers less than 2022 have digits that sum to two?

76. How many times does $\frac{1}{22}$ go into $\frac{1}{12}$? Express your answer as a common fraction.

77. In order to earn her black belt, Sara needs to train for 12 weeks with each week having 2 classes. Sara just finished a third of her classes. How many classes does Sara have left to go before she can earn her black belt?

78. Evaluate: $4^1 + 3^2 + 2^3 + 1^4$.

79. Suppose that $x^2 + 8y = 11z$. If $x = 10$ and $z = 12$, what is y?

80. What is the product of the GCD and the LCM of 50 and 55?

Answers
12313

Sprint Round

1. 9	11. 12	21. 18
2. 12.6	12. $\frac{1520}{39}$	22. 46
3. 270	13. 7025	23. 7
4. $2\frac{1}{4}$	14. 0	24. 12
5. 6	15. 0	25. $\frac{5}{16}$
6. 64	16. 41	26. 18
7. 10	17. 5	27. 256
8. 23	18. 35	28. $\frac{115}{16}$
9. $\frac{1}{3}$	19. $\frac{25}{12}$	29. 3
10. 35	20. 72	30. 21

Target Round

1. 25
2. 4
3. 9
4. 118
5. 24
6. 79461
7. 168
8. 81

Team Round

1. 0.255
2. 99
3. 16
4. 14
5. 42
6. 528
7. 15
8. 104
9. 56
10. 252

Countdown

1. $\frac{31}{64}$	21. 1011	41. $36 + 18\sqrt{3}$	61. 48
2. 12	22. 0	42. 2	62. 165
3. $\frac{1}{4}$	23. 440π	43. $\frac{1}{15}$	63. 2024
4. 4	24. $\sqrt{281}$	44. $n+1$	64. 822.6
5. 75π	25. 40	45. 24	65. 289
6. 21	26. $\frac{5}{9}$	46. 16500	66. $9\frac{1}{2}$
7. 211	27. 16	47. 8	67. 91
8. 97	28. 7	48. $\frac{3}{4}$	68. 3.5
9. 40	29. 26	49. 20	69. 1913.27
10. 232	30. 150	50. 198	70. 36
11. $\frac{1}{3}$	31. 8	51. 9	71. 59
12. -4	32. $168\sqrt{3}$	52. 192	72. 0.75
13. 0.91	33. 122	53. 0	73. 60
14. 10	34. 20	54. 6	74. 402
15. 216	35. 3	55. 12	75. 4
16. $\frac{4}{3}$	36. 79	56. 86	76. $\frac{11}{6}$
17. 12π	37. 1247	57. 275	77. 16
18. 4	38. 15	58. 110	78. 22
19. $\frac{4}{5}$	39. $\frac{180}{17}$	59. 4	79. 4
20. 4	40. 2	60. 6	80. 2750

Sprint Round Solutions

1. Eric's pack has a total of $4 \cdot 5 = 20$ water bottles. Because 11 of them are used by the players, the water bottle back has $20 - 11 = \boxed{9}$ water bottles remaining.

2. Carter walked $2.4 + 3.9 = 6.3$ kilometers to get from his apartment to the museum. Since he took the same route home, Carter walked a total of $6.3 + 6.3 = \boxed{12.6}$ kilometers.

3. Since there are six faces in a cube, and all of its faces are squares with the same area, the answer is $6 \cdot 45 = \boxed{270}$.

4. Juliet needs to make $8 + 2 \cdot 2 = 12$ servings of pancakes. We can then set up a proportion and let x be the number of cups of flour. Our proportion is $\frac{x}{12} = \frac{1\frac{1}{2}}{8}$, and so $x = \frac{12}{8} \cdot \frac{3}{2} = \frac{9}{4}$. Converting $\frac{9}{4}$ to a mixed number results in $\boxed{2\frac{1}{4}}$.

5. After the letter M gets placed, there are 3 remaining squares for where the A can get placed. Then, there will be 2 remaining squares for where the T can get placed, and finally, there will be 1 remaining square for where the H can get placed. Thus, the answer is $3 \cdot 2 \cdot 1 = \boxed{6}$.

6. The length of the radius was originally 10 since $10^2 \cdot \pi = 100\pi$. When the length of its diameter decreases by 4, the length of its radius decreases by 2. Then, the radius will become 8, so the area will become $8^2 \cdot \pi = 64\pi$, so $a = \boxed{64}$.

7. Since we are considering empty seats, we need to consider remainders. There are a total of 40 pairs of people in line, and in each session, at most 7 pairs, or 14 people, can be on the merry-go-round. Since each person in line goes in pairs, Sarah will have one empty seat each time 14 people are on the merry-go-round. This happens 5 times, and on the sixth time, the remaining 10 people go on the merry-go-round, leaving 5 empty seats. This means that across all her sessions with people, there are $\boxed{10}$ empty seats.

8. If the number 3 appears exactly two times, then the number 4 appears at least three times, so it can appear 3, 4, 5, or 6 times. Since we want to minimize the average of the eight numbers, we must minimize the number of times the number 4 appears, so we let it appear 3 times. Then, we want to maximize the number of times the number 1 appears, while still having more 2s than 1s. This is accomplished by having one 1 and two 2s. This gives us a sum of $1 \cdot 1 + 2 \cdot 2 + 3 \cdot 2 + 4 \cdot 3 = \boxed{23}$.

9. Suppose there are t total marbles in the bag, so that $\frac{3t}{5}$ are red and $\frac{2t}{5}$ are blue. Then, $\frac{t}{5}$ marbles must be removed, or $\boxed{\dfrac{1}{3}}$ of the red marbles.

10. Since the relation between the snowfall and the day number is linear, we can find that on the nth day of the blizzard, exactly $n + 1$ centimeters of snow fall on the ground. During the blizzard, the number of centimeters of snow that accumulate is $2 + 3 + \cdots + 8 = 35$ (use the triangular sum formula if necessary). But 7 of these centimeteres have already been removed; thus, it will take 28 more days on top of the 7 blizzard days, which is a total of $\boxed{35}$ days.

11. We can approach by using casework based on the largest coin or banknote used. Megan can either use a 10-rupee coin or a 10-rupee banknote, resulting in 2 possibilities. Otherwise, she can use two, one, or zero 5-rupee coins. There is 1 possibility when using two 5-rupee coins. However, when using one 5-rupee coin, she can either use two, one, or zero 2-rupee coins and cover the rest with 1-rupee coins, for a total of 3 possibilities. Finally, when using zero 5-rupee coins, she can either use five, four, three, two, one, or zero 2-rupee coins and cover the rest with 1-rupee coins, for a total of 6 possibiliites. In summary, there are $2 + 1 + 3 + 6 = \boxed{12}$ possibilities.

12. Let t and j denote Tamsin's and Joanie's heights in 2017, respectively. Then, we have that $t = \frac{19}{20}j$ and $j + 15 = \frac{19}{20}(t + 20) = \frac{19}{20}t + 19$, so $j = \frac{361}{400}j + 4$ and $j = \frac{1600}{39}$. Then, $t = \boxed{\dfrac{1520}{39}}$.

13. We could determine the coordinates of the vertices of $A'B'C'$, but it is easier to note that rotations preserve distances. This means that we only need to compare the distances from each of the vertices of triangle ABC to the origin. By applying the Distance Formula, we can see that the distance from A to the origin is $\sqrt{25^2 + 80^2} = \sqrt{7025}$, and the distance from B to the origin is $\sqrt{30^2 + 70^2} = \sqrt{5800}$. As the square of the distance from C to the origin is $82^2 = 6724$, the square of the furthest distance from a vertex of $A'B'C'$ to the origin is $\boxed{7025}$.

14. Let a, b, c, d, e, f be the first six terms of the arithmetic sequence, in that order. Note that $a + b + c = 3b$ and $d + e + f = 3e$, so $b = 4e$. Then, the common difference of the sequence is $\frac{e - b}{3} = -e$. Thus, we have that f, or the sixth term, is equal to $e - e = \boxed{0}$.

15. Let $a = \frac{x}{y}$, so that $a + \frac{1}{a} = 2$, or $a^2 - 2a + 1 = 0$. As $a^2 - 2a + 1 = (a - 1)^2$, it follows that $a = 1$ is the only solution, or $x = y$. Then, $|x - y| = \boxed{0}$.

16. There are two cases: in June, the first Tuesday comes before the first Thursday, or the first Thursday comes before the first Tuesday. Suppose the first Tuesday of June came on day x. If the first Tuesday came before the first Thursday, then the first Thursday came on day $x + 2$ which means the fourth Thursday came on day $x + 23$. There are then $(x + 23) - x + 1 = 24$ days on which he tried the level. If the first Thursday comes before the first Tuesday, then the first Thursday came on day $x - 5$ which means the fourth Thursday came on day $x + 16$. There are then $(x + 16) - x + 1 = 17$ days on which he tried the level so the answer is $24 + 17 = \boxed{41}$.

17. Both of these divisors must be odd, so we start from $3 \cdot 5$, and list out $5 \cdot 7$, $11 \cdot 13$, $17 \cdot 19$, and $29 \cdot 31$, since we certainly want the lower factor to be less than $\sqrt{1000} \approx 31$. This gives $\boxed{5}$ such numbers under 1000.

18. Any number that satisfies the conditions in the problem has 10 digits in binary, and the first digit must be 1 and the last two digits must be 0 (because the five powers of 2 have to be at least 4). Among the seven digits that can be either 1 or 0, exactly four must be 0. There are then $\binom{7}{4} = \boxed{35}$ such whole numbers.

19. The greatest possible time difference between any two places in the world is $14 - (-12) = 26$ hours. Since $26 > 24$, the Baker Islands and Kiribati are guaranteed to always have different dates, so the number of distinct dates is at least 2. However, there is a two-hour window between $10:00$ p.m. and $12:00$ a.m. in the Baker Islands when the Baker Islands are two calendar days behind Kiribati, and in some other location, for instance Ghana, it is the day in between. The probability that there are three simultaneous dates is then $\frac{2}{24}$, and with a minimum of two simultaneous dates at all times, the expected number of distinct dates around the world is $3 \cdot \frac{2}{24} + 2 \cdot \frac{22}{24} = \boxed{\dfrac{25}{12}}$.

20. Note that a triangle with side lengths $2\sqrt{3}$, $2\sqrt{3}$, and 6 is exactly one third of an equilateral triangle with side length 6. Thus, if we attach 3 of these triangles together, then we will get an equilateral triangle with side length 6. Then, it remains to find how many equilateral triangles with side length 6 can fit in a regular hexagon with side length 12. Note that the regular hexagon is composed of 6 equilateral triangles with side length 12, and each equilateral triangle with side length 12 is composed of 4 equilateral triangles with side length 6. Thus, the answer is $6 \cdot 4 \cdot 3 = \boxed{72}$.

21. If *EVER* occupies the first four spots, then the E, S, and T can be arranged in any of 6 ways. Let X, Y, and Z be placeholder letters for the E, S, and T, which are not used in the word *EVER*. If we have *XEVERYZ*, then the E cannot go in the first slot, but positions are otherwise unrestricted, giving 4 arrangements. If we have *XYEVERZ*, then the same holds, giving 4 arrangements, and if we have *XYZEVER*, then we once again have 4 arrangements. This yields a total of $\boxed{18}$ arrangements.

22. We can rewrite the expression as $\left(\frac{2}{5}\right)^{20} \cdot \left(\frac{3}{8}\right)^{22} = \frac{3^{22}}{2^{46} \cdot 5^{20}}$. Note that the number of digits to the right of the decimal point excluding trailing zeroes is the exponent of the smallest power of 10 that we can multiply to the expression to result in a whole number. Looking at $2^{46} \cdot 5^{20}$, we see that $46 > 20$, so if we multiply the expression by 10^{46}, then the result will be a whole number. Thus, the answer is $\boxed{46}$.

23. Let the radius of the circle be r. Then, we have that $BQ = 2r$ and $PC = 2r$. Since the circle is tangent to side $\overline{AC}$, we know that the perpendicular from P to side $\overline{AC}$ with foot R has length r. This means that $\angle ACB = 30°$ by 30-60-90 properties. We are also given that $AB = 3$ and $\frac{PC}{BC} = \frac{2}{3}$, so by similar triangles, $BC = 6$ and $r = 2$. Finally, by 30-60-90 properties, we have that $AC = 3\sqrt{3}$, so $AR = \sqrt{3}$. Finally, by the Pythagorean Theorem, $AP^2 = \boxed{7}$.

24. Without loss of generality, let $a > b$ and denote $a - b$ by x. Then, we can factor $a^3 - b^3$ as $(a - b)(a^2 + ab + b^2) = 2022$ so $a^2 + ab + b^2 = \frac{2022}{x}$. Note that $a^2 + ab + b^2 = x^2 + 3ab$ so $ab = \frac{1}{3} \cdot \left(\frac{2022}{x} - x^2\right)$. Since a and b are positive but don't have to be integers, the only restriction on x is that $ab > 0$ since we can keep lowering a and b to satisfy the product. Therefore, we only need $\frac{2022}{x} - x^2 > 0$ or $2022 > x^3$ which means x can be from 1 to 12 inclusive. We can then find $(a + b)^2 = (a - b)^2 + 4ab$ and since $a + b$ must be the positive square root, each x yields exactly one possible $a + b$ meaning the number of possible values of $(a + b)$ is $\boxed{12}$.

25. Since Tina can only earn one or two points each turn, she must have either 4 or 5 points immediately after the turn in which she first earns at least 4 points. Note that the only way to reach 5 points without reaching 4 points is if Tina eventually has 3 points and then earns two more points with a $\frac{1}{2}$ probability. We can end up with 3 points with three 1-point turns or one 1-point turn and one 2-point turn in either order, giving a $\frac{1}{8} + 2 \cdot \frac{1}{4} = \frac{5}{8}$ probability of eventually having 3 points. Then, there is a $\frac{1}{2}$ chance of going from 3 points to 5 points, so our probability is $\frac{5}{8} \cdot \frac{1}{2} = \boxed{\dfrac{5}{16}}$.

26. Note that in general, we can draw six lines, as there are three midpoints, and there are two different directions in which the lines can be tangent to the circle. Thus, if there are fewer than five lines, then at least two of the lines must connect a midpoint to another midpoint. Suppose that one line connects A and B, and the other line connects B and C. Then, the circle must be tangent to both of these lines. Draw the line connecting A and C for reference. We now have three cases: the circle does not touch this line, the circle is tangent to this line, and the circle intersects this line at two points. We can draw diagrams to find n for each case. For the first case, we see that $n = 8$. Next, for the second case, we see that $n = 4$. Finally, for the third case, we see that $n = 6$. Thus, the answer is $4 + 6 + 8 = \boxed{18}$.

27. Note that $144 = 2^4 \cdot 3^2$, so the only possible prime factors of either greatest common divisor are 2 and 3. Next, note that if a number whose only prime factor is 2 and another number whose only prime factor is 3 are in the same subset, then their greatest common divisor would be 1, regardless of what other numbers are in the subset. Thus, we must have one subset contain all the powers of 2 and the other subset contain all the powers of 3. Then, we are left with the numbers whose prime factors are 2 and 3. In order for such a number to be a divisor of 144, we must have the exponent of 2 be between 1 and 4, inclusive, and we must have the exponent of 3 be between 1 and 2, inclusive. This gives us 8 total numbers. For each number, there are two choices for which subset it can go into. Thus, the answer is $2^8 = \boxed{256}$.

28. We approach by considering the face that gets rolled first.

   - With probability $\frac{1}{4}$, the face with one dot will have its dot removed. From there, with probability $\frac{9}{16}$, we never roll the dot-less face, with probability $\frac{3}{8}$, we roll it once, and there will only be two dots removed, and with probability $\frac{1}{16}$, we will roll it twice and there will only be one dot removed.
   - With probability $\frac{1}{4}$, we remove one dot from the face with two dots and end up with a die with faces with 1, 1, 3, and 4 dots. With probability $\frac{1}{2}$, we turn the face with one dot into a dot-less face, from which the expected number of dots removed will be $2 \cdot \frac{3}{4}$.
   - With probability $\frac{1}{2}$, on the other hand, the expected number of dots removed will be 3, since no third roll can come up with a dot-less face. If the face with three of four dots is rolled at first, with probability $\frac{1}{4}$, then the expected number of dots removed will be $2 \cdot \frac{3}{4}$, and with probability $\frac{3}{4}$, the expected number of dots removed will be 3.

   As such, the total expected number of dots removed is $\frac{1}{4}\left(3 \cdot \frac{9}{16} + 2 \cdot \frac{3}{8} + 1 \cdot \frac{1}{16}\right) + \frac{1}{4}\left(\frac{1}{2} \cdot \frac{11}{4} + \frac{1}{2} \cdot 3\right) + \frac{1}{2}\left(\frac{1}{4} \cdot \frac{11}{4} + \frac{3}{4} \cdot 3\right) = \frac{45}{16}$. Then, the expected number of dots remaining is $10 - \frac{45}{16} = \boxed{\dfrac{115}{16}}$.

29. Subtracting x from both sides and squaring gives $5 - x^2 = n^2 - 2nx + x^2$, or $2x^2 - 2nx + (n^2 - 5) = 0$. Then, the solutions x are $x = \frac{2n \pm \sqrt{40 - 4n^2}}{4} = \frac{n \pm \sqrt{10 - n^2}}{2}$. We note that neither of these can be outside the interval $[-\sqrt{5}, \sqrt{5}]$, so, in particular, $n + \sqrt{10 - n^2} < 2\sqrt{5}$. This is only possible if $n = 3$ because if $n = 2$, we get $\frac{2 + \sqrt{6}}{2} > \sqrt{5}$. This is true because $\sqrt{6} > 2\sqrt{5} - 2$, as can be seen from squaring both sides to obtain $6 > 24 - 8\sqrt{5}$, or $8\sqrt{5} < 18$. Square once more to get that $320 < 324$, a true statement. Also, for $-2 \leq n \leq 1$, plugging in the positive value of x does not work, so $n = \boxed{3}$ is indeed unique.

30. Call each of the $10 \cdot 3 = 30$ colors associated with a student a student-color tie. Let each color have 1 student-color tie to start. Since there are 24 total colors, we have $30 - 24 = 6$ remaining student-color ties. Let $\{a_n\}$ be a sequence of positive whole numbers, where $a_1 + a_2 + \cdots + a_n = 6$. We optimally let any two students have at most one common favorite color, and for each color where we need to add additional student-color ties, we optimally have the a_k additional student-color ties be all associated with different students. Then, for each favorite color that is shared by more than one student, a_k is how many more students than 1 have that favorite color. For every color that $a_k + 1$ students have as their favorite, $\binom{a_k + 1}{2}$ is how many handshakes are held between every possible pair of students. Then, the approach is to find a sequence a_n that maximizes the sum $\binom{a_1 + 1}{2} + \binom{a_2 + 1}{2} + \cdots + \binom{a_n + 1}{2}$. By inspection, this sum is maximized by letting $n = 1$ and $a_n = 6$. Thus, we have that the maximum number of handshakes is $\binom{7}{2} = \boxed{21}$.

Target Round Solutions

1. We can identify the coordinates of the four other islands as $(11, 9)$, $(11, 19)$, $(6, 14)$, and $(16, 14)$. We can then mark the center to find that $(11, 14)$ satisfies the condition, and the sum of the coordinates is $\boxed{25}$.

2. Let our fractions be $\frac{a}{6}$ and $\frac{b}{10}$. Then, their product is equal to $\frac{ab}{60}$. Since the fractions are common fractions, we have that $\gcd(a, 6) = 1$ and $\gcd(b, 10) = 1$. Thus, we only have $a = 1, 5$ and $b = 1, 3, 7, 9$ as possibilities. Since 60 only contains prime factors of 2, 3, and 5, we should let $a = 5$ and $b = 3$ (or 9) in order for the denominator to be less than 60 and minimized. Then, the denominator of the product will be $\frac{60}{3 \cdot 5} = \boxed{4}$.

3. Expanding $(5x^4 + 4x^2)(3x + 2)$ gives us $15x^5 + 10x^4 + 12x^3 + 8x^2$. Thus, our answer is $15 - 10 + 12 - 8 = \boxed{9}$.

4. The square that Anna writes the number 380 in will be in the 18th row from the top, since $374 = 17 \cdot 22 < 380 \le 18 \cdot 22 = 396$, and it will be the sixth square from the left in that row. Thus, the number that Beth writes will be equal to $5 \cdot 20 + 18 = \boxed{118}$.

5. Note that since the reflex angle at D is $270°$, the exterior angle is $90°$. Thus, we have that $\triangle ACD$ has right angle $\angle ADC$. By the Pythagorean Theorem, we get that $AC = 5$. This means that $\triangle ABC$ is a $5 - 12 - 13$ triangle, so it has a right angle at $\angle BAC$. Finally, the area of $ABCD$ is the area of $\triangle ABC$ minus the area of $\triangle ACD$. By the base-height area formula, this is $\frac{1}{2} \cdot 5 \cdot 12 - \frac{1}{2} \cdot 3 \cdot 4 = \boxed{24}$.

6. The number cannot contain more than two zeroes. If it contains exactly two zeroes, then they must be the thousands digit and the tens digit. The other three digits can be any of the digits from 1 to 9, giving $9^3 = 729$ numbers in total for this case. If the number contains exactly one zero, then we have three choices for its placement (thousands digit, hundreds digit, tens digit), and we have $9^4 = 6561$ choices for the other digits, giving another $3 \cdot 6561 = 19683$ numbers. Finally, if the number does not contain any zeros, then we have $9^5 = 59049$ possible numbers. This gives a total of $729 + 19683 + 59049 = \boxed{79461}$ five-digit positive whole numbers with the specified property.

7. We can do casework where we treat the ruby and sapphire as a 1×2 or 2×1 unit. There are a total of 7 ways to place the units, and for each unit placement, there are 2 ways to arrange the ruby and sapphire and $4 \cdot 3 = 12$ ways to arrange the amethyst and pearl. Thus, there are a total of $7 \cdot 2 \cdot 12 = \boxed{168}$ ways to put the crystal gems in the box.

8. Rearranging the equation, we get $\sqrt{mn} - \sqrt{m} + \sqrt{n} = 5$. Subtracting one from both sides and using Simon's Favorite Factoring Trick, we get $(\sqrt{m} + 1)(\sqrt{n} - 1) = 4$. Note that since the right hand side is a whole number, we need $\sqrt{m} + 1$ and $\sqrt{n} - 1$ to either be whole numbers or radical conjugates. If they are both whole numbers, then since $\sqrt{m} > 0$, we have that $\sqrt{m} + 1 > 1$, so the smallest whole number that $\sqrt{m} + 1$ can be is 2. Then, we have 2 and 4 as possibilities for $\sqrt{m} + 1$, giving us $m = 1, 9$ as possibilities. The corresponding values for $\sqrt{n} - 1$ are 2 and 1, respectively, giving us $n = 9, 4$ as possibilities. If they are radical conjugates, then $m = n$, so we have $(\sqrt{m} + 1)(\sqrt{n} - 1) = 4$, which becomes $m - 1 = 4$, or $m = 5$. Thus, we have that $(m, n) = (5, 5)$. From the ordered pairs $(1, 9)$, $(9, 4)$, and $(5, 5)$, we obtain values for $3m + 2n$ of 21, 35, and 25, respectively, for a sum of $21 + 35 + 25 = \boxed{81}$.

Team Round Solutions

1. The 4th place finisher finished in $34.391 + 0.137 = 34.528$ seconds. The difference in time between the 1st place finisher and the 4th place finisher is $34.528 - 34.273 = \boxed{0.255}$ seconds.

2. The worst-case scenario is when every single seat that is not the middle seat is occupied. There are a total of $25 \cdot 2 \cdot 2 = 100$ seats that are not middle seats, so if all of them are occupied, Tanya has to sit in a middle seat. This means that if there are only $\boxed{99}$ passengers already on the plane, then there would be at least one seat that is not a middle seat that Tanya could sit in.

3. Finn will take 90 seconds to climb every 5 flights of stairs, whereas taking the elevator only takes 50 seconds. We can thus solve the linear equation $120 + 50x = 90x$, where x is the number of multiples of 5 that evenly go into the number of floors that Finn must travel. This yields $x = 3$, so Finn takes an equal amount of time to go 15 floors up on the stairs and the elevator. However, 16 floors up, the elevator begins to have the advantage, as it only takes 10 more seconds to reach the sixteenth floor, whereas Finn takes an additional 15 seconds to reach the sixteenth floor. Thus, Finn's apartment should be at least $\boxed{16}$ floors above the lobby.

4. Plot point E such that $ABDE$ is a rectangle. Note that $AE^2 = BD^2 = 13^2 - 3^2 = 160$ by the Pythagorean Theorem. Since $\angle AEC = 90°$, $AC^2 = AE^2 + EC^2 = AE^2 + (2 \cdot CD)^2 = 160 + 36 = 196$. Thus, $AC = \sqrt{196}$, or $\boxed{14}$.

5. Such a substring must begin and end with C. The C's must be 1 or 2 apart, since if they are 3 or 4 apart, then there would need to be 2 of the same letter between them, which is not possible. If they are 1 apart, then we have 4 ways to place them and 6 ways to arrange the H, E, and K. If they are 2 apart, then we have 3 ways to place them and 6 ways to arrange the H, E, and K, so there are $4 \cdot 6 + 3 \cdot 6 = \boxed{42}$ arrangements of $CHECK$ with a palindromic substring.

6. Rewrite the equation as $f((x-1)^2) = (x^2-1)^2$. Then, $(x-1)^2 = 36$, but since x must be negative, we have $x = -5$. Then, $f(36) = 24^2$. Then, if we want to plug 24^2 into f, we must have that $(x-1)^2 = 24^2$, and since x must be negative, we have $x = -23$. Then, $f(576) = 528^2$, the square root of which is $\boxed{528}$.

7. The diagonal passes through $m+n-\gcd(m,n)$ of the interiors of the squares. First note that $\gcd(m,n)$ must be a factor of $m+n$, as if both m and n are multiples of $\gcd(m,n)$ (by definition), then so is $m+n$. If $\gcd(m,n) = 1$, then $m+n = 11$, giving 10 distinct ordered pairs (m,n) ranging from $(1,10)$ to $(10,1)$. If $\gcd(m,n) = 2$, then $m+n = 12$ and $(m,n) = (2,10),(10,2)$. If $\gcd(m,n) = 5$, $m+n = 15$ and $(m,n) = (5,10),(10,5)$. Finally, $\gcd(m,n) = 10$ and $m+n = 20$ gives the single pair $(m,n) = (10,10)$. There are $\boxed{15}$ ordered pairs (m,n) in total.

8. Since the distance from building A to building E is $\frac{1}{2}$ mile, Carawyn can make the trip in 3.75 minutes without any stops. If she does not get the coffee, she can rest for a total of up to 6 minutes. By sticks-and-stones, there are $\binom{6+3-1}{3-1} = \binom{8}{2}$ ways for her to make stops that sum to 6 minutes, $\binom{7}{2}$ ways for her to stop a total of 5 minutes, and so forth, until $\binom{2}{2} = 1$ way for her to not stop at all. By the hockey stick identity, she has $\binom{9}{3} = 84$ possible ways to rest for up to 6 minutes. On the other hand, should she decide to grab a coffee, she can only rest for a total of up to 3 minutes. This gives her an additional $\binom{5}{2} + \binom{4}{2} + \binom{3}{2} + \binom{2}{2} = \binom{6}{3} = 20$ ways to make the rests. Altogether, she has $84 + 20 = \boxed{104}$ possible ways to make the walk without running late.

9. Extend $\overline{BO}$ past B to a point C such that $CO = 16$. Then, we have that $\overline{AB}$ is a median of $\triangle AOC$, and P is the centroid, or the intersection of the medians of $\triangle AOC$. Then, since $AO = CO$, we have that $\overline{OP} \perp \overline{AC}$. Let lines OP and AC intersect at a point Q. By properties of the centroid, we find that $\frac{OP}{PQ} = 2$, so $PQ = 4$, and so $OQ = 12$. By the Pythagorean Theorem, we have that $AQ = \sqrt{AO^2 - OQ^2}$, or $AQ = 4\sqrt{7}$. Then, by the Pythagorean Theorem again, we have that $AP = \sqrt{PQ^2 + AQ^2}$, or $AP = 8\sqrt{2}$. By properties of the centroid, we find that $BP = 4\sqrt{2}$. Finally, since the circle is tangent to $\overline{AB}$, we must have that the foot of the perpendicular from O to $\overline{AB}$, which we will call X, is such that OX is the radius of the circle. Since $BO = OP$, we have that X is the midpoint of $\overline{BP}$. Thus, by the Pythagorean Theorem, the radius of the circle is $\sqrt{OP^2 - PX^2} = 2\sqrt{14}$, the square of which is $\boxed{56}$.

10. Note that if $p = 2$, then $2p+1$ is a prime, while $4p+1$ is composite, and if $p = 3$, then both $2p+1$ and $4p+1$ are primes. If $p > 3$, then p can only be 1 or 5 modulo 6. If p is 1 modulo 6, then $2p+1$ is divisible by 3, and $4p+1$ is 5 modulo 6. If p is 5 modulo 6, then $2p+1$ is 5 modulo 6, and $4p+1$ is divisible by 3. We are now looking for odd multiples of 3 less than 140, which we will call n, such that either both $\frac{n-1}{2}$ and $2n-1$ or both $\frac{n-1}{4}$ and $\frac{n+1}{2}$ are prime. Testing $n = 135$, we see that both $\frac{n-1}{2} = 67$ and $2n-1 = 269$ are prime. Testing $n = 129$, we see that $\frac{n-1}{2} = 64$ and $\frac{n+1}{2} = 65$ are not prime. Testing $n = 123$, we see that $2n-1 = 245$ and $\frac{n+1}{2} = 62$ are not prime. Testing $n = 117$, we see that both $\frac{n-1}{4} = 29$ and $\frac{n+1}{2} = 59$ are prime. Since 117 and 135 both satisfy the conditions, we may finish testing values of n. Thus, the answer is $117 + 135 = \boxed{252}$.

Sprint Round
12314

Place ID Sticker
Inside This Box

Name _____

Grade _____

School _____

1.	2.	3.	4.	5.
6.	7.	8.	9.	10.
11.	12.	13.	14.	15.
16.	17.	18.	19.	20.
21.	22.	23.	24.	25.
26.	27.	28.	29.	30.

1. Nayeli wants to buy three tacos, and each taco costs $5. She has paid $11 so far. How many dollars does Nayeli still need to pay?

2. Aikawa has 7 apples, and Aisaka has 11 apples. If Aikawa takes 5 of Aisaka's apples, how many more apples will Aikawa have than Aisaka afterwards?

3. One square has a perimeter twice as large as the perimeter of a smaller square. If the area of the smaller square is 25, what is the area of the larger square?

4. Austin recorded the probabilities of each of the five best gigantic monsters winning the battle royale simulation, which can only have one winner, in the table below. Based on the data, what is the probability that none of the five monsters win in the simulation? Express your answer as a common fraction.

Gigantic Monster ID	Probability of Winning
131	30%
892	30%
6	12%
861	8%
858	8%

5. Audrina can read a 270-page novel in 6 hours. The audiobook takes 9 hours to finish the same novel. The reading rates per page for both Audrina and the audiobook remain constant. If she starts reading the novel and listening to the audiobook version at the same time, how many hours will it take for Audrina to have read and listened to a combined total of 100 pages? Express your answer as a common fraction.

6. A video is 4 minutes and 55 seconds long. The point on the number line below marks the percentage of the video that Matthew watched so far. Given that Matthew watched a whole number of minutes, how many seconds does Matthew still need to watch to finish the video?

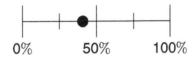

7. A rectangular prism with whole number side lengths has two faces with areas 12 and 21. What is the smallest possible volume of the rectangular prism?

8. Andrew is working on the crossword below with 49 small squares, including some shaded. Only the unshaded small squares may have a letter. Of the unshaded squares, there are 6 more squares with letters than squares without letters. What fraction of all the small squares, both shaded and unshaded, have letters? Express your answer as a common fraction.

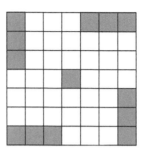

9. Philemon is making four towers of tiles. His first tower has the most tiles, and all other towers each have the same number of tiles. The range of the number of tiles in his towers is 1, and the average number of tiles in his towers is $4\frac{1}{4}$. How many tiles are in the tower with the most tiles?

10. Let $\triangle ABC$ be an isosceles triangle with $AB = AC$, and let X be a point on side $\overline{AB}$. Line segment $\overline{CX}$ is extended past X to a point Y such that $\overline{AY} \parallel \overline{BC}$. If $\angle AYC = 45°$ and $\angle ACY = 30°$, how many degrees is the measure of $\angle AXC$?

11. For real numbers a, h, and k, the graph of the function $f(x) = a|x - h| + k$ has a line of symmetry at $x = -25$, has exactly one point on the line $y = -75$, and passes through the point $(50, 150)$. What is the value of $f(-125)$?

12. How many ways are there to fit two identical 3×1 rectangular tiles, one 2×1 rectangular tile, and one 1×1 square tile entirely within a 3×3 square such that no two tiles overlap, and rotations and reflections of an arrangement are considered distinct?

13. If y is a positive real number for which the two values of $y \pm \sqrt{y^2 - 72}$ differ by 14, what is the value of y?

14. What is the probability that a randomly chosen positive divisor of 10206 is less than 101? Express your answer as a common fraction.

15. Let a, b, and c be positive whole numbers, where $a > c$. If both $a - b$ and $c - b$ are prime numbers, and $a + c = 2019$, what is the greatest possible value of b?

16. A permutation of a string of ℓ letters is called *opposite* if all pairs of identical letters are in opposite positions k and $\ell - k + 1$ in the string for some $1 \leq k \leq \ell$. For example, the permutation *LEAGEU* is opposite, but *MAITHEAICTNAM* is not. How many permutations of the word *OPPOSITE* are opposite?

17. Six congruent gray circles, each internally tangent to a circle with radius 14, are drawn such that their centers form a regular hexagon with side length 11. Next, a seventh gray circle is drawn, inside the circle with radius 14 and externally tangent to each of the six gray circles. The area inside the circle with radius 14 and outside of the seven gray circles can be written as $a\pi$. What is the value of a?

18. What is the smallest positive whole number greater than 1 that contains only the digits 0 or 1 in both its base 4 and base 8 representations?

19. Given that $\frac{x}{x+1} = \frac{1}{x^2+x} + 3$, what is the sum of all possible values of x^2? Express your answer as a common fraction.

20. Rectangle $ABCD$ and triangle ABE share side $\overline{AB}$ and do not overlap. If $AB = 5$, $AE = 4$, $BE = 3$, and the area of triangle CDE is equal to 21, what is BC?

21. Let m and n be positive whole numbers such that m^2n is a factor of 9, mn^2 is a factor of 12, and m^2n^2 is a factor of 18. What is the sum of all possible values of $3m + 2n$?

22. Given a circle with radius 3 and center O, line segment $\overline{AB}$ of length 8 is tangent to the circle at A. Let M be the midpoint of $\overline{AB}$, and let segment $\overline{MO}$ intersect the circle at a point P. What is the area of $\triangle BMP$? Express your answer as a common fraction.

23. Yiming has five fair coins. He flips each of them once, and he removes any coins that landed on heads. Then, he flips each of his remaining coins again, and he removes any coins that landed on tails. What is the probability that Yiming now has at least three coins left? Express your answer as a common fraction.

24. What is the smallest three-digit whole number n such that n is a multiple of 6, and the numbers of positive divisors of n, $2n$, and $3n$ form an arithmetic sequence in that order?

25. What is the greatest whole number n such that $\sqrt{n+1} - \sqrt{n} > \frac{1}{20}$?

26. On a plane, points A, B, C, and D lie on a line in that order. Let there be a point P on the same plane such that $\angle APC = 90°$ and $\angle BPC = \angle CPD$. If $BC = 3$ and $CD = 5$, what is AB?

27. What is the remainder when 10^{2023} is divided by 9801?

28. Say a positive whole number is *bizarre* if all of its digits are odd and its digit sum is prime. For example, 353 is bizarre, but neither 121 nor 171 are bizarre. How many three-digit whole numbers are bizarre?

29. Given that a and b are positive whole numbers that satisfy $9a^2 + 8b^3 = 27a^3 + 4b^2$ and $ab = 24$, what is the sum of all possible values of $a^2 + b^2$?

30. A circle has a diameter $\overline{AB}$ of length 16. A second circle in the same plane intersects the first circle at point A and another point C, where $AC > BC$. The line parallel to $\overline{AB}$ passing through C intersects the first and second circles at points D and E, respectively, both distinct from C. If $\triangle ADE$ is equilateral, what is BE^2?

Name _____

Grade _____

School _____

Problems 1 & 2

1. Ava currently has 20 spaces in her satchel. Barbara offers to increase Ava's satchel space efficiently but at a price. The first increase by one space only costs $150, but each following increase of one space costs $100 more than the previous increase. Ava does not want to spend more than $2000 to increase satchel storage. What is the greatest possible number of spaces that Ava could have in total once she finishes buying more satchel storage?

1.

2. A line with y-intercept $(0, 6)$ and slope -2 intersects a line with y-intercept $(0, 1)$ and slope m at a point on the line $y = x$. What is the value of m? Express your answer as a common fraction.

2.

Place ID Sticker
Inside This Box

Name _____

Grade _____

School _____

Problems 3 & 4

3. Diana and Victoria plan to meet up on Monday, but they have very busy schedules! On Monday, Diana is only available from 11:30 AM to 12:30 PM and from 3 PM to 6 PM, while Victoria is only available from 10:45 AM to 11:45 AM and from 2:45 PM to 3:15 PM and from 5:15 PM to 6:15 PM. How many minutes of the day are Diana and Victoria both available for meeting up?

3.

4. A set of three distinct single-digit whole numbers is such that exactly one of the numbers is a divisor of 36, exactly one of the numbers is a divisor of 42, and exactly one of the numbers is a divisor of 48, but the numbers satisfying each condition may not necessarily be distinct. What is the sum of all possible products of the numbers in the set?

4.

Place ID Sticker
Inside This Box

Name _____

Grade _____

School _____

Problems 5 & 6

5. Ayuna, Benji, Chitose, Daisuke, and Emi are standing in a straight line, where Ayuna and Benji are the greatest distance apart out of any two people, at 12 meters apart. If Ayuna and Chitose are 9 meters apart, Benji and Daisuke are 5 meters apart, and Chitose and Emi are 7 meters apart, how many meters apart are Daisuke and Emi?

5.

6. The number 88 has the special property that it can be expressed as a product of palindromes because $88 = 11 \cdot 2 \cdot 2 \cdot 2$. How many positive integers less than or equal to 50 have this property?

6.

Place ID Sticker
Inside This Box

Name _____

Grade _____

School _____

Problems 7 & 8

7. Call a positive whole number *wavy* if each pair of adjacent digits differ by exactly 1. How many five-digit multiples of 5 are wavy?

7.

8. Two circles have radii 25 and 12 and are internally tangent to each other at a point P. A diameter of the circle with radius 25 is drawn, tangent to the circle with radius 12 at a point Q. Let segment $\overline{PQ}$ be extended past Q to intersect the circle with radius 25 at a point R. What is QR^2?

8.

School or Team

Name _____

Name _____

Name _____

Name _____

Place ID Sticker
Inside This Box

Place ID Sticker
Inside This Box

Place ID Sticker
Inside This Box

Place ID Sticker
Inside This Box

1.	2.	3.	4.	5.

6.	7.	8.	9.	10.

1. In equilateral triangle *ABC* with side length 8, let points *D* and *E* lie on sides $\overline{AC}$ and $\overline{AB}$, respectively, so that triangle *ADE* is an equilateral triangle with side length 5. What is the perimeter of quadrilateral *BCDE*?

2. At a library, each book is assigned exactly one genre, and the number of books per genre is shown in the table below. Amee wants to select one book from the genre with the most books and one book from the genre with the fewest books. How many ways can Amee select the books?

Genre	Number of Books
Mystery	60
Fantasy	45
Biography	35
Reference	50
Science Fiction	40

3. Jessica is launching a bottle rocket with a parachute from 10 meters below sea level. Exactly 1 minute and 10 seconds after the launch, the bottle rocket reached the maximum height of 123 meters above sea level and deployed the parachute. What is the average number of meters gained in elevation per second of Jessica's bottle rocket from the time the rocket launched to the time the rocket deployed the parachute? Express your answer as a decimal without trailing zeroes.

4. A cake is a cylinder with a radius of 4 centimeters and a height of 4 centimeters. MacKenzie makes straight cuts perpendicular to the top and bottom circular faces such that each cut is a radius of the circular faces, and the cuts divide the cake into equally-sized cake slices, where the surface area of each cake slice is $8\pi + 32$ square centimeters. MacKenzie finds that among a group of some number of teammates, she can give one slice to every teammate except for one. Including the teammate who did not get cake, how many teammates are in the group?

5. The sum of two odd whole numbers with 3 and 4 positive divisors is a whole number with 7 positive divisors. What is the greatest possible value of the number with 4 positive divisors?

6. Let a, b, and c be real numbers (possibly zero) and n a positive whole number. If $(x - 8)(ax^2 + bx + c) + 8c = x^n$, what is the sum of all possible values of $a + b + c + n$?

7. From the vertices of a regular 2023-gon, choose 1011 of the vertices at random, without replacement. In how many ways can vertices be chosen such that no chosen vertex is immediately adjacent to another? Note that rotations are considered distinct.

8. Let $\triangle ABC$ with $\angle A$ acute be inscribed in a circle with center O. Let M be the midpoint of $\overline{BC}$, and let ray $\overrightarrow{OM}$ intersect the circle at P. Let segments $\overline{AP}$ and $\overline{BC}$ intersect at Q. If $AP = 30$, $MP = \frac{15}{2}$, and $MQ = 4$, what is BC^2?

9. For positive whole numbers n, the value of $\frac{n+5}{n^2+10n+100}$ can be written as $\frac{p}{q}$, where p and q are relatively prime positive whole numbers. What is the smallest possible value of $p + q$ over all positive whole numbers n?

10. Adam, Bob, Chris, and David each roll a fair six-sided die once. The numbers on Adam's die are the whole numbers from 1 to 6, inclusive, the numbers on Bob's die are the whole numbers from 7 to 12, inclusive, the numbers on Chris' die are the whole numbers from 13 to 18, inclusive, and the numbers on David's die are the whole numbers from 19 to 24, inclusive. What is the probability that the sum of the two numbers showing on Adam and David's dice is strictly greater than the sum of the two numbers showing on Bob and Chris' dice? Express your answer as a common fraction.

Countdown Round
12314

1. Annie wants to buy exactly 36 novels and 1 word-search book for her magic tree house. Each word-search book costs $1, and she can either buy novels individually for $5 each or buy any five novels for $24. What is the minimum number of dollars that Annie needs to buy the novels and word-search book?

2. David is writing a comic book about a dog superhero. So far, on an 8.5×11 paper, he drew three 2×2 square panels and two 8×2.5 rectangular panels. What is the area of the paper *not* occupied by any panels? Express your answer as a decimal without trailing zeroes.

3. What positive whole number value for x can satisfy the equation $x^3 - 3x^2 + 3x - 1 = 64$?

4. Charlotte is weaving a web that consists of three regular octagons with the same center. The vertices of the two smaller octagons trisect all line segments going from the center to the vertices of the larger octagon. The sum of the perimeters of the three octagons is 72 centimeters. How many millimeters is the side length of the largest octagon?

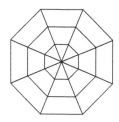

5. Christine is raising funds for women in education. So far she raised $31250, which is $12\frac{1}{2}\%$ of the fundraising goal. How many dollars is the fundraising goal?

6. Three rectangles have whole number side lengths and equal area. One side of the first rectangle has length 22, one side of the second rectangle has length 12, and one side of the third rectangle has length 15. What is the least possible value of the perimeter of one of the rectangles?

7. Jose is digging a cylindrical hole that has a radius of 3 feet. So far, the cylindrical hole has a depth of 1 foot. When digging, Jose can increase the volume of the hole at the rate of 3π cubic feet per minute. How many minutes will it take Jose to get the cylindrical hole to have a depth of 3 feet?

8. Find the sum: $1! - \frac{2!}{2} + \frac{3!}{3} - \frac{4!}{4}$.

9. What is the area of a triangle with side lengths 14, 25, and 25?

10. Charlie made the following pie chart that models last year's sales of the four chocolate bars from his factory. The milk chocolate was the most popular at 80000 bars sold. The fudge mallow and whipped delight were tied in sales and together made up half the bars sold. The least popular bar was the nut crunch. How many nut crunch bars were sold last year?

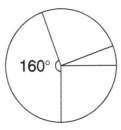

11. For what value of x is $f(x) = -|3x - 51| + 12^3$ maximized?

12. Jessica plans six bridges across three different islands such that for any two islands, there is at least one bridge connecting them. If two bridges that connect the same islands are considered identical, how many ways can Jessica build the six bridges?

13. What is the remainder when 3^{10} is divided by 80?

14. If the radius of semicircle A is half the length of the radius of circle B, what is the ratio of the area of the circle to that of the semicircle?

15. The number 11663 has exactly two prime factors, and the positive difference between the two prime factors is 2. What is the larger prime factor?

16. When a group sings a song a cappella, its key shifts half a step sharp by the end. They sing this song 10 times in a row, each time starting in the key that they ended in previously. At the end of the 10th time, how many steps sharp are they from the original key?

17. How many five-digit palindromes end with a 0?

18. A poem collection has 123 poems. Justin and Ben read different poems, but Justin read two more poems than Ben. They finished all but one poem. If Justin randomly picked a poem he read, what is a probability that he did not pick his favorite one he read, which is about a sidewalk ending? Express your answer as a common fraction.

19. Three positive whole numbers have a product of 108. What is the smallest possible value of their sum?

20. The three solutions to the equation $x^3 - ax^2 + bx - 49 = 0$ are $x = 7, r_1, r_2$. What is $r_1 r_2$?

21. How many ways are there to arrange 7 books lined up in a row if 4 of them are indistinguishable?

22. Jake and Rachel each plan to randomly choose one of the following 6 animals: an eagle, a tiger, a leopard, a falcon, a horse, and a wolf. However, Rachel instead randomly chooses any animal that is not an eagle or a falcon. What is the probability that Jake and Rachel choose the same animal? Express your answer as a common fraction.

23. Simplify: $3^4 + 2^3 + 1^2$.

24. Find the positive difference between the third-largest and third-smallest five-digit palindromes.

25. Gear A with 16 teeth is connected to Gear B with 24 teeth, which in turn is connected to Gear C with 30 teeth. How many revolutions will Gear C make in the time that Gear A makes 90 revolutions?

26. How many real solutions are there to the equation $|x^2 - 3| = 3$?

27. What is the largest perfect square that divides 12221?

28. John observes that one ring is a cylinder with diameter 2 centimeters and height 0.5 centimeters but with a cylindrical hole with diameter 1.5 centimeters going through one of the faces, as shown below. John then finds that the volume is $a\pi$ cubic centimeters. What is the value of a? Express your answer as a common fraction.

29. How many arrangements of a subset of the letters of *BOOKS* are palindromes with at least two letters?

30. There exists an x such that $y = 3x - 5$ and $y = -2x + 16$. Find y, expressing your answer as a common fraction.

31. Evaluate $125^{-\frac{2}{3}}$. Express your answer as a common fraction.

32. In a 5×5 square maze shown below, Min runs from the upper left point to the bottom left point while only staying on the edges drawn. If Min takes 3 minutes to run through an edge that directly connects two vertices, at least how many minutes will it take Min to reach the bottom right point?

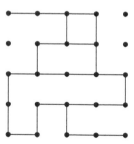

33. One side of a rectangle has length 6. For how many possible whole number lengths for the other side is the length of the diagonal also a whole number?

34. In how many ways can the letters in the word *READ* be arranged if the *E* and the *A* must be adjacent?

35. Lily sketches a beehive where each section of the beehive corresponds to a regular hexagon. Initially, all sections had the same number of bees. Afterward, 25 more bees entered the hive, and as a result, there are 145 bees in the entire beehive. How many bees were in each section initially?

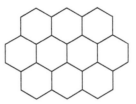

36. The kilowatt-hour is a unit of energy used for electricity that is equivalent to 1000 watts of power running for 1 hour. Andrea observed that a boy inventor created a windmill with a power of 12 watts from junk parts. If two of these windmills run for 120 minutes, how many kilowatt-hours of energy are produced from both windmills? Express your answer as a decimal without trailing zeroes.

37. Parallelogram $ABCD$ is similar to parallelogram $BCEF$. If $AB = 9$ and $BC = 6$, what is CE?

38. Brian encountered a large log and plans on using his hatchet to make pieces of wood for his wilderness dwelling. If he makes each piece 8 feet long, he will have 6 fewer pieces than if he makes each piece 5 feet long. How many feet long is the large log?

39. If the ratio of $a : b$ is $5 : 4$, what is the ratio of $b : 5a$? Express your answer as a common fraction.

40. What is the units digit of 2^{80}?

41. Julian wrote in a diary that a stinky piece of cheese is equidistant from three vertical poles. Additionally, any two poles can be connected by a string used for papeles picados that is exactly 20 meters long. How many meters is the stinky piece of cheese from any of the three poles? Express your answer in simplest radical form.

42. In triangle ABC, $AB = 20$, $BC = 23$, and $\angle B = 43°$. How many possible values are there for the perimeter of ABC?

43. James models the radius of his spherical giant peach as a linear function of days elapsed since he first saw the peach in the graph below. The y-intercept and slope are both multiples of 3. After 7 days have passed since James first saw the peach, how many cubic meters is the volume of the peach? Express your answer in terms of π.

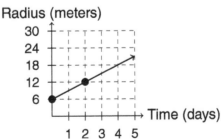

44. The interior angles of a certain 22-sided polygon all measure either 90° or 270°. How many of the interior angles measure 270°?

45. What is the smallest whole number greater than 1 such that the remainder when 210 is divided by it is a prime number?

46. Three pigs each built the same number of cubic wooden houses. However, the big bad wolf blew off the top face of each house, leaving only 1125 faces across all the houses. How many houses did each pig build?

47. An isosceles trapezoid has side lengths $20, 10, 36, 10$. Find its area.

48. Rick surveyed campers in Long Island about Olympic sports. He found that 48% of the campers like archery, 54% of the campers like swimming, and 34% of the campers do not like archery or swimming. If 90 campers like both archery and swimming, how many campers did Rick survey?

49. The formula for the number of edges of an n-dimensional cube can be modeled by the function $f(n) = n \cdot 2^{n-1}$, where $f(n)$ is the number of edges. A k-dimensional cube has 48 more edges than a tesseract, which is a 4-dimensional cube. Given that k is a positive integer, what is the value of k?

50. A *perfect number* satisfies the property that the sum of the proper divisors of the number equals the number itself. What is the sum of the reciprocals of the divisors of the perfect number 8128?

51. Two interior angles of a convex quadrilateral measure $40°$, and one of the remaining two interior angles has a measure $46°$ greater than the measure of the other. How many degrees is the measure of the largest interior angle of the quadrilateral?

52. Simplify: $\frac{4}{7} \times 39 - \frac{4}{7} \times 4$.

53. Solve for a: $a \div 4 + a \div 5 = 27$.

54. What is the sum of the sixth and eleventh primes?

55. What integer is closest to the value of 4.49×8.98?

56. 60% of what number is 20% of 150?

57. Evaluate: 99×19.

58. A total of 50 mice scurried into a formation with more than one row, and each row had the same number of mice. Peter observes that one row had more than 7 mice but less than 12 mice. How many rows were in the formation?

59. Find $\gcd(28, 16) \cdot \text{lcm}(28, 16)$.

60. What is the sum of the median and the mode of the following list?

$$23, 37, 10, 29, 8, 19, 37$$

61. A coin is flipped and a fair six-sided die is rolled. What is the probability that the coin shows tails and the die shows 3? Express your answer as a common fraction.

62. Express in scientific notation: $\frac{3 \times 10^2}{4 \times 10^5}$.

63. Jack observes that eight ducks of different ages lined up in random order. What is the probability that the duck in the front is the oldest and the duck in the back is the youngest? Express your answer as a common fraction.

64. Two fair six-sided dice are rolled. What is the probability that the sum of numbers facing up is 8? Express your answer as a common fraction.

65. Daniel found that AJ's entry in the database for the number of classes taken at a weird school is off by one while the other two students had the right number. After correcting AJ's entry, Daniel found that the average number of classes taken by the three students is a positive whole number. How many classes did AJ actually take?

Student	Number of Classes
AJ	11
Andrea	13
Emily	16

66. A field is a regular hexagon that has a side length of 120 meters. The lion could roam anywhere except the section that has poppies, which make up $3600\sqrt{3}$ square meters of the field. What fraction of the field could the lion roam around? Express your answer as a common fraction.

67. Compute: $\frac{21}{3} + 2 \cdot 3$.

68. Maxim observes wild creatures in the jungle and can classify them as either flying or water but not both. He found that the ratio of flying creatures to water creatures is 3 : 2, and there are 15 more flying creatures than water creatures. If Maxim plans on giving one bowl of supper to each of the wild creatures, how many bowls of supper should he give?

69. A circle has an area of 25π. If the diameter is increased by 4 units, what would the new area be? Express your answer in terms of π.

70. On January 14, Lauren gave a mouse a cookie for the first time. On January 15, Lauren gave a mouse a haircut. On January 16, Lauren gave a mouse a drawing. Lauren then cycles between giving a mouse a cookie, a haircut, and a drawing over the rest of the days of January. By the end of January 31, how many days did Lauren give a mouse a cookie?

71. What is the smallest integer n such that $3n - 2 > -23$?

72. Line segments $\overline{AB}$ and $\overline{CD}$ intersect at point E. Given that $\angle AEC = 23°$, how many degrees is the measure of $\angle AED$?

73. Ben is tasked with putting photos of his uncle's fabulous adventures in a logbook such that he will fill up 4 pages where each page has 5 rows and each row has 2 photos. Of the photos on the four pages, 15 of them are about the kingdom of fantasy. What common fraction of the photos on the four pages are about the kingdom of fantasy?

74. Express $\frac{4}{7} + \frac{7}{4}$ as a common fraction.

75. Amanda has a red book, an orange book, a yellow book, a green book, a blue book, and a purple book. She plans on reading three of the books in order. How many ways could she do that?

76. Solve for a: $128 = 2^a$.

77. Sam visited a train station and found that a total of 27 people ate doughnuts, a total of 29 people drank lemonade, and 13 people ate doughnuts and drank lemonade. Sam then gave 2 carrots to each person who ate doughnuts or drank lemonade. How many carrots did Sam give out?

78. If $f(x) = 5x + 12$, then find $f(13)$.

79. What is the sum of the prime numbers between 30 and 40?

80. A mouse uses a 21-centimeter-long piece of red thread to measure a motorcycle trip that starts at town S, passes through another town, and finishes at town F, as shown in the map below. One centimeter of red thread corresponds to 5 kilometers in real life. How many kilometers apart are the towns S and F?

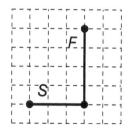

Sprint Round

1. 4	11. 225	21. 16	
2. 6	12. 12	22. $\frac{12}{5}$	
3. 100	13. 11	23. $\frac{53}{512}$	
4. $\frac{3}{25}$	14. $\frac{1}{2}$	24. 120	
5. $\frac{4}{3}$	15. 1007	25. 99	
6. 175	16. 288	26. 12	
7. 84	17. 78	27. 1198	
8. $\frac{3}{7}$	18. 64	28. 82	
9. 5	19. $\frac{1}{4}$	29. 52	
10. 120	20. 6	30. 448	

Target Round

1. 25
2. $\frac{1}{2}$
3. 75
4. 644
5. 5
6. 35
7. 20
8. 650

Team Round

1. 19
2. 2100
3. 1.9
4. 9
5. 55
6. 89
7. 2023
8. 795
9. 21
10. $\frac{575}{1296}$

Countdown

1. 174	21. 210	41. $\frac{20\sqrt{3}}{3}$	61. $\frac{1}{12}$
2. 41.5	22. $\frac{1}{6}$	42. 1	62. $7.5 \cdot 10^{-4}$
3. 5	23. 90	43. 26244π	63. $\frac{1}{56}$
4. 45	24. 89598	44. 9	64. $\frac{5}{36}$
5. 250000	25. 48	45. 4	65. 10
6. 104	26. 3	46. 225	66. $\frac{5}{6}$
7. 6	27. 121	47. 168	67. 13
8. -4	28. $\frac{7}{32}$	48. 250	68. 75
9. 168	29. 4	49. 5	69. 49π
10. 10000	30. $\frac{38}{5}$	50. 2	70. 6
11. 17	31. $\frac{1}{25}$	51. 163	71. -6
12. 10	32. 36	52. 20	72. 157
13. 9	33. 1	53. 60	73. $\frac{3}{8}$
14. 8	34. 12	54. 44	74. $\frac{65}{28}$
15. 109	35. 12	55. 40	75. 120
16. 5	36. 0.048	56. 50	76. 7
17. 0	37. 4	57. 1881	77. 86
18. $\frac{61}{62}$	38. 80	58. 5	78. 77
19. 15	39. $\frac{4}{25}$	59. 448	79. 68
20. 7	40. 6	60. 60	80. 75

Sprint Round Solutions

1. One taco costs \$5, so three tacos cost \$15. Since Nayeli has paid \$11 already, she still needs to pay \$ $\boxed{4}$.

2. After Aikawa takes 5 of Aisaka's apples, she will have $7+5 = 12$ apples, and Aisaka will have $11-5 = 6$ apples. Afterwards, Aikawa will have $12 - 6 = \boxed{6}$ more apples than Aisaka.

3. If the area of a square is 25, then the side length is 5, meaning that the perimeter is $5 \cdot 4 = 20$. Then, the larger square has a perimeter of $20 \cdot 2 = 40$, so it has a side length of $\frac{40}{4} = 10$. Then the larger square has an area of $10 \cdot 10 = \boxed{100}$.

4. Recall that probabilities of all events have to add up to 1, or 100%. As the battle royale simulation only has one winner, the probabilities of gigantic monsters winning the simulation are disjoint, meaning that no two of them can happen at the same time. Thus, we can add up the probabilities to get that the probability of any of the five monsters winning is 88%, meaning that the probability that none of the five monsters win the simulation is 12%, which as a fraction is $\frac{12}{100} = \boxed{\frac{3}{25}}$.

5. In one hour, Audrina can read 45 pages and listen to 30 pages, so she can get through a combined total of 75 pages. This means that it will take her $\frac{100}{75} = \boxed{\frac{4}{3}}$ hours to get through a total of 100 pages.

6. We know that Matthew watched at least 25% of the video but less than 50% of the video. Now, we could test out percentages, but we could note that 4 minutes and 55 seconds is close to 5 minutes, and the percentage information means that we can conclude that Matthew watched 2 minutes. Since the video is 295 seconds long and Matthew watched 120 seconds, Matthew still needs to watch $295-120 = \boxed{175}$ seconds of the video.

7. Let the side lengths of the rectangular prism be a, b, and c. Then, suppose that $ab = 12$ and $bc = 21$, so $ab^2c = 252$. The volume is the product of the side lengths abc, which we can also use the previous equation to write as $abc = \frac{252}{b}$. Thus, we want to maximize b. This is accomplished by having b be the greatest common divisor of 12 and 21, which is 3. Therefore, the volume will be $\frac{252}{3} = \boxed{84}$.

8. Let x be the number of unshaded squares with letters and y be the number of unshaded squares without letters. The crossword has 36 smaller squares that are unshaded, so $x + y = 36$. From the given information, we can write $x = y + 6$. By substitution, we can find that $x = 21$ and $y = 15$. The fraction of all the squares that have letters is $\frac{21}{49} = \boxed{\frac{3}{7}}$.

9. Let x be the number of tiles in Philemon's tallest tower. Since the range of the number of towers is 1, each of the other tiles has $x - 1$ tiles. By taking the average, we can set up the equation $\frac{x + 3(x-1)}{4} = 4\frac{1}{4}$. We can solve the linear equation by properties of equality to get $4x - 3 = 17$, or $x = \boxed{5}$.

10. By parallel lines, we get that $\angle BCY = \angle AYC$, so $\angle BCY = 45°$, and $\angle ACB = 75°$. Now, since $\triangle ABC$ is isosceles, we have that $\angle ABC = \angle ACB$, so $\angle ABC = 75°$, so $\angle BAC = 30°$. Finally, we have that $\angle AXC = 180° - m\angle XAC - m\angle ACX = 180° - 30° - 30° = \boxed{120}°$.

11. We notice that the function is in the form of an absolute value function. By observing the properties of the vertex (h, k) of an absolute value function, we find that $x = h$ is the line of symmetry, and the graph of the absolute value function intersects $y = k$ exactly one time. This means that $(-25, -75)$ is the vertex of this absolute value function. Additionally, the slope of the function if $x > -25$ is -1 times that of the same function if $x < -25$. Now, we could compute slopes, but we could also observe from numbers being multiples of 25 that if we add 25 three times to get from -25 to 50, we add 25 nine times to get from -75 to 150. This means that if we subtract 25 four times to get from -25 to -125, we add 25 twelve times to get from -75 to $\boxed{225}$.

12. Note that once we orient a 3×1 rectangle inside the square, either vertically or horizontally, the other 3×1 rectangle has to have the same orientation. There are two orientations, and within each one, there are 3 ways to arrange the two 3×1 rectangles. Then, in the remaining 3×1 rectangle space, there are 2 ways to place the 2×1 rectangle and the 1×1 square. Thus, there are $2 \cdot 3 \cdot 2 = \boxed{12}$ ways to fill in the 3×3 square.

13. Note that $(y + \sqrt{y^2 - 72}) - (y - \sqrt{y^2 - 72}) = 2\sqrt{y^2 - 72}$ is equal to 14, so $\sqrt{y^2 - 72} = 7$. Squaring both sides yields $y^2 - 72 = 49$, or $y^2 = 121$. As $y > 0$, we pick $y = \boxed{11}$.

14. For a positive number n that is not a perfect square, exactly half of the positive divisors are less than $\sqrt{n}$. Since 10206 is not a perfect square, half of the positive divisors of 10206 will be less than $\sqrt{10206} \approx 101.025$. Clearly, there are no positive divisors between 101 and $\sqrt{10206}$ and 101 is not a divisor of 10206, so half of the positive divisors of 10206 are less than 101. Thus, the probability is $\boxed{\frac{1}{2}}$.

15. Note that 2019 is odd, so one of a and c must be even. Since $a > c$, $a \geq 1010$. If $a = 1010$, then $c = 1009$. Then we can set $b = 1007$ to obtain $a - b = 3$ and $c - b = 2$, which are both prime numbers. To show that $b = 1007$ is optimal, note that increasing the value of a decreases the value of c in order to still satisfy $a + c = 2019$. Then b must also increase because $a - b$ and $c - b$ leave different remainders when divided by 2. Since 2 is the only even prime and is smaller than every odd prime, we must have that $c - b = 2$. Thus, the greatest possible value of b is indeed $\boxed{1007}$.

16. The identical pairs are the two Os and the two Ps, which can be positioned in $4 \cdot 3 = 12$ ways, as placing one O in the first four positions forces the second O into the opposite position. Then there are $4! = 24$ ways to permute the other four distinct letters: S, I, T, and E. The total number of opposite permutations of the word *OPPOSITE* is $\boxed{288}$.

17. Consider two of the six congruent circles that are next to each other and call their radius r and their centers O and Q. Then, we have that $OQ = 11$. Let the center of the drawn circle be X, and call its radius R. Then, we have by internal tangency that $R + 2r = 14$. Next, we see that X is the center of the regular hexagon by symmetry. Thus, we have that $\angle OXQ = \frac{360°}{6}$, or $60°$. Since $OX = QX$, we have that $\triangle OQX$ is equilateral. Thus, we have that $R + r = 11$. Finally, solving for r and R gives us $r = 3$ and $R = 8$. The sum of the areas of the seven gray circles is $64\pi + 6 \cdot 9\pi = 118\pi$, so the area inside the circle with radius 14 and outside of the seven gray circles is $196\pi - 118\pi = 78\pi$, for an answer of $\boxed{78}$.

18. First, let us consider the numbers in the base 8 representation. Note that $8 = 2^3$, or $2 \cdot 4$, so if the second-to-last digit of the base 8 representation of the number is equal to 1, then the second-to-last-digit of the base 4 representation of the number would be equal to 2, which we do not want. Then, note that $8^2 = 64$, or 4^3, which yields the digit 1 in the 4^3 digit of the base 4 representation. This gives us the number $\boxed{64}$, which indeed works.

19. Note that $\frac{x}{x+1} = \frac{x^2}{x^2+x}$, so we get that $\frac{x^2-1}{x^2+x} = 3$. As $x \neq -1$, we can divide out the $x + 1$ factor to get $\frac{x-1}{x} = 3$. From here, we get that $x - 1 = 3x$, from which we get that $x = -\frac{1}{2}$, so $x^2 = \frac{1}{4}$. Since this is the only possible value, our answer is $\boxed{\dfrac{1}{4}}$.

20. Drop an altitude from E to side $\overline{CD}$ and call the foot P. Call the intersection of this altitude and $\overline{AB}$ point Q. Then, $EP = BC + EQ$. Note that EQ is the length of the altitude of 3-4-5 right triangle ABE from the side with length 5. Since the area of the triangle is $\frac{3 \cdot 4}{2} = 6$, we have $\frac{5 \cdot EQ}{2} = 6$, which gives $EQ = \frac{12}{5}$. Then, by the base-height area formula, $\frac{1}{2} \cdot \left(BC + \frac{12}{5}\right) \cdot 5 = 21$. Solving for BC gives us $BC = \boxed{6}$.

21. From the fact that $m^2 n^2$ divides 18, we look for perfect square divisors of 18 and find 1 and 9. We see that 1 can be obtained with $m = 1$ and $n = 1$, which works, and we see that 9 can be obtained with $(m, n) = (1, 3), (3, 1)$. Checking each ordered pair, we see that $(3, 1)$ works, but $(1, 3)$ does not work since $mn^2 = 9$, but 9 does not divide 12. Thus, $3m + 2n$ can equal $3 + 2 = 5$ or $9 + 2 = 11$, for a sum of $5 + 11 = \boxed{16}$.

22. We have that $AM = 4$ and $BM = 4$. By the Pythagorean Theorem, we have that $MO = 5$. Since $\overline{OP}$ is a radius of the circle, we have that $OP = 3$. Then, $MP = 2$. We know that the areas of $\triangle AMO$ and $\triangle BMO$ are equal by length ratios, and by the base-height area formula, this area is $\frac{1}{2} \cdot 3 \cdot 4 = 6$. Finally, the ratio of the area of $\triangle BMP$ to that of $\triangle BMO$ is $2 : 5$ since $\frac{MP}{MO} = \frac{2}{5}$. Thus, the area of $\triangle BMP$ is $\frac{2}{5} \cdot 6 = \boxed{\dfrac{12}{5}}$.

23. For now, let us suppose that every coin is flipped twice. Then, for each coin, we have the outcomes HH, TT, HT, and TH, where H denotes heads and T denotes tails. Of these, the only outcome that allows the coin to remain is TH, so there is a $\frac{1}{4}$ chance that it remains and a $\frac{3}{4}$ chance that it gets removed at some point. Thus, there is a $\frac{3^2 \cdot \binom{5}{2} + 3^1 \cdot \binom{5}{1} + 3^0 \cdot \binom{5}{0}}{4^5} = \boxed{\frac{53}{512}}$ chance that Yiming now has at least three coins left.

24. Let $n = 2^a \cdot 3^b \cdot m$, where a and b are positive whole numbers, and m is a positive whole number relatively prime to 2 and 3. Since we are only multiplying by 2 and 3, we do not care about the number of positive divisors of m, so let m have k positive divisors. The numbers of positive divisors of n, $2n$, and $3n$ are $(a+1)(b+1)k$, $(a+2)(b+1)k$, and $(a+1)(b+2)k$ in that order. Then we must have that $2(a+2)(b+1)k = (a+1)(b+1)k + (a+1)(b+2)k$, which simplifies to $a = 2b+1$. Finding possible values of a and b gives us $(a,b) = (3,1), (5,2), (7,3)$, and so on. For $(a,b) = (3,1)$, the smallest three-digit positive whole number n is 120 with $m = 5$, and m is not divisible by 2 or 3. Now $(a,b) = (5,2)$ gives us $2^5 \cdot 3^2 = 288$, which is larger than 120, and any larger pairs of (a,b) will also be too large. Thus, the answer is $\boxed{120}$.

25. Take the reciprocal of both sides to get $\sqrt{n+1} + \sqrt{n} < 20$. Then, note that if $n = 99$, then $\sqrt{n+1} = 10$ and $\sqrt{n} < 10$, so this works. However, if $n = 100$, then $\sqrt{n+1} > 10$ and $\sqrt{n} = 10$, so this does not work. Thus, the answer is $\boxed{99}$.

26. By the Angle Bisector Theorem, we know that $\frac{BP}{DP} = \frac{3}{5}$. Let $BP = 3x$ so that $DP = 5x$. Next, let Q be the point on segment $\overline{DP}$ such that $\overline{AP} \parallel \overline{BQ}$, which in turn gives $\overline{BQ} \perp \overline{PC}$. Since $\angle BPC = \angle CPD$, it follows that $BP = PQ$. Then, we have that $PQ = 3x$ and $DQ = 2x$. Finally, note that $\triangle BDQ \sim \triangle ADP$. This means that $\frac{DP}{DQ} = \frac{AD}{BD}$, so $\frac{AD}{BD} = \frac{2}{5}$. Since $BD = 8$ and $AB = AD - BD$, we have that $AB = \boxed{12}$.

27. First, note that $9801 = 99^2$. Then, we can write 10^{2023} as $10 \cdot 100^{1011} = 10 \cdot (99 + 1)^{1011}$. By the Binomial Theorem, modulo 99^2, this reduces to $10(1011 \cdot 99 + 1) \equiv 10(21 \cdot 99 + 1) = 20800$. Thus, our answer is $20800 - 2 \cdot 9801 = \boxed{1198}$.

28. The digit sum may be 3, 5, 7, 11, 13, 17, 19, or 23. Respectively, these are twice 0, 1, 2, 4, 5, 7, 8, and 10, plus 3. Beginning with 111, we may add 0, 1, 2, 4, 5, 7, 8, and 10 twos to the digits to form a bizarre number. This can be done in $\binom{0+3-1}{3-1} + \binom{1+3-1}{3-1} + \binom{2+3-1}{3-1} + \binom{4+3-1}{3-1} = 25$ ways for adding up to 4 twos, by sticks-and-stones. For adding 5 twos, we have $\binom{5+3-1}{3-1} - 3 = 18$ ways, since we cannot add 10 to a digit. For adding 7, 8, and 10 twos, we may consider the complement problem of subtracting 5, 4, and 2 twos from 999, to get another $18 + 15 + 6 = 39$ bizarre numbers. Altogether, there are $25 + 18 + 39 = \boxed{82}$ bizarre three-digit numbers.

29. Rearranging the equation, we get $9a^2 - 4b^2 = 27a^3 - 8b^3$, which factors as $(3a + 2b)(3a - 2b) = (3a - 2b)(9a^2 + 6ab + 4b^2)$. Assuming that $3a \neq 2b$ and dividing both sides by $3a - 2b$, we get $3a + 2b = 9a^2 + 6ab + 4b^2$. Note that $9a^2 + 6ab + 4b^2 = (3a + 2b)^2 - 6ab$, so our equation becomes $3a + 2b = (3a + 2b)^2 - 6ab$, and given that $ab = 24$, this becomes $3a + 2b = (3a + 2b)^2 - 144$, which rearranges to $(3a + 2b)^2 - (3a + 2b) - 144 = 0$. However, solving for $3a + 2b$ gives us no whole number solutions. Thus, we must have that $3a = 2b$ and $ab = 24$, which gives us $(a,b) = (4,6)$ as our only positive whole number solution. Then $a^2 + b^2 = \boxed{52}$.

30. Since $\triangle ADE$ is equilateral, we have that $\angle ADE$, $\angle AED$, and $\angle DAE$ all have measure $60°$. Since $\overline{AB} \parallel \overline{CE}$, we have that $\angle DAB = 60°$. Then, $\angle BAE = 120°$. Since $\overline{AB} \parallel \overline{CD}$, and they are both chords of the first circle, we have that $ABCD$ is an isosceles trapezoid with $AD = BC$. Thus, $\angle ABC = 60°$ and $\angle DAB = 60°$. Since the sum of the interior angles of a quadrilateral is $360°$, we get that $\angle BCE = 120°$. Thus, we have that $ABCE$ is a parallelogram. This means that $CE = 16$ since $AB = 16$. We also know that $\angle ACB = 90°$ since $\overline{AB}$ is a diameter, and $\angle ABC = 60°$, so $AC = 8\sqrt{3}$ and $BC = 8$ by 30-60-90 properties. Then, since $ABCE$ is a parallelogram, we find that $AE = 8$. Finally, dropping a perpendicular from B to line AE and calling it F, we have a right triangle BFE with $BF = 8\sqrt{3}$ and $EF = 16$, after noticing that $\triangle ABF$ is a 30-60-90 right triangle. By the Pythagorean Theorem, $BE^2 = \boxed{448}$.

Target Round Solutions

1. The first increase costs $150, the second increase costs $250, the third increase costs $350, and so on. We can keep adding the costs and stop when the cost gets above $2000. We find that five increases costs $1750, but six increases costs $2400. Thus, Ava can get at most 5 more spaces, and the total number of spaces that she could have is $\boxed{25}$.

2. The line with y-intercept $(0, 6)$ and slope -2 goes down two units for every one unit to the right it goes. Thus, this line intersects the point $(2, 2)$, which is on the line $y = x$. Then, the line with y-intercept $(0, 1)$ must pass through $(2, 2)$, for a slope of $\frac{2-1}{2-0} = \boxed{\frac{1}{2}}$.

3. Diana and Victoria are both available from 11:30 AM to 11:45 AM, from 3:00 PM to 3:15 PM, and from 5:15 PM to 6 PM. Therefore, there are $15 + 15 + 45 = \boxed{75}$ minutes in which both of them are available to meet up that day.

4. First, we list all of the single-digit divisors of 36, 42, and 48: 36 gives $1, 2, 3, 4, 6, 9$, 42 gives $1, 2, 3, 6, 7$, and 48 gives $1, 2, 3, 4, 6, 8$. We claim that none of the numbers $1, 2, 3, 6$ can be in the set. If one of these numbers was in the set, then the other two numbers must not be a divisor of any of 36, 42, and 48. However, the only such single-digit number is 5, and we cannot have two of the same number in the set. Then, we are left with $4, 5, 7, 8, 9$. Now we need a number that divides 42, so 7 must be one of the numbers. This leaves 4 and 9 for 36 as well as 4 and 8 for 48. We then get that the two sets $\{4, 5, 7\}$ and $\{7, 8, 9\}$ work, for an answer of $140 + 504 = \boxed{644}$.

5. Let points A, B, C, D, and E denote the points where Ayuna, Benji, Chitose, Daisuke, and Emi are standing, respectively. Given that $AB = 12$, $AC = 9$, and $BD = 5$, we have that $AD = 7$ and $BC = 3$. Next, given that $CE = 7$, we know that $CE > BC$, which means that B and E must be on opposite sides of point C. Thus, $BE = 3 + 7$, so $BE = 10$. Since $BE = BD + DE$, we have that $DE = BE - BD$, which gives $DE = \boxed{5}$.

6. All the palindromes less than 100 are either single-digit positive integers or multiples of 11. Therefore, the given property amounts to having only a subset of 2, 3, 5, 7, and 11 as prime factors. It is easier to consider the numbers that don't have the special property, where the numbers have a prime factor that is at least 13. The multiples of 13 include 13, 26, and 39. The multiples of 17 include 17 and 34. The multiples of 19 include 19 and 38. The multiples of 23 include 23 and 46. Finally, we have the primes 29, 31, 37, 41, 43, and 47. Altogether, there are 15 numbers that do not have the special property, and so there are $50 - 15 = \boxed{35}$ numbers that have the special property.

7. A multiple of 5 must end in 0 or 5, so there are two cases to consider. If the fifth digit is 0, then the fourth digit is 1, and the third digit is either 0 or 2. From here, there are not many possibilities, so we can list all of them out: 21010, 21210, 23210, and 43210. As such, there are a total of 4 numbers from this case. Now if the fifth digit is a 5, then the fourth, third, second, and first digits may increase or decrease by 1 from the digit to its right without any restrictions, for a total of $2^4 = 16$ numbers from this case. The total number of five-digit wavy multiples of 5 is $4 + 16 = \boxed{20}$.

8. Let A and B be the centers of the circles with radii 25 and 12, respectively, and let M and N be the endpoints of the drawn diameter, with M closer to Q than N is. Since $\overline{BQ}$ is a radius and $\overline{MN}$ is a tangent line, we have $\overline{BQ}$ perpendicular to $\overline{MN}$. Since $\overline{AP}$ is a radius of the circle with radius 25, $AP = 25$. Since $\overline{BP}$ and $\overline{BQ}$ are radii of the circle with radius 12, $BP = 12$ and $BQ = 12$. Thus, $AB = 13$. By the Pythagorean Theorem, $AQ = 5$.

Additionally, as both $\triangle APR$ and $\triangle BPQ$ are isosceles triangles that share an angle, these two triangles are similar, making $\angle ARP = \angle BQP$. Now observe that $\angle BQP + \angle PQM = 90°$ and that $\angle PQM = \angle AQR$ by the Vertical Angle Theorem. This means that we can do a substitution to show that $\angle AQR + \angle QRA = 90°$, and so $\angle RAQ = 90°$. Finally, by using the Pythagorean Theorem, $QR^2 = 25^2 + 5^2 = \boxed{650}$.

Team Round Solutions

1. From the fact that triangles ABC and ADE are equilateral triangles, we see that $BC = 8$ and $DE = 5$. Also, since triangle ADE is an equilateral triangle, we have that $AD = 5$ and $AE = 5$, which means that $BE = 3$ and $CD = 3$. This means that the perimeter of quadrilateral $BCDE$ is $8 + 3 + 5 + 3 = \boxed{19}$.

2. The genre with the most books is mystery, at 60 books. The genre with the least books is biography, at 35 books. For each mystery book that Amee can pick, she can pick from any of the 35 biography books. This means that Amee has $60 \cdot 35 = \boxed{2100}$ ways to pick the books.

3. The starting location is 10 meters below sea level, so sea level is 10 meters above the starting location. Since the maximum height is 123 meters above sea level, Jessica's bottle rocket gained a total of $123 + 10 = 133$ meters in elevation. Since 1 minute equals 60 seconds, the rocket flew for 70 seconds before deploying the parachute. Therefore, the average gain in elevation of Jessica's bottle rocket is $\frac{133}{70} = \boxed{1.9}$ meters per second.

4. Let k be the number of slices of cake. For the surface area of the cake slice, we can observe that each cake slice would have two sector faces, two rectangular faces, and part of the outer wrap of the original cylinder. This means that the surface area is $\frac{1}{k} \cdot 2 \cdot 16\pi + \frac{1}{k} \cdot 8\pi \cdot 4 + 2 \cdot 16$ square centimeters, which we know is equal to $8\pi + 32$ square centimeters. Setting the two quantities equal, we find that $\frac{64\pi}{k} + 32 = 8\pi + 32$. Therefore, $k = 8$, and including the one who did not get cake, we find that there are $\boxed{9}$ teammates in the group.

5. We know that the sum of two odd whole numbers is an even whole number, and this whole number has 7 positive divisors. Since 7 is prime, we know that this number is equal to p^6 for a prime p. The only even prime number is 2, so the number must be $2^6 = 64$. Then, since 3 is also prime, we know that one of the odd numbers must be equal to q^2 for a prime q. Then, we have that the odd number with 4 positive divisors is equal to $64 - q^2$. Testing $q = 3$, we get $55 = 5 \cdot 11$, which indeed has 4 positive divisors. Thus, the greatest possible value is $\boxed{55}$.

6. Note that the degree of $x - 8$ is one and the degree of $ax^2 + bx + c$ is at most two, so the degree of x^n must be at most $1 + 2 = 3$. Then, we are left with $n = 1, 2, 3$. If $n = 1$, then we need $a = 0$ and $b = 0$. Then, we need $c = 1$. This gives us $a + b + c + n = 2$. If $n = 2$, then we need $a = 0$. Then, we need $b = 1$. Finally, in order for the product to only have two terms, we need $c = 8$. This gives us $a + b + c + n = 11$. If $n = 3$, then we need $a = 1$. Then, $(x - 8)(x^2 + bx + c) = x^3 + (b - 8)x^2 + (c - 8b)x - 8c$. We need $b - 8 = 0$ and $c - 8b = 0$. This gives us $b = 8$ and $c = 64$. This gives us $a + b + c + n = 76$. Thus, the answer is $2 + 11 + 76 = \boxed{89}$.

7. We can label the vertices with the positive integers from 1 to 2023, inclusive. Consider the vertices that are not chosen, where at least one vertex not chosen must go between two vertices that are chosen. If we just insert one unchosen vertex between two chosen vertices, we would have $1011 + 1011 = 2022$ vertices, with one vertex left over. Therefore, there must be exactly one part involving two unchosen vertices going between two chosen vertices. By symmetry, we can then consider the labels of the two consecutive vertices that are not chosen, which consist of 1 and 2, 2 and 3, and so on, until 2023 and 1. Thus, there are $\boxed{2023}$ possibilities in total.

8. Note that $\overline{OP} \perp \overline{BC}$, so $\triangle MPQ$ is a right triangle. By the Pythagorean Theorem, $PQ = \frac{17}{2}$. Let N be the midpoint of $\overline{AP}$, so that $NP = 15$. Since $AO = OP$, $\overline{ON} \perp \overline{AP}$. Thus, $\triangle ONP$ is a right triangle. Thus, $\triangle MPQ \sim \triangle NPO$. Then, we find that $OP = 17$. Thus, $OM = \frac{19}{2}$. Then, $BO = 17$ since it is also a radius. Finally, by the Pythagorean Theorem, $\frac{BC}{2} = \sqrt{17^2 - \left(\frac{19}{2}\right)^2}$, so $BC = \sqrt{795}$, so $BC^2 = \boxed{795}$.

9. First, we note that the value of $p + q$ for a fraction and its reciprocal should be equal since the numerator and denominator of the fraction are merely switched. Then, we have $\frac{n^2 + 10n + 100}{n + 5}$. Next, by polynomial division (or observing that $(n + 5)^2 = n^2 + 10n + 25$, which is really similar), we get that $\frac{n^2 + 10n + 100}{n + 5} = n + 5 + \frac{75}{n + 5}$. Let $m = n + 5$. Then, we want to minimize the value of $p + q$ for the fraction $m + \frac{75}{m}$, where m is a whole number at least 6. We see that $m + \frac{75}{m} = \frac{m^2 + 75}{m}$. Then, the value of $p + q$ for this fraction would be $\frac{m^2 + m + 75}{\gcd(m, 75)}$. Then, we want to maximize the value of $\gcd(m, 75)$ while minimizing the value of $m^2 + m + 75$.

We see that the set of all possible values of $\gcd(m, 75)$ is $\{1, 3, 5, 15, 25, 75\}$. In order to minimize the value of $p + q$, we want to find the smallest value of m such that $\gcd(m, 75)$ covers the corresponding value. If $\gcd(m, 75) = 3$, then the smallest m is 6, giving $p + q = 39$. If $\gcd(m, 75) = 5$, then the smallest m is 10, giving $p + q = 37$. For $\gcd(m, 75) = 15, 25, 75$, the smallest m is $15, 25, 75$, respectively, giving $p + q = 21, 29, 77$, respectively. Of these, the smallest possible value of $p + q$ is $\boxed{21}$.

10. Let a, b, c, and d be the numbers showing on Adam's, Bob's, Chris', and David's dice. Then, consider the substitution $b' = b - 6$, $c' = c - 12$, and $d' = d - 18$, where a, b', c', and d' are each whole numbers between 1 and 6, inclusive. Then, we have that $a + d > b + c$ becomes $a + d' > b' + c'$. By symmetry, it follows that the number of possibilities where $a + d > b + c$ is $\frac{6^4 - (2(1^2 + 2^2 + 3^2 + 4^2 + 5^2) + 6^2)}{2} = 575$. Since 575 is not divisible by 2 or 3, it follows that the probability is $\boxed{\dfrac{575}{1296}}$.

Sprint Round
12315

Place ID Sticker
Inside This Box

Name _____

Grade _____

School _____

1.	2.	3.	4.	5.
6.	7.	8.	9.	10.
11.	12.	13.	14.	15.
16.	17.	18.	19.	20.
21.	22.	23.	24.	25.
26.	27.	28.	29.	30.

1. On Saturday, Usha saw 12 legendary birds and 15 legendary dogs. On Sunday, she saw 21 legendary birds and 9 legendary dogs. On the day that Usha saw more legendary dogs than legendary birds, how many legendary creatures did Usha see altogether?

2. Raichi is writing a math contest consisting of 10 problems. She has already written the first nine problems, with each problem containing 20 words. If the combined number of words in all ten problems cannot be greater than 500, at most how many words can the tenth problem have?

3. A building is shaped like a rectangular prism with dimensions 3 meters by 8 meters by 24 meters. Edward observes that a mural covers one of the two largest external faces of the building. How many square meters is the area of the mural?

4. What is the sum of all positive whole numbers less than or equal to 15 that evenly divide neither of 14 and 15?

5. In the sequence $-2, 2, 6, \ldots$, any two consecutive terms have the same difference from left to right. What is the value of the fifteenth term of this sequence?

6. Elise is watching two 10-minute portions of a game show. The first portion starts at 4:46 PM, and the second one ends at 5:09 PM the same day. The two parts of the show are separated by 4 commercials of equal length. How many seconds does each commercial last?

7. In the diagram below, point O is on line AG, and five additional rays are drawn from point O such that $\angle AOG$ is split into angles of equal measure. How many ways can two distinct rays with a vertex at O be selected such that the smaller angle formed between them is acute?

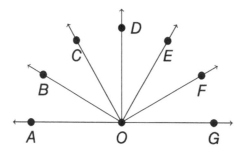

8. What is the sum of all non-negative single-digit whole numbers d such that d^n has units digit d for all positive whole numbers n?

9. Shuwen's red string is just long enough to make a circular loop with diameter 1 meter. She plans on putting lake beads of length 2 centimeters on the string with at least half a centimeter of space between each bead. What is the greatest number of beads that Shuwen can put on the string?

10. A whole number a between 1 and 10, inclusive, is chosen at random. What is the probability that $\left(\frac{2}{3}\right)^{-a} < 3$? Express your answer as a common fraction.

11. The first term of a particular sequence is 1, and every term thereafter is equal to one more than the sum of the previous term and the square of the previous term. What is the units digit of the sum of the first 2023 terms of the sequence?

12. Isabel plans on making boxes that are cubes from pieces of cardboard that are each 8 feet by 6 feet. She has two ways to cut out and fold a net as shown below, and she leaves behind unused quadrilaterals each time. The total volume of all her boxes is 80 cubic feet, and $\frac{2}{7}$ of the unused quadrilaterals are squares. How many unused quadrilaterals are squares?

13. Let $f(x) = \frac{x}{2x+1}$. What is the sum of all positive whole numbers x for which $f(x) \leq \frac{\sqrt{6}}{5}$?

14. Lisa has a list of four consecutive whole numbers. If she increases one of the numbers by two and decreases a different number by two, then the resulting list is $4, 4, n, n$ in some order. What is the sum of all possible values of n?

15. A typical license plate in Mathleaguia has a two-digit number consisting of a digit chosen from 1, 2, and 3 followed by a digit chosen from 4, 5, and 6. If there is only one license plate for each two-digit number, how many unordered groups of three different license plates are there such that all of the digits from 1 to 6, inclusive, appear on at least one of the license plates?

16. Starting from the year 2022, the smartphone company Cherry will come out with n "new" iterations of the c-Phone in the year $2021 + n$ for all $n \geq 1$. In what year will the 1000th iteration of the c-Phone come out?

17. Given that $2x + 3y + 4z = 24$, $4x + 3y + 2z = 48$, and $yz = -72$, what is the greatest possible value of x?

18. Parallelogram $ABCD$ has $AB = 10$. Let there be a point E on side $\overline{CD}$ such that $AE = 13$ and $BE = 13$. If the area of $\triangle ADE$ is 36, what is the area of $\triangle BCE$?

19. How many different sequences of four positive whole numbers have a first term of 2, a last term no more than 20, and the property that every term after the first is at least twice as large as the term before it?

20. Let a and b be distinct divisors of the number 225. If the product ab is *not* a divisor of 225, what is the smallest possible value of $a + b$?

21. For how many ordered pairs (a, b) of positive whole numbers less than or equal to 20 does $\sqrt{a + b\sqrt{3}}$ have simplest form $c + d\sqrt{3}$ for some positive whole numbers c and d?

22. Sammy rolls three standard six-sided dice. What is the probability that the sum of the numbers rolled is between 7 and 14, inclusive? Express your answer as a common fraction.

23. How many ordered pairs (m, n) of positive whole numbers are there such that $\sqrt{m} + \sqrt{n} = \sqrt{192}$?

24. Given rectangle $ABCD$ with $AB = 12$ and $BC = 5$, let P be the point outside of $ABCD$ such that $\overline{DP} \parallel \overline{AC}$ and $\angle BPD = 90°$. What is the length of $\overline{DP}$? Express your answer as a common fraction.

25. Three of the digits in the number $m = 121212$ are replaced with the digit 9 to form a number n. What is the largest possible value of $\gcd(m, n)$?

26. Triangle ABC has whole-number side lengths $n + 1$, $n + 2$, and $n + 3$ for some positive whole number n. Points are drawn along each edge of the triangle, including at the vertices, to split the sides into segments of length 1. Let $f(n)$ be a polynomial in terms of n that calculates the number of triangles with positive area that can be formed from the points on triangle ABC. What is the sum of the coefficients of $f(n)$?

27. Let a and b be real numbers less than 1 such that $a + \sqrt{1 - b} = \frac{1}{2}$ and $b + \sqrt{1 - a} = \frac{1}{2}$. Given that exactly one ordered pair (a, b) satisfies these conditions, what is the value of ab? Express your answer as a common fraction.

28. In a regular 200-sided polygon $A_1 A_2 \ldots A_{200}$, diagonals $\overline{A_7 A_{77}}$ and $\overline{A_{11} A_{111}}$ intersect at a point P. For some unique positive whole numbers m and n, with $m < n$, the diagonal $\overline{A_m A_n}$ passes through P. What is $n - m$?

29. When the base 10 fraction $\frac{1}{1536}$ is converted into base 12, the result is $0.a_1 a_2 \ldots a_n$, where each a_i is a digit in base 12. What is the value of the base 10 sum $a_1 + a_2 + \cdots + a_n$?

30. In regular octagon $MATHLEGU$, point I lies on segment $\overline{UH}$ so that $\overline{AI} \parallel \overline{ME}$. If the area of $\triangle LIE$ is equal to 4, what is the square of the area of $\triangle AIM$?

Place ID Sticker
Inside This Box

Name _____

Grade _____

School _____

Problems 1 & 2

1. The stadium of Victoria's favorite football team has six floors of 20 sections each, with each section containing 200 seats. The table below lists the fan attendance at the last six games. How many seats were empty at the game with the most occupied seats?

Game	Seats Occupied
1	14827
2	18592
3	16492
4	18255
5	18946
6	16396

1.

2. Zhengzhe has a scale model of a skyscraper shaped like a rectangular prism. In the model, 1 centimeter represents 3 miles. Zhengzhe knows that the top of the skyscraper is a square with area 36 square miles, and he notices that a vertical face of his scale model has an area of 24 square centimeters. How many cubic centimeters is the volume of the scale model?

2.

Place ID Sticker
Inside This Box

Name _____

Grade _____

School _____

Problems 3 & 4

3. Claudia is making tule boats. She has 50 small bundles of tule reeds, 30 long sticks, and 500 pieces of big rope. It takes 2 small bundles of tule reeds and a long stick to make one section of a tule boat, and each full boat contains three sections connected by 20 pieces of big rope. Claudia needs 15 minutes to make each tule boat, and she makes boats until she no longer has enough materials to make another whole boat. How many minutes will Claudia work?

3.

4. Two fair standard six-sided dice are rolled. What is the probability that the sum of the reciprocals of the numbers rolled is at least $\frac{1}{2}$? Express your answer as a common fraction.

4.

Place ID Sticker
Inside This Box

Name _____

Grade _____

School _____

Problems 5 & 6

5. How many sets of two distinct whole numbers between 1 and 8, inclusive, exist such that the product of the two numbers is odd?

5.

6. The line $y = ax + 2$ intersects the parabola $y = 20x^2 + 22x + a$ at two points whose x-coordinates differ by 20. The greater of the two possible values of a may be written in the form $p + q\sqrt{r}$, where p, q, and r are positive whole numbers, and r is not divisible by the square of a prime number. What is $p + q + r$?

6.

Place ID Sticker
Inside This Box

Name _____

Grade _____

School _____

Problems 7 & 8

7. Two concentric circles have radii 8 and 17. A chord of the larger circle with whole-number length intersects the smaller circle at least once. How many values are possible for the length of the chord?

7.

8. Let a and b be relatively prime positive whole numbers. If exactly two of the numbers $a - 3b$, $3a - 5b$, and $5a - 7b$ are positive, and exactly one of the numbers $a \div 3b$, $3a \div 5b$, and $5a \div 7b$ is a whole number, what is the sum of all possible values of $a + b$?

8.

Team Round
12315

School or Team	Name _____
	Name _____
	Name _____
	Name _____

Place ID Sticker
Inside This Box

Place ID Sticker
Inside This Box

Place ID Sticker
Inside This Box

Place ID Sticker
Inside This Box

1.	2.	3.	4.	5.
6.	7.	8.	9.	10.

1. Ellen bought a lot of frozen yogurt: 15 servings of chocolate, 16 servings of vanilla, 14 servings of strawberry, and 12 servings of cookie dough. Her friends ate some whole number servings of frozen yogurt, and of what remains, the probability that a randomly chosen serving is strawberry is 100%. At least how many servings did her friends eat?

2. Let a, b, and c be positive whole numbers. If b is 180 percent larger than a, c is 100 percent larger than b, and c is p percent larger than a, what is the smallest possible value of $a + b + c + p$?

3. Fey and Tak cannot fall asleep late at night, so they take turns counting sheep in a particular manner. Fey starts by saying "two sheep," and then Tak says "five sheep." For each turn after that, one of them says the sum of the two numbers of sheep from the last two turns. For example, Fey will say "seven sheep" on her next turn, and then Tak will say "twelve sheep." At some point, one of them says "$(n+3)$ sheep," after which the other person says "$(2n-6)$ sheep," for some positive whole number n. What is n?

4. On Evelyn's map, the side length of a unit square represents 5 kilometers, and the shaded areas represent six islands of equal area. She knows that there is treasure at the centers of two islands that each have $180°$ but not $90°$ rotational symmetry. If the real-life distance between the two treasures is $\sqrt{N}$ kilometers, what is the value of N?

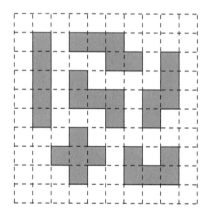

5. What is the sum of all three-digit whole numbers beginning with 5 which still have 5 as their leftmost digit when multiplied by 9?

6. Marcie has a box of 16 chocolates, two each of eight different flavors. She randomly selects eight chocolates from her box without replacement. What is the probability that Marcie selects both chocolates of at most two flavors? Express your answer as a common fraction.

7. In $\triangle ABC$, $\angle ACB = 90°$, and the altitude from point C to $\overline{AB}$ intersects $\overline{AB}$ at D such that the lengths AD and BD are both whole numbers. Given that $AC^2 - BC^2 = 19$, the area of $\triangle ABC$ is $\frac{m\sqrt{n}}{p}$, where m, n, and p are positive whole numbers such that m and p are relatively prime, and n is not divisible by the square of any prime. What is $m + n + p$?

8. Let S be the sum of all perfect squares less than or equal to 2022^2 that are multiples of 30 but not 40. What is $\frac{S}{900}$?

9. In the 3×3 grid below, a positive whole number from 1 to 9, inclusive, is written in each square. No number appears twice, and the sum of the numbers in each column is the same. In addition, the sum of the numbers in the top row is 6, and the sum of the numbers in the bottom row is 24. How many ways can the grid be filled with numbers?

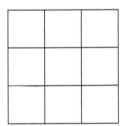

10. Trina boards a train from Snoozeville to Sleepytown at 12:00 PM. The train travels at a constant rate for the first part of the journey, but at some point, it starts raining, and the train's speed is reduced by half. Exactly 90 minutes after it starts raining, the rain stops, and the train returns to its original speed. Trina arrives in Sleepytown at 3:15 PM. Let r be the ratio of the total distance covered before it stopped raining to the total distance covered after it started raining, and let s be the ratio of the total time before it stopped raining to the total time after it started raining. If $\frac{r}{s} = \frac{21}{20}$, how many minutes into the ride did it start raining?

1. Cary and Michael are designing a simulation that shows the relative sizes of objects in the universe. A red blood cell has a diameter of 7 micrometers, and a moon has a diameter of 3500 kilometers. In scientific notation, how many times wider is the moon than the red blood cell? Note that one meter equals one million micrometers.

2. If $20x + 400 + x = 80 + 2(300 + x) - 3$, what is the value of x? Express your answer as a common fraction.

3. Simplify: $(45 + \sqrt{2763})(45 - \sqrt{2763})$.

4. The price of school supplies at a store is shown below. Roxana plans on buying exactly one pack of binder paper and at least one mechanical pencil at the store. If she spends a total of 20 dollars, how many combinations of mechanical pencils and pencil lead can Roxana buy?

Item	Price
Mechanical Pencil	$2
Pencil Lead	$0.50
Binder Paper Pack	$3

5. Madeline is participating in a sparring match. Each match involves some number of rounds where the winner of the match is the first one to win two rounds. If the probability that Madeline wins a round is $\frac{3}{5}$, what is the probability that Madeline wins the match? Express your answer as a common fraction.

6. What is the area of the region bounded by the x-axis, y-axis, and the line $2x + 3y = 12$?

7. If two square numbers have a difference of 40, what is the largest possible sum of those square numbers?

8. Jeff bought three pieces of bubble gum that each have the same price by using a penny (1 cent), a nickel (5 cents), a dime (10 cents), a quarter (25 cents), and a dollar from his mother. How many cents does each piece of bubble gum cost?

9. Find 2^x if $\left(\frac{1}{2}\right)^{x+1} = 2763$. Express your answer as a common fraction.

10. Express $\sqrt{4.84}$ as a decimal to the nearest tenth.

11. Evaluate: $7 - 8 + 9 - 10 + \cdots + 99 - 100$.

12. Cheyenne arranges 99 ice cubes that each have an edge length of 1 unit so that they form a rectangle, and exactly 36 of these ice cubes lie along the edges of the rectangle. What is the positive difference between the side lengths of the rectangle, in units?

13. How many different ways are there to arrange the letters in the word *ANIMATE*, if no two vowels (*A, E, I, O,* or *U*) can be next to each other?

14. Three regular hexagons with the same side length do not intersect internally but share a common vertex. The perimeter of the shape formed by the three hexagons is 144. What is the side length of one of the hexagons?

15. In the Needy Knitting Session, Lois provides bundles of red yarn, green yarn, and white yarn for four friends. In how many ways can each friend select between one and three different colors of yarn for their knitting session?

16. Simplify: $\left(1 - \frac{1}{2}\right)\left(1 - \frac{1}{3}\right)\left(1 - \frac{1}{4}\right) \cdots \left(1 - \frac{1}{12}\right)$. Express your answer as a common fraction.

17. On an exam day that requires all students to have at least one blue pen or at least one black pen, 72% of the students have a blue pen and 38% of the students have a black pen. If 15 students have a blue pen and a black pen, how many students showed up to the exam?

18. How many two-digit numbers are divisible by 5 or 7 but not both?

19. What is the sum of the units and tens digits of 2763^2?

20. How many different sets of prime numbers sum to 22 if numbers may not appear more than once in any particular set and the order of numbers in the set does not matter?

21. What is the sum of the solutions of the equation $|2x + 7| = 63$?

22. How many elements are in the union of $\{A, C, D, E, F\}$ and $\{B, D, F, G, H\}$?

23. If $y^{1/2} = x^{1/3}$, then $y^{216} = x^k$. What is k?

24. A positive integer n less than or equal to 60 is randomly selected. What is the probability that $\gcd(n, 60) > 1$? Express your answer as a common fraction.

25. If $f(x) = x^2 + 3$ and $g(x) = 2x + 4$, then what is $f(g(4))$?

26. If $x, y, z \neq 0$ and $x + 2y = 4z$, then what is the value of $\frac{x^3 + 8y^3 - 64z^3}{xyz}$?

27. If $y = 2x - 3$ and $y = -4x + 11$, what is the value of x? Express your answer as a common fraction.

28. How many 4-digit numbers have no even digits?

29. What is the value of $\frac{(\sqrt{27})^{\frac{1}{15}} + \sqrt[5]{\sqrt[6]{27}}}{(\sqrt[3]{9})^{\frac{3}{20}}}$?

30. An eraser with a volume of 1.296 cubic centimeters has only four rectangular faces. The other two faces are parallelograms with two parallel sides of length 1.8 centimeters that are 1.2 centimeters apart. How many centimeters apart are the two non-rectangular faces? Express your answer as a decimal without trailing zeroes.

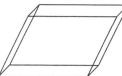

31. The perimeter of a regular octagon is 2^{48}. If the side length of the octagon is 2^x, what is the value of x?

32. When converting 2763_9 to base 3, how many digits are non-zero?

33. A pirate ship has 10 wooden planks arranged in a row. John randomly picks five planks to drop. If the leftmost and rightmost planks are not dropped, what is the probability that the five dropped planks are all next to each other? Express your answer as a common fraction.

34. What is the smallest fully simplified fraction whose numerator and denominator are each a two-digit whole number whose digits are in strictly decreasing order? Express your answer as a common fraction.

35. Two interior angles of a convex quadrilateral measure 40°, and one of the remaining two interior angles has a measure 40° greater than the measure of the other. How many degrees is the measure of the largest interior angle of the quadrilateral?

36. The table below partially shows the number of two-point shots and three-point attempts that Curtis did over the last few basketball games. Curtis scored a total of 124 points from successful attempts and did a total of 92 attempts. If Daniel blocked 35% of Curtis's missed attempts, how many attempts did Daniel block?

	Success	Missed
Two-Point	32	
Three-Point		24

37. How many of the numbers that can be expressed as the factorial of a positive whole number are not divisible by 10?

38. If $p(x)$ and $q(x)$ are distinct polynomials of degree 5, then how many possible values are there for the degree of the polynomial $p(x) - q(x)$?

39. Harrison is running from a giant rock, which is tumbling at a speed of 7.5 meters per second towards him. Harrison is currently 500 meters ahead of the rock, and the exit is 100 meters ahead of him. At least how many centimeters per second must Harrison run to reach the exit?

40. How many seconds does it take the hour hand on a clock to rotate 20 degrees?

41. For what value of x is $f(x) = |3x - 15| - 2021^2$ minimized?

42. Dillon is making a snowman with two spherical snowballs, where each radius is a whole number of meters. The volume of the snowman is $\frac{364}{3}\pi$ cubic meters, and the sum of the diameters of the snowballs is 14 meters. How many meters long is the radius of the larger snowball?

43. What is the largest integer x such that 2^x divides 1152?

44. Elise did some putting at a flat mini-golf course. In her first stroke, her golf ball went 25 meters east from the starting point. In her second stroke, her golf ball then went 11 meters south. The golf ball is now 35 meters west from the hole. How many meters is the starting point from the hole?

45. If the value of $2x^2 + (2x)^2 + 4(-x)^2 + (-4x)^2$ is 234, what is the smallest possible value of x?

46. Skye gives 3 tennis balls to each player of every two-player team in a doubles tennis tournament. After each game, exactly one team wins and remains in the tournament and one team loses and gets eliminated. The tournament has a total of 15 doubles games before the winner of the last game is announced. How many tennis balls does Skye give?

47. Compute: $\frac{27^2 - 63^2}{6^2}$.

48. What is $\binom{10}{0} + \binom{10}{2} + \binom{10}{4} + \binom{10}{6} + \binom{10}{8} + \binom{10}{10}$?

49. At a flower market, roses come in bundles of three, and violets come in bundles of four. Joy bought two of each bundle for $28, and the violet bundle costs $2 more than the rose bundle. If Joy instead got the same number of roses as violets by buying the smallest possible positive whole number of each bundle, how many dollars would she pay?

50. What is the degree measure of the supplement of an angle whose complement has a measure of 27.63 degrees? Express your answer as a decimal without trailing zeroes.

51. Evaluate: $\sqrt{32} \cdot \sqrt{128}$.

52. A cylinder has a radius of 6 and a surface area of 156π. What is the height of the cylinder?

53. What is the median of the numbers in the following list? Express your answer as a decimal to the nearest hundredth.
$$\{0.12, 0.034, 5.6, 0.78\}$$

54. A list of three consecutive whole numbers sums to 2763. What is the smallest number in the list?

55. What is the sum of the units and hundreds digits of $101 \times 202 \times 404$?

56. Simplify: $10000 - 2763$.

57. An octagon is created by placing four equilateral triangles with sides of length 4 around a square with a side length of 4. What is the area of the octagon? Express your answer in simplest radical form.

58. The measure of two exterior angles of a triangle are $142°$ and $78°$. How many degrees is the measure of the third exterior angle?

59. Evaluate: 51×90.

60. Express as a mixed number: $2\frac{1}{2} + 5\frac{1}{5} + 10\frac{1}{10}$.

61. What is the quotient when 28 is divided by $\frac{1}{4}$?

62. Compute: $0.8289 \div 27.63$. Round your answer to the nearest hundredth.

63. Evaluate: $64^{-1/3}$. Express your answer as a common fraction.

64. Calculate: $2763 \cdot 101$.

65. Thomas's sponge is a rectangular prism with dimensions of 1 centimeter, 4 centimeters, and 8 centimeters. Thomas observes that for each square centimeter on the surface of the sponge, there are 3 holes. How many holes are on Thomas's sponge?

66. The number 2023 is 2 less than a perfect square. The number 2023 is how much greater than the greatest perfect square less than 2023?

67. How many distinct prime factors does 92 have?

68. Quincy flips a fair coin 5 times, and it lands on heads 3 times. What is the positive difference between Quincy's experimental probability of landing on heads and the theoretical probability of landing on heads? Express your answer as a common fraction.

69. Jared recorded the number of pins he knocked down for his first nine frames in the table below. A frame during which 10 pins are knocked down is considered either a spare or a strike. Across all frames that are not strikes or spares, how many pins did he knock down?

Frame	1	2	3	4	5	6	7	8	9
Attempt 1	9	8	7	8	0	10	10	9	7
Attempt 2	0	2	3	1	10	0	0	0	0

70. The number 2763 has six positive factors. What is the greatest prime factor of 2763?

71. Find the 9th term in the arithmetic sequence: $27, 63, 99, \ldots$.

72. A drawing of a teardrop is formed by attaching a semicircle of radius 3 to the longest side of an isosceles triangle where two of the sides have length 5. To the nearest whole number, what is the area of the teardrop?

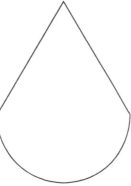

73. What is the units digit of the product $187 \times 709 \times 667 \times 781$?

74. How many ways are there to split 5 identical balls among 3 friends?

75. The radius of circle A is 30% of the radius of circle B. The area of circle A is what percent of the area of circle B?

76. A mathleague.org online problem video that was released at 5:00:00 PM EST is 2 minutes and 30 seconds long. David started watching the video, and at 7:15:00 PM EST on the same day, David still had 90 seconds to go before finishing the video. How many minutes after the release did David start watching the video?

77. A hexagon has five sides of length 6 and a perimeter of 42. What is the length of the sixth side?

78. What is the smallest possible value of x that satisfies $x^2 = 1024$?

79. Cassie is estimating the area of a leaf by laying it on a grid with 100 unit squares, as shown below. How many unit squares are completely inside the leaf?

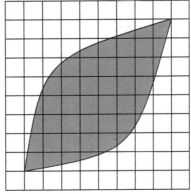

80. Bryce's patrol is having s'mores at a campfire. Each s'more consists of one marshmallow and two crackers. The patrol started with 40 marshmallows and some number of crackers such that, once half the marshmallows are used for s'mores, the same number of crackers and marshmallows remain. How many crackers did the patrol start with?

Sprint Round

1. 27	11. 7	21. 6
2. 320	12. 8	22. $\frac{22}{27}$
3. 192	13. 300	23. 7
4. 73	14. 16	24. $\frac{119}{13}$
5. 54	15. 6	25. 40404
6. 45	16. 2066	26. 69
7. 11	17. 18	27. $\frac{3}{4}$
8. 12	18. 24	28. 130
9. 125	19. 10	29. 8
10. $\frac{1}{5}$	20. 12	30. 32

Target Round

1. 5054
2. 48
3. 120
4. $\frac{7}{9}$
5. 6
6. 204
7. 5
8. 23

Team Round

1. 43
2. 507
3. 28
4. 250
5. 25410
6. $\frac{32}{39}$
7. 69
8. 52394
9. 12
10. 60

Countdown

1. $5 \cdot 10^{11}$	21. -7	41. 5	61. 112
2. $\frac{277}{19}$	22. 8	42. 4	62. 0.03
3. -738	23. 144	43. 7	63. $\frac{1}{4}$
4. 8	24. $\frac{11}{15}$	44. 61	64. 279063
5. $\frac{81}{125}$	25. 147	45. -3	65. 264
6. 12	26. -24	46. 96	66. 87
7. 202	27. $\frac{7}{3}$	47. -90	67. 2
8. 47	28. 625	48. 512	68. $\frac{1}{10}$
9. $\frac{1}{5526}$	29. 2	49. 48	69. 34
10. 2.2	30. 0.6	50. 117.63	70. 307
11. -47	31. 45	51. 64	71. 315
12. 2	32. 5	52. 7	72. 26
13. 72	33. $\frac{1}{14}$	53. 0.45	73. 1
14. 12	34. $\frac{10}{97}$	54. 920	74. 21
15. 2401	35. 160	55. 12	75. 9
16. $\frac{1}{12}$	36. 14	56. 7237	76. 134
17. 150	37. 4	57. $16 + 16\sqrt{3}$	77. 12
18. 27	38. 6	58. 140	78. -32
19. 15	39. 125	59. 4590	79. 22
20. 4	40. 2400	60. $17\frac{4}{5}$	80. 60

Sprint Round Solutions

1. Usha saw more legendary dogs than legendary birds on Saturday. That day, she saw $12 + 15 = \boxed{27}$ legendary creatures in total.

2. The first nine problems have a total of $9 \cdot 20 = 180$ words. Thus, the greatest number of words that the tenth problem could have is $500 - 180 = \boxed{320}$.

3. The largest face is the one with dimensions 8 meters by 24 meters and has an area of $24 \cdot 8 = \boxed{192}$ square meters.

4. The factors of 14 are 1, 2, 7, and 14, and the factors of 15 are 1, 3, 5, and 15. The sum of the whole numbers from 1 through 15, inclusive, that are factors of neither 14 nor 15 is then $4 + 6 + 8 + 9 + 10 + 11 + 12 + 13 = \boxed{73}$.

5. Notice that the second term is equal to 4 plus the first term, the third term is equal to 8 plus the first term, and so on. Then the 15th term is equal to $14 \cdot 4 = 56$ plus the first term, so the 15th term is $-2 + 56 = \boxed{54}$.

6. The first commercial starts at 4:56 PM while the last one ends at 4:59 PM. This means that there are three minutes, or 180 seconds, of time equally divided among 4 commercials. Thus, the commercials each last $\frac{180}{4} = \boxed{45}$ seconds.

7. Note that the rays split $\angle AOG$ into 6 smaller angles each measuring $\frac{180°}{6} = 30°$. By the Angle Addition Postulate, we can also put together two adjacent $30°$ angles to form a $60°$ angle, of which there are 5. Adding more $30°$ angles would result in an angle measure of $90°$ or more, which makes the resulting angle no longer acute. Thus, the number of pairs of rays with an acute angle between them is $6 + 5 = \boxed{11}$.

8. We check each digit from 0 to 9, inclusive. By inspection, 0 and 1 work as $0^n = 0$ and $1^n = 1$ for all positive whole numbers n. However, 2, 3, and 4 do not meet our criterion since $2^2 = 4$, $3^2 = 9$, and $4^2 = 16$, respectively. Similarly, 7, 8, and 9 do not work. That leaves 5 and 6, both of which meet the given requirement. For instance, $5^2 = 25$, $6^2 = 36$, $5^3 = 125$, $6^3 = 216$, and so on. Thus, the sum of the non-negative whole numbers whose positive whole number powers have the same units digit as themselves is $0 + 1 + 5 + 6 = \boxed{12}$.

9. The length of Shuwen's string is 100π centimeters, which equals the circumference of a circle with diameter 1 meter. We can then pair each lake bead with an adjacent space into units of length 2.5 centimeters. The maximum number of such bead-space units on the string is $\frac{100\pi}{2.5} = 40\pi$, so the greatest number of beads Shuwen can put on the string is the largest whole number less than 40π, or $\boxed{125}$.

10. Note that $\left(\frac{2}{3}\right)^{-a} = \left(\frac{3}{2}\right)^a$, so we want all $1 \le a \le 10$ such that $\left(\frac{3}{2}\right)^a < 3$. Testing values of a, we find that only $a = 1$ and $a = 2$ work as $\left(\frac{3}{2}\right)^3 = \frac{27}{8}$, which is greater than 3, and increasing a will also increase the value of $\left(\frac{3}{2}\right)^a$. The probability that a randomly chosen positive whole number less than or equal to 10 satisfies $\left(\frac{2}{3}\right)^{-a} < 3$ is then $\frac{2}{10} = \boxed{\frac{1}{5}}$.

11. Note that only the units digit of each term is relevant. The second term of the sequence is $1+1+1^2 = 3$, and the third term is $1 + 3 + 3^2 = 13$, which also has a units digit of 3. Iterating further reveals that all of the terms in the sequence except for the first have a units digit of 3. Thus, the sum of the first 2023 terms of this sequence has a units digit equal to the remainder when $1 + 3 \cdot 2022 = 6067$ is divided by 10, or $\boxed{7}$.

12. Let x be the number of pieces that use the net on the left and y be the number of pieces that use the net on the right. Both nets would result in a cube with a side length of 2 feet, so the volume of each cube is 8 cubic feet. Thus, Isabel makes 10 boxes, so $x+y = 10$. Additionally, the net on the left leaves behind $2x$ squares and $2x$ non-squares, and the net on the right leaves behind $2y$ non-squares. It follows that $\frac{2x}{4x+2y} = \frac{2}{7}$, which we can rewrite as $3x = 2y$ by cross multiplication and simplification. Now we have a system of equations, and solving gives $x = 4$ and $y = 6$. The number of unused quadrilaterals that are squares is $4 \cdot 2 = \boxed{8}$.

13. We square both sides of the inequality $\frac{x}{2x+1} \le \frac{\sqrt{6}}{5}$ to obtain $\frac{x^2}{4x^2+4x+1} \le \frac{6}{25}$, so $25x^2 \le 24x^2 + 24x + 6$ by cross multiplication. Simplifying yields $x^2 \le 24x + 6$ or $x(x - 24) \le 6$, so $1 \le x \le 24$. The sum of all possible values of x is then $\frac{24 \cdot 25}{2} = \boxed{300}$.

14. Working backwards, we see that one of the 4s and one of the ns must have changed. Otherwise, if the two changed numbers are both 4 or both n, then the other two numbers would be the same, which we do not want. Then, we can either have new numbers $4 - 2 = 2$ and $n+2$, or $4+2 = 6$ and $n-2$, giving us $2, 4, n, n+2$ or $4, 6, n-2, n$. Of these, we see that both options have valid solutions. In particular, the first option has solutions $n = 1$ and $n = 3$, and the second option has solutions $n = 5$ and $n = 7$. The sum of these values is $1 + 3 + 5 + 7 = \boxed{16}$.

15. Since each license plate has exactly two digits, there are six total digits across three license plates. Since we want all digits from 1 to 6, inclusive, to appear, each digit must appear exactly once. If we fix the digits 1, 2, and 3, then there are $3! = 6$ ways to pair them with the digits 4, 5, and 6. Thus, the answer is $\boxed{6}$.

16. Note that 1000 is slightly greater than $1 + 2 + 3 + \cdots + 44 = 990$, so $n = 45$, and the 1000th c-Phone will come out in the year $2021 + 45 = \boxed{2066}$.

17. We multiply the first equation by 2 to get $4x + 6y + 8z = 48$. The difference between that and the second equation is then $3y + 6z = 0$, so $y = -2z$. Substituting $y = -2z$ into $yz = -72$, we get $-2z^2 = -72$, which solves to $z = \pm 6$. Now we plug $y = -2z$ into $2x + 3y + 4z = 24$ to obtain $2x - 2z = 24$ or $x - z = 12$. Finally, since we want to maximize x, we let $z = 6$ so that $x = \boxed{18}$.

18. By the base-height area formula, the area of $\triangle ABE$ is half the area of $ABCD$. Then note that $\triangle ABE$ is composed of two 5-12-13 right triangles, each having an area of $\frac{1}{2} \cdot 5 \cdot 12 = 30$. Thus, the area of $\triangle ABE$ is 60, and the area of $ABCD$ is 120. The sum of the areas of $\triangle ADE$ and $\triangle BCE$ must then also be 60, so the area of $\triangle BCE$ is $60 - 36 = \boxed{24}$.

19. All such sequences have the ordered form $2, 4 + a, 8 + 2a + b, 16 + 4a + 2b + c$ for some non-negative whole numbers a, b, and c. Since $16 + 4a + 2b + c \leq 20$, we know that $4a + 2b + c \leq 4$.
    - If $a = 0$, then $2b + c \leq 4$, which yields $b = 0$ and $c = 0, 1, 2, 3, 4$; $b = 1$ and $c = 0, 1, 2$; or $b = 2$ and $c = 0$, for a total of 9 possible sequences.
    - If $a = 1$, then $2b + c \leq 0$, so $b = 0$ and $c = 0$. This yields 1 additional sequence.
    - If $a \geq 2$, there are no non-negative whole number solutions of the inequality $4a + 2b + c \leq 4$ for b and c.

    Thus, there are $9 + 1 = \boxed{10}$ possible sequences.

20. Note that $225 = 3^2 \cdot 5^2$. For ab not to be a divisor of 225, the exponent of at least one of 3 and 5 in the prime factorization of ab must be greater than 2. The smallest possible value for ab is then $3^3 = 27$. Since $a + b$ is minimized when a and b are closer together, we pick 3 and 9, both divisors of 225, as a and b. Thus, the smallest possible value of $a + b$ is $3 + 9 = \boxed{12}$.

21. Writing $\sqrt{a + b\sqrt{3}} = c + d\sqrt{3}$ and squaring both sides, we get $a + b\sqrt{3} = (c^2 + 3d^2) + 2cd\sqrt{3}$, so $a = c^2 + 3d$ and $b = 2cd$. Then $c^2 + 3d^2 \leq 20$ and $cd \leq 10$. The first inequality implies $d \leq 2$. If $d = 1$, then $1 \leq c \leq 4$, and if $d = 2$, then $1 \leq c \leq 2$. All of these pairs satisfy $cd \leq 10$, so there are $4 + 2 = \boxed{6}$ possible ordered pairs (a, b).

22. Let n be the sum of the numbers that Sammy rolls, and let $P(n)$ denote the probability of obtaining a sum of n. Then we have that $P(3) = P(18)$, $P(4) = P(17)$, $P(5) = P(16)$, and $P(6) = P(15)$. By sticks-and-stones, $P(3) = \frac{\binom{2}{2}}{216}$, $P(4) = \frac{\binom{3}{2}}{216}$, $P(5) = \frac{\binom{4}{2}}{216}$, and $P(6) = \frac{\binom{5}{2}}{216}$; so $P(3) + P(4) + P(5) + P(6) = P(15) + P(16) + P(17) + P(18) = \frac{5}{54}$. Consequently, the probability that n is not between 7 and 14, inclusive, is $2 \cdot \frac{5}{54} = \frac{5}{27}$, and the probability that $7 \leq n \leq 14$ is $1 - \frac{5}{27} = \boxed{\frac{22}{27}}$.

23. Note that $\sqrt{192} = 8\sqrt{3}$, so we have $\sqrt{m} = 8\sqrt{3} - \sqrt{n}$ and $\sqrt{n} = 8\sqrt{3} - \sqrt{m}$. Squaring these equations yields $m = 192 + n - 16\sqrt{3n}$ and $n = 192 + m - 16\sqrt{3m}$. This means that $3m$ and $3n$ are perfect squares, so $m = 3j^2$ and $n = 3k^2$ for some whole numbers j and k. Then $\sqrt{m} + \sqrt{n} = (j + k)\sqrt{3} = 8\sqrt{3}$, which yields $j + k = 8$. Since j and k must be positive whole numbers, we have $\boxed{7}$ such ordered pairs.

24. Let E and F be the feet of the perpendiculars from B and D, respectively, to diagonal $\overline{AC}$. We see that $DFEP$ is a rectangle since $\angle DFE = 90°$, $\angle DPE = 90°$, and $\overline{DP} \parallel \overline{EF}$. Thus, $DP = EF = AC - AF - CE$. Note that $AF = CE$ by symmetry, so it suffices to find one of them. By the Pythagorean Theorem, $AC = 13$. Since $\triangle BEC \sim \triangle ABC$, we can write $\frac{BC}{CE} = \frac{AC}{BC}$, which yields $CE = \frac{25}{13}$. Thus, $EF = 13 - 2 \cdot \frac{25}{13}$, giving us $DP = \boxed{\dfrac{119}{13}}$.

25. Note that $121212 = 12 \cdot 10101$. If we replace the 1s in m with 9s, we get the number $n = 929292$. Since $929292 = 92 \cdot 10101$, we find that $\gcd(m, n) = 4 \cdot 10101 = 40404$, which equals $\frac{121212}{3}$. We must now show that $\gcd(m, n)$ cannot be greater than 40404. This is possible if and only if $\gcd(m, n)$ equals $\frac{121212}{2} = 60606$ or 121212. It is impossible to create a multiple of 121212 by replacing 3 digits with 9s, so $\gcd(m, n) \neq 121212$. For $\gcd(m, n)$ to equal 60606, the difference between n and 121212 must be divisible by 60606. This means that either all of the 1s or all of the 2s in m are replaced with the digit 9. Having already considered the former, we find that replacing the 2s with 9s forms the number 191919, which differs from 121212 by 70707, not a multiple of 60606. Thus, the largest possible value of $\gcd(m, n)$ is $\boxed{40404}$.

26. In total, we have $(n + 1 - 1) + (n + 2 - 1) + (n + 3 - 1) + 3 = 3n + 6$ points on triangle ABC, including the vertices. There are $\binom{3n+6}{3}$ triangles that can be formed from these vertices. However, $\binom{n+2}{3} + \binom{n+3}{3} + \binom{n+4}{3}$ of these are degenerate triangles along a single edge, so we discount them. This leaves a total of $f(n) = \binom{3n+6}{3} - \left[\binom{n+2}{3} + \binom{n+3}{3} + \binom{n+4}{3} \right]$ non-degenerate triangles. The sum of the coefficients of $f(n)$ is then $f(1)$, which evaluates to $\binom{9}{3} - \left(\binom{3}{3} + \binom{4}{3} + \binom{5}{3} \right) = \boxed{69}$.

27. The given equations are symmetric with respect to a and b and only have one ordered pair solution, so we let $a = b$. Then a and b both equal the solution to $x + \sqrt{1 - x} = \frac{1}{2}$. Expanding, we have $1 - x = (\frac{1}{2} - x)^2$, or $1 - x = \frac{1}{4} - x + x^2$. Hence, $x^2 = \frac{3}{4}$, so $ab = \boxed{\dfrac{3}{4}}$. Note that $a = b = -\frac{\sqrt{3}}{2}$ since $\frac{\sqrt{3}}{2} > \frac{1}{2}$.

28. Inscribe the 200-sided polygon in a circle. We see that $\overline{A_{11}A_{111}}$ is a diameter of this circle because $111 - 11 = 100$, which is half the number of vertices. We can then reflect chord $\overline{A_7A_{77}}$ over this diameter. To do this, we add $11 - 7 = 4$ to 11 to get 15 and $111 - 77 = 34$ to 111 to get 145. Thus, $m = 15$ and $n = 145$, so the answer is $n - m = \boxed{130}$.

29. The key idea is to multiply the fraction by 12, keep the whole number part, and iteratively repeat this process on the fractional part. Since $1536 = 2^9 \cdot 3$, we have $\frac{12^3}{1536} = \frac{9}{8} = 1.125$, so $a_3 = 1$. Then $\frac{12}{8} = \frac{3}{2} = 1.5$, so $a_4 = 1$. Lastly, $\frac{12}{2} = 6$, so $a_5 = 6$. It follows that $a_1 + a_2 + \cdots + a_5 = 0 + 0 + 0 + 1 + 1 + 6 = \boxed{8}$.

30. Note that $\overline{UH}$ and $\overline{AE}$ are perpendicular and intersect at their midpoints, so I lies on the perpendicular bisector of $\overline{AE}$. We also know that I lies on segment $\overline{AL}$. Since $\overline{AL}$ and $\overline{ET}$ intersect on $\overline{UH}$ by symmetry, we can conclude that I also lies on $\overline{ET}$. Next, we note that $\triangle ATI \cong \triangle ELI$ by symmetry. Additionally, both of these triangles are 45-45-90 right triangles. Thus, since the area of $\triangle LIE$ is equal to 4, we find that $\triangle ATI$ and $\triangle ELI$ have legs of length $2\sqrt{2}$ and a hypotenuse of length 4. We also see that $\angle MAI = 90°$. That gives us $MA = 2\sqrt{2}$ and $AI = 4$, so the area of $\triangle AIM$ is $\frac{1}{2} \cdot 2\sqrt{2} \cdot 4 = 4\sqrt{2}$, the square of which is $\boxed{32}$.

Target Round Solutions

1. The football stadium has a total of $6 \cdot 20 \cdot 200 = 24000$ seats. The maximum attendance occurred during Game 5, with 18946 occupied seats. This means that there were $24000 - 18946 = \boxed{5054}$ empty seats.

2. Since 1 centimeter corresponds to 3 miles, 1 square centimeter represents $3^2 = 9$ square miles. Then the top face of the scale model has an area of $\frac{36}{9} = 4$ square centimeters. The top face is a square, so the side length of the square top in the model is $\sqrt{4} = 2$ centimeters. Finally, each vertical face of the scale model has an area of 24 square centimeters, so the height of the scale model is $\frac{24}{2} = 12$ centimeters. Finally, the volume of the scale model is $2 \cdot 2 \cdot 12 = \boxed{48}$ cubic centimeters.

3. One tule boat needs 20 pieces of big rope, $3 \cdot 2 = 6$ small tule reed bundles, and $3 \cdot 1 = 3$ long sticks. Claudia can make $\frac{500}{20} = 25$ tule boats from 500 pieces of big rope, $\frac{30}{3} = 10$ tule boats from 30 long sticks, and $\lfloor \frac{50}{6} \rfloor = 8$ tule boats from 50 small tule reed bundles. The limiting resource is tule reeds, so Claudia will make 8 tule boats, which takes her $8 \cdot 15 = \boxed{120}$ minutes.

4. Let the numbers rolled be a and b. The sum of their reciprocals is $\frac{a+b}{ab}$, so $\frac{a+b}{ab} \geq \frac{1}{2}$, or $ab - 2a - 2b \leq 0$. By Simon's Favorite Factoring Trick, $(a-2)(b-2) \leq 4$, which holds except when $(a, b) = (4, 5), (4, 6), (5, 4), (5, 5), (5, 6), (6, 4), (6, 5),$ or $(6, 6)$. Thus, in all but 8 out of $6^2 = 36$ cases, the sum of the reciprocals of the numbers rolled is at least $\frac{1}{2}$, giving us a probability of $1 - \frac{8}{36} = \boxed{\frac{7}{9}}$.

5. In order for the product of two numbers to be odd, both numbers must be odd. The only odd numbers between 1 and 8, inclusive, are 1, 3, 5, and 7, so we can form the unordered sets $\{1, 3\}$, $\{1, 5\}$, $\{1, 7\}$, $\{3, 5\}$, $\{3, 7\}$, and $\{5, 7\}$. Therefore, the answer is $\boxed{6}$.

6. We have that $ax + 2 = 20x^2 + 22x + a$, which rearranges to $20x^2 + (22 - a)x + (a - 2) = 0$. By the Quadratic Formula, $x = \frac{(a-22) \pm \sqrt{(22-a)^2 - 80(a-2)}}{40}$. We need $\frac{\sqrt{(22-a)^2 - 80(a-2)}}{20} = 20$. Expanding and combining like terms, we get $a^2 - 124a - 159356 = 0$. Using the Quadratic Formula again gives us $a = 62 \pm 40\sqrt{102}$. Thus, $p + q + r = \boxed{204}$.

7. The chord obtains its minimum length when it is tangent to the circle with radius 8. By the Pythagorean Theorem, the length of the chord is twice $\sqrt{17^2 - 8^2} = 15$, or 30. Similarly, the chord obtains its maximum length when it passes through the center of both circles as a diameter of the larger circle. In this case, the chord has length $17 \cdot 2 = 34$, so there are a total of $34 - 30 + 1 = \boxed{5}$ possible lengths for the chord.

8. From the subtraction conditions, exactly two of $a - 3b > 0$, $3a - 5b > 0$, and $5a - 7b > 0$ are true. These simplify to $\frac{a}{b} > 3$, $\frac{a}{b} > \frac{5}{3}$, and $\frac{a}{b} > \frac{7}{5}$, respectively. Since $3 > \frac{5}{3} > \frac{7}{5}$, the last two conditions hold but not the first. This gives us $\frac{5}{3} < \frac{a}{b} \leq 3$. From the division conditions, exactly one of the numbers $\frac{1}{3} \cdot \frac{a}{b}$, $\frac{3}{5} \cdot \frac{a}{b}$, and $\frac{5}{7} \cdot \frac{a}{b}$ is a whole number. We know that $\frac{5}{3} < \frac{a}{b} \leq 3$, so it follows that $\frac{5}{9} < \frac{1}{3} \cdot \frac{a}{b} \leq 1$, $1 < \frac{3}{5} \cdot \frac{a}{b} \leq \frac{9}{5}$, or $\frac{25}{21} < \frac{5}{7} \cdot \frac{a}{b} \leq \frac{15}{7}$. The whole-number solutions for $\frac{a}{b}$ for these inequalities are 1, no solution, and 2, respectively. Thus, $\frac{1}{3} \cdot \frac{a}{b} = 1$ or $\frac{5}{7} \cdot \frac{a}{b} = 2$, so $\frac{a}{b} = \{3, \frac{14}{5}\}$, which yields $a = 3b$ or $5a = 14b$. Finally, since a and b are relatively prime, our only solutions are $(a, b) = \{(3, 1), (14, 5)\}$. This gives us $a + b = \{4, 19\}$, and the sum of all possible values of $a + b$ is $\boxed{23}$.

Team Round Solutions

1. For a 100% probability that a randomly chosen serving is strawberry, all remaining servings must be strawberry. This means that, at minimum, Ellen's friends ate all servings of the other flavors, of which there are $15 + 16 + 12 = \boxed{43}$.

2. We have $b = (1 + \frac{180}{100}) \times a = \frac{14}{5}a$ and $c = (1 + \frac{100}{100}) \times b = 2b = \frac{28}{5}a$, so c is $100 \times (\frac{28}{5} - 1) = 460$ percent larger than a. For a to be a positive whole number, a must be a positive multiple of 5, so $a \geq 5$. Then $b \geq 14$ and $c \geq 28$, so the smallest possible value of $a + b + c + p$ is $5 + 14 + 28 + 460 = \boxed{507}$.

3. We can work backwards. The person who says "$2n - 6$ sheep" would have last said $2n - 6 - (n+3) =$ "$(n - 9)$ sheep," and the person who says "$n + 3$ sheep" said $n + 3 - (n - 9) =$ "12 sheep" before that. From the given information, we find that Tak says "12 sheep," then Fey says "19 sheep." This means that $n - 9 = 19$, so $n = \boxed{28}$.

4. Recall that a shape with 180° rotational symmetry can be rotated 180° about its center and result in an identical shape. Of the islands on the map below, the lighter-colored shapes have 180° have rotational symmetry. However, the plus sign-shaped island also has 90° rotational symmetry, so we know the rectangular and S-shaped islands have treasure. We then plot these islands' centers and connect them as shown.

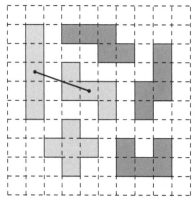

   Now observe that Evelyn can get from the center of the rectangular island to the center of the S-shaped island by moving 3 units to the right and 1 unit down. By the Pythagorean Theorem, this distance is $\sqrt{3^2 + 1^2} = \sqrt{10}$ units. As 1 unit corresponds to 5 kilometers, this represents $5\sqrt{10} = \sqrt{250}$ kilometers, so $N = \boxed{250}$.

5. We seek all three-digit whole numbers x such that $500 \leq x \leq 599$ and $5000 \leq 9x \leq 5999$. From the second inequality, $\frac{5000}{9} \leq x \leq \frac{5999}{9}$, or $556 \leq x \leq 666$ since x is a whole number. However, $x \leq 599$, so $556 \leq x \leq 599$. The sum of all possible values of x is then $(599 - 556 + 1) \times \frac{556+599}{2} = \boxed{25410}$.

6. For $0 \leq n \leq 4$, the number of ways in which Marcie can select n pairs of chocolates of the same flavor from 8 pairs of different flavors is $\binom{8}{n}\binom{8-n}{8-2n}2^{8-2n}$. Thus, the probability that Marcie selects at most two flavor pairs is $\dfrac{\sum_{n=0}^{2}\binom{8}{n}\binom{8-n}{8-2n}2^{8-2n}}{\binom{16}{8}} = \dfrac{32}{39}$. Alternatively, we use complementary probability to compute the desired probability to be $1 - \dfrac{\sum_{n=3}^{4}\binom{8}{n}\binom{8-n}{8-2n}2^{8-2n}}{\binom{16}{8}} = 1 - \dfrac{7}{39}$, which indeed equals $\boxed{\dfrac{32}{39}}$.

7. Let $AD = a$ and $BD = b$. The altitude from C to $\overline{AB}$ has length $\sqrt{ab}$, so $AC = \sqrt{a^2 + ab}$ and $BC = \sqrt{b^2 + ab}$ by the Pythagorean Theorem. Since $AC^2 - BC^2 = 19$, $a^2 - b^2 = 19$. This has the unique solution over positive whole numbers of $(a, b) = (10, 9)$ since 19 is prime, and the area of $\triangle ABC$ is $\frac{1}{2} \cdot (a+b) \cdot \sqrt{ab} = \frac{19\sqrt{90}}{2} = \frac{57\sqrt{10}}{2}$. Thus, we have that $m = 57$, $n = 10$, and $p = 2$, so $m+n+p = \boxed{69}$.

8. For a positive integer x, $x^2 \equiv 0 \bmod 30$ if and only if $x \equiv 0 \bmod 30$ because $30 = 2 \cdot 3 \cdot 5$, so x must have 2, 3, and 5 as prime factors. However, $x^2 \equiv 0 \bmod 40$ is true whenever $x \equiv 0 \bmod 20$ as $40 = 2^3 \cdot 5$, and x need only have 2 factors of 2 and one factor of 5 in its prime factorization. Thus, S contains the squares of all positive integers x such that $x \leq 2022$ and $x \equiv 30 \bmod 60$. The sum of all such squares is $S = 30^2 + 90^2 + 150^2 + \cdots + 2010^2$. Thus, $\frac{S}{900} = \frac{S}{30^2} = 1^2 + 3^2 + 5^2 + \cdots + 67^2$. This sum yields $(1^2 + 2^2 + 3^2 + \cdots + 67^2) - (2^2 + 4^2 + 6^2 + \cdots + 66^2) = \frac{67 \cdot 68 \cdot 135}{6} - 2^2 \cdot \frac{33 \cdot 34 \cdot 67}{6} = \frac{67 \cdot 68 \cdot (135 - 2 \cdot 33)}{6} = 67 \cdot 34 \cdot 23 = \boxed{52394}$.

9. The sum of the numbers in each column is $\frac{1}{3} \cdot \frac{9 \cdot (1+9)}{2} = 15$. Without loss of generality, we start with the first row, which must contain 1, 2, and 3 in some order. This order does not matter, so there are $3! = 6$ ways to fill the first row. Similarly, the bottom row must contain 7, 8, and 9. Note that the middle row contains 4, 5, and 6, so any given column cannot contain both 1 and 7 or both 3 and 9 since $15 - (1 + 7) > 6$ and $15 - (3 + 9) < 4$. Therefore, the columns containing 1, 2, and 3 must contain 8, 9, and 7; or 9, 7, and 8, respectively. After filling in the bottom row, there is only one way to complete the middle row, so we can fill the grid in $3! \cdot 2 \cdot 1 = \boxed{12}$ ways.

10. While it is raining, the train goes at half its regular speed for 90 minutes, so it covers the same distance as it would traveling at its regular speed for 45 minutes. Since it travels at its regular speed for 105 minutes in sunny weather, it follows that the distance the train travels in the rain is $\frac{45}{105+45} = \frac{3}{10}$ of the total distance, and the train can travel the distance from Snoozeville to Sleepytown in 150 minutes in sunny weather. Let d be the portion of the journey completed when it starts raining, where d is a number between 0 and 1, inclusive. Thus, r is equal to $d + \frac{3}{10(1-d)} = \frac{10d+3}{10-10d}$, and s is equal to $\frac{150d+90}{90+150(1-(d+\frac{3}{10}))} = \frac{150d+90}{195-150d}$. Then we have $\frac{r}{s}$ equals $\frac{(10d+3)(195-150d)}{(10-10d)(150d+90)} = \frac{(10d+3)(13-10d)}{(2-2d)(50d+30)}$.

We can expand and simplify to get $\frac{100d-100d^2+39}{40d+60-100d^2} = \frac{21}{20}$, or $2000d - 2000d^2 + 780 = 840d + 1260 - 2100d^2$. Then $100d^2 + 1160d - 480 = 0$, or $5d^2 + 58d - 24 = 0$. Solving for d using the quadratic formula, we get $d = \frac{-58 \pm \sqrt{58^2 + 480}}{10}$, which simplifies to $\frac{-58 \pm 62}{10}$. Only $d = \frac{2}{5}$ works since $d > 0$, so it began raining $\frac{2}{5}$ of the way into the journey, or after $150 \cdot \frac{2}{5} = \boxed{60}$ minutes.

Sprint Round
12316

Place ID Sticker
Inside This Box

Name _____

Grade _____

School _____

1.	2.	3.	4.	5.
6.	7.	8.	9.	10.
11.	12.	13.	14.	15.
16.	17.	18.	19.	20.
21.	22.	23.	24.	25.
26.	27.	28.	29.	30.

1. Juliana is filling out the playoff bracket below for the last four basketball teams in a tournament. To do so, she needs to pick a winner from the upper pair of teams, a winner from the lower pair of teams, and a bracket winner from the two first-round winners. How many possible brackets can Juliana make?

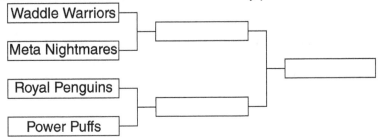

2. Andy sorts 200 tomatoes at a food bank and finds that 15% of them are rotten. He places all of the tomatoes that are not rotten into containers that each hold up to six tomatoes. What is the smallest number of containers that Andy needs?

3. In the diagram below, a square of side length 36 is divided into nine equally sized squares, and one of the smaller squares is further divided into nine equally sized squares. What is the area of the shaded region?

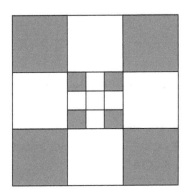

4. Jeri and Brandi are 120 meters apart in a paddleboarding area, and they start paddleboarding towards each other. Brandi paddleboards twice as fast as Jeri, and they reach each other in 150 seconds. How many meters does the slower paddleboarder travel per minute?

5. Two positive whole numbers greater than 1 multiply to 576 and have no common factors other than 1. What is the sum of those two numbers?

6. Each of the sides and diagonals of a regular hexagon *ABCDEF* are drawn. Then, each of the sides and diagonals of quadrilateral *ABDE* are colored red. How many sides and diagonals of *ABCDEF* are *not* colored red?

7. Four not necessarily distinct positive whole number multiples of 4 have squares summing to a multiple of 10. What is the smallest possible sum of these multiples of 4?

8. The difference between the third term and the tenth term of an increasing arithmetic sequence is 28. What is the value of the common difference of this sequence?

9. Aidan's ball course is composed of two concentric semicircular arcs of radii 7 and 10 that are cut off by collinear line segments as shown below. In addition, the course has a circular hole that is just large enough to fit a spherical ball with volume $\frac{4}{3}\pi$. The area of Aidan's ball course excluding the hole is $a\pi$. What is the value of a? Express your answer as a common fraction.

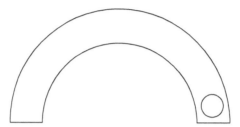

10. What is the probability that a randomly picked positive whole number between 1 and 1000, inclusive, has a fourth root no more than 4 and a fifth root no less than 3? Express your answer as a common fraction.

11. A rectangular pool table has vertices at $(0,0)$, $(0,3)$, $(3,3)$, and $(3,0)$ in the xy-plane. Zara shoots a billiard ball from the origin so that the ball initially travels along the line $y = \frac{3}{4}x$. Every time the ball bounces off of an edge of the table, the slope of its path is multiplied by -1. This process continues indefinitely until the ball goes into a corner of the table. How many times will it bounce off of an edge of the table before the ball reaches a corner?

12. The product of the page numbers of the middle two pages in a book leaves a remainder of 6 when divided by 10. What is the remainder when the number of pages in the book is divided by 10?

13. The *look-and-say sequence* begins with the term 1. Each term is then obtained from reading out the digits in the previous term out loud from left to right. For instance, 1 is read as "one one" or 11, 11 is read as "two one(s)" or 21, 21 is read as "one two, one one" or 1211, and so on to produce the sequence $\{1, 11, 21, 1211, \ldots\}$. If we change the first term of the look-and-say sequence to 7 without changing the method for obtaining subsequent terms, what is the sum of the units digits of the first 20 terms of the new sequence?

14. Three consecutive positive whole numbers have the property that the smallest number is a multiple of 6, the middle number is a multiple of 7, and the largest number is a multiple of 8. What is the second-smallest possible median of a set of three such numbers?

15. A bag contains 3 red and 5 blue marbles, and a second bag contains 2 red and 6 blue marbles. Two marbles are drawn at random from the first bag and placed into the second bag. A marble is then drawn from the second bag at random. What is the probability that this marble is red? Express your answer as a common fraction.

16. To reach Krakaton Peak, a climber must ascend a mountain with two distinct sections, each with constant slope: first a section angled at $45°$ angle above the horizontal and then a second section angled $60°$ above the horizontal. The summit lies 10000 feet above the ground, and in ascending to the peak, a climber will have traveled a horizontal distance of 8000 feet. In simplest radical form, the horizontal distance the climber travels during the first section of the ascent can be expressed in the form $a - b\sqrt{c}$ for positive integers a, b, and c, with c not divisible by the square of any prime number. What is $a + b + c$?

17. Let $a_n = \frac{3^n + 1}{2}$ for all whole numbers $n \geq 0$. What is the sum of the possible units digits of $a_n + a_{n+1}$?

18. How many positive whole numbers s have the property that $\frac{(s+2)^2 - (s+1)^2}{(s+3)^2 - (s+1)^2} < \frac{49}{100}$?

19. What is the sum of the distinct roots of the polynomial $(x^3 + 10x^2 + 25x + 18)(x^3 + 9x^2 + 17x + 9)$?

20. The *numerical semigroup* of three pairwise relatively prime positive whole numbers a, b, and c is the set of all whole numbers that can be expressed as a sum of positive multiples of a, b, and c. What is the largest whole number that is *not* in the numerical semigroup of $\{4, 7, 9\}$?

21. Selena counts the number of ways she can arrange 18 threes, 6 ones, and a 0 in a line. Talar counts the number of ways she can arrange 19 threes and 6 ones in a line. What is Selena's number divided by Talar's number?

22. Susana has a non-square rectangular garden of lily pads. If the number of lily pads in her garden is 24 times the sum of the number of lily pads in the length and width of the garden, what is the smallest possible number of lily pads in Susana's garden?

23. Points A and B lie outside of circle O with radius 6 such that $AO = 12$, $BO = 9$, and $\overline{AB}$ is tangent to circle O. Then AB can be written as $\sqrt{m} + \sqrt{n}$, where m and n are positive whole numbers. What is $m + n$?

24. The square root of a positive whole number n is not a whole number and has exactly 2023 digits to the left of the decimal point. However, the cube root of n is a whole number. Excluding leading and trailing zeroes, how many of the digits of the smallest possible value of n are zero?

25. Let x, y, and z be single-digit positive whole numbers with $xyz = 108$. How many possibilities are there for the ordered triple (x, y, z)?

26. Two six-sided dice are initially blank on all six faces. A total of six dots are painted on the 12 faces of the dice, with each face having 0 or 1 dot. Assuming each face is equally likely to have a dot, what is the probability that at least one of the two dice has a dot on its top face? Express your answer as a common fraction.

27. The number 2022 is an example of a positive whole number whose non-zero digits are all powers of 2. What is the average of all such four-digit whole numbers?

28. Three numbers are selected at random with replacement from the set $\{1, 2, 3, 4, 5\}$. They are placed in non-descending order with $a \leq b \leq c$, and the sum of $b - a$ and $c - b$ is calculated. What is the probability that this sum is at most 2? Express your answer as a common fraction.

29. Six points are equally spaced on a circle with radius 1 and center O. Consider a random selection of four of the six points, which are labeled A, B, C, and D in clockwise order. Chords $\overline{AC}$ and $\overline{BD}$ intersect at a point P. The expected shortest distance from O to P is $\frac{a+b\sqrt{c}}{d}$, where a, b, c, and d are positive whole numbers, $\gcd(a, b, d) = 1$, and c is not divisible by the square of any prime. What is $a + b + c + d$?

30. What is the smallest positive whole number n for which $n + \sqrt{n^2 - 2022} + \sqrt{n - \sqrt{n^2 - 2022}} \geq 2022$?

Name _____

Grade _____

School _____

Problems 1 & 2

1. The edges of rectangles with dimensions 2×3, 2×8, and 3×6 are glued together wihtout overlap to create a larger rectangle. What is the perimeter of the larger rectangle?

1.

2. Four different positive whole numbers have the property that the largest number is 20% greater than the smallest number, and the other two numbers are both multiples of 3. What is the smallest possible sum of the four numbers?

2.

Target Round
12316

Place ID Sticker
Inside This Box

Name _____

Grade _____

School _____

Problems 3 & 4

3. Raichi is writing a new math contest consisting of 15 problems. She wants to include a diagram for 3 to 6 problems, inclusive, and she wants 4 to 7 problems, inclusive, to be geometry problems. However, she does not want any non-geometry problems to have diagrams. What is the greatest possible number of geometry problems that do not have diagrams?

3. [   ]

4. Rika wants to color each of the 40 squares in the figure below red, yellow, or blue such that any two squares whose sides touch have different colors. How many ways can Rika color the squares?

4. [   ]

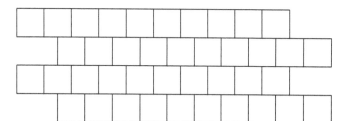

Place ID Sticker
Inside This Box

Name _____

Grade _____

School _____

Problems 5 & 6

---

5. What is the smallest whole number that is four less than a perfect square and five greater than a positive multiple of three?

5.

6. How many coefficients in the expansion of $(100x^{100} + 99x^{99} + 98x^{98} + \cdots + 2x^2 + x)^2$ are even?

6.

Place ID Sticker
Inside This Box

Name _____

Grade _____

School _____

Problems 7 & 8

7. How many ways are there to order the first seven positive whole numbers such that the positive difference between any two consecutive numbers is odd?

7.

8. In convex quadrilateral *ABCD* with right angles ∠*ABC* and ∠*ACD*, *AC* = 6, and *AB* · *AD* = 36, let diagonals $\overline{AC}$ and $\overline{BD}$ intersect at a point *E*. If *BE* : *DE* = 4 : 9, what is the square of the area of *ABCD*?

8.

Team Round
12316

School or Team	Name _____
	Name _____
	Name _____
	Name _____

Place ID Sticker Inside This Box

Place ID Sticker Inside This Box

Place ID Sticker Inside This Box

Place ID Sticker Inside This Box

1.	2.	3.	4.	5.

6.	7.	8.	9.	10.

1. On March 13, 2023, TJ woke up and saw that his alarm clock read 7 AM, but he forgot to adjust his clock one hour forward for Daylight Saving Time! TJ's school, which set its clocks correctly, starts at 8:45 AM. If TJ needs 23 minutes to get dressed and eat breakfast before heading to school, at most how many minutes can he take to get to school and still arrive on time?

2. Ellen is navigating a mall with 4 restaurants as shown below. She is currently 30 meters west and 45 meters north of Restaurante de Excellente, which is 90 meters east of Kay's Cafe. To the nearest whole number, how many meters away is Ellen from the closest restaurant?

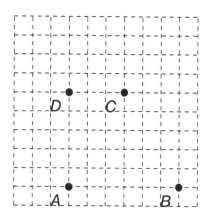

Point	Location
A	Kay's Cafe
B	Restaurante de Excellente
C	Ruben's Types Tacos
D	Simplex Subs

3. Ivy is walking with her brother Griff from home to school at a constant speed. At this speed, they can make the trip in 15 minutes. At some point during the walk, Ivy realizes that she forgot her homework, so she jogs back home twice as quickly as she walks and then sprints to school three times as quickly as she walks. While Ivy gets her homework, Griff continues walking to school, and they arrive at school at the same time. How many minutes after leaving home did Ivy realize that she forgot her homework? Express your answer as a common fraction.

4. In the equation $\overline{PIE} \cdot \overline{TAU} = 314628$, each letter represents a distinct digit. What is the sum of all possible values for the sum $P + I + E + T + A + U$?

5. Seventy-two people are seated in a room with chairs arranged in a 5×15 rectangular grid. The unoccupied chairs are decorated with flowers, and no two unoccupied chairs can be in the same row or column. How many ways can the decorated chairs be located in the grid?

6. Triangle ABC has integer side lengths, one of which is $AB = 43$. Let F be the foot of the altitude from C to $\overline{AB}$ with $AF = 20$ and $BF = 23$. What is CF^2?

7. Let a and b be positive whole numbers such that $a \cdot b$ has 52 divisors and $\gcd(a, b)$ has 5 divisors. What is the least possible number of divisors that $\text{lcm}(a, b)$ could have?

8. Below is a 5×5 grid of unit squares. Josh wants to shade two unit squares such that the following conditions hold.
   - One of the shaded squares must share an edge with the 5×5 square, and the other shaded square must share an edge with either the prior shaded square or the 5×5 square.
   - Every unshaded square must share an edge with at least one other unshaded square.

   How many ways can Josh shade two unit squares if the order in which he does so is irrelevant?

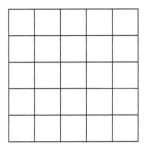

9. Lily brought some money to a flower market whose flower prices are shown below. If she buys exactly one tulip, then there are 37 ways for her to buy some combination of the other two types of flowers with none, some, or all of her remaining money. If she does not buy a tulip, then she can either spend all of her money on orchids or buy as many roses as possible and have $2 remaining. How many dollars did Lily bring to the market?

Flower	Price
Orchid	$4
Rose	$6
Tulip	$8

10. In convex quadrilateral $ABCD$ with $AB = 20$ and $BC = 23$, let points M and N trisect diagonal $\overline{AC}$ so that A, M, N, and C lie in that order. If $\angle BNC = \angle CMD$, $\angle ABN = 60°$, and $\angle CDM = 30°$, what is the square of the area of $ABCD$?

1. A regular polygon with 18 sides of length 2 is split up into some number of equilateral triangles with side length 2. As shown below, some of the triangles are shaded. In simplest radical form, what is the area of the unshaded region within the 18-sided polygon?

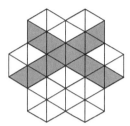

2. What is the value of the base-2 expression $111_2 \cdot 1010_2^{10_2} + 1000_2 \cdot 1010_2 + 101_2$ in base 10?

3. What is the units digit of the number $7^{210} + 8$?

4. Evan has some number of buckets, and 60% of the buckets are occupied. Only when Evan fills three more buckets will at least 70% of the buckets be occupied. If Evan then doubles the total number of buckets, what is the greatest possible number of buckets that Evan will have as a result?

5. A collection of 40 identical 1×1 square tiles is arranged, without overlapping and with no empty space between tiles, into a polygon. What is the least possible perimeter of that polygon?

6. Point A has coordinates $(3, 5)$, and the midpoint of AB is $(1, -1)$. What is the product of the coordinates of B?

7. The ratio of likes to dislikes for a rewind video is 1 to 8. Out of the 225 million users who watched that rewind video, a total of 22.5 million users did either a like or a dislike, and no users did both. What common fraction of the users who watched the rewind video disliked the video?

8. What is 160 decreased by 35%?

9. IPv4 addresses use 32 bits, where each bit can be a 0 or a 1. IPv6 addresses use 128 bits, where each bit can be a 0 or 1. Given that the number of possible IPv4 addresses is between 4 billion and 5 billion, the number that equals the number of possible IPv6 addresses has how many digits?

10. How many sides does a polygon with 54 diagonals have?

11. Hannah's first day of CS tutoring is April 3, 2023, and her last day is June 9, 2023. Across all days of tutoring, she helps an average of 10 students per day and an average of 45 lines of code per student. How many lines of code does Hannah review from the students?

12. A region with two semicircles of radius 5 is attached to a rectangle with width 10 and length 15. Additionally, there are three unshaded circular regions that each have a radius of 3, resulting in the figure below. To the nearest whole number, what is the area of the shaded region?

13. What is the slope of the line $x = \frac{2}{5}y + 6$? Express your answer as a common fraction.

14. The ratio of the measures of two supplementary angles is 5:7. What is the difference between the measures of the two angles, in degrees?

15. Elise checks to see if any of the following four inputs into $f(x) = 3x + 4$ result in the desired outputs shown below. How many inputs result in the desired output?

Input	Wanted Output
6	21
14	45
25	78
36	111

16. The mean of three numbers is 5. If the smallest of the three numbers is replaced by 6, the mean will increase by 4. What is the smallest of the three numbers?

17. Hannah puts four cups in numbered positions as shown below, with a ball in the cup in position 3. She then swaps the cups in positions 1 and 3, then positions 2 and 4, and finally positions 1 and 2. What number position does the cup with a ball end at?

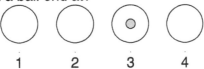

      1   2   3   4

18. How many numbers in the arithmetic sequence $102, 106, 110, \cdots, 390$ are greater than 246?

19. Ellen starts at one of twelve signposts labeled with whole numbers from 1 to 12 in clockwise order. At any point, if she is not at signposts 4, 5, or 7, then she runs clockwise to the next signpost. Given that Ellen finishes at signpost 4, what is the sum of all possible signpost numbers she starts at?

20. The base-16 digits, in order, are $0, 1, 2, 3, \ldots, 9, A, B, C, D, E, F$. What is the base-16 number $4C_{16}$, in base 10?

21. If the length of a rectangle is 3 feet less than three times its width and its perimeter is 50 feet, what is the area of the rectangle?

22. Yuelei and Youran are playing a game. In this game, Yuelei picks an integer between 1 and 2021, inclusive, and Youran tries to guess it. After each guess, Yuelei tells Youran whether his guess was greater than, less than, or equal to her number. What is the minimum number of guesses that Youran needs to guarantee that his last guess is Yuelei's number?

23. Two integers have a product of -96 and a positive difference of 22. What is the larger possible value of their sum?

24. A positive integer n less than or equal to 50 is selected at random. What is the probability that $\gcd(n, 50) > 1$? Express your answer as a common fraction.

25. In the diagram below, lines ℓ and m are parallel, and two of the angles are labeled as shown. What is the value of x? Express your answer as a common fraction.

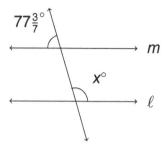

26. How many positive whole numbers less than or equal to 35 are factors of 1932?

27. Three fair six-sided dice are rolled. What is the probability that each pair of results has a positive difference of at least 2? Express your answer as a common fraction.

28. What is the least positive whole number that has exactly 28 positive whole number divisors?

29. The average of six consecutive integers is 5.5. What is the smallest of the six integers?

30. Adam and Bob randomly select positive whole numbers $a, b \leq 5$ (a and b are not necessarily distinct). Charles then chooses one of the four basic arithmetic operators (addition, subtraction, multiplication, division), and David performs the calculation a (operator) b. What is the probability that David's result is positive? Express your answer as a common fraction.

31. How many square units are in the area bounded by $x + 2y = 8$, the x-axis, and the y-axis?

32. Which perfect square rounds to 2000 when rounding to the nearest hundred?

33. Amy uses a timely ocarina to navigate through three regions of the lost woods. The table below shows which region she ends up at after singing either song A or song B. Given that Amy starts at region 1, how many ways can she sing three songs to end up at region 3?

Current Region	Region 1	Region 2	Region 3
Next Region After Song A	1	3	2
Next Region After Song B	2	3	3

34. Suppose x and y are positive numbers such that $xy = x + 2$ and $5x = y - 4$. Find x. Express your answer as a common fraction.

35. Set A has 8 elements and set B has 11 elements. The union of set A and B has 13 elements. How many elements are in the intersection of set A and B?

36. Jessalyn is thinking of a 5-digit positive integer. If the number has two digits that are zero and three distinct digits other than zero, what is the eighth-smallest number Jessalyn could be thinking of?

37. What is the area of a triangle with side lengths of 5, $4\sqrt{2}$, and 7?

38. Carson and Riley are currently on two vertices of a square field with perimeter 400 meters. They both start running clockwise at the same rate along the perimeter of the field. How many meters is the shortest possible distance between the two? Express your answer in simplest radical form.

39. What is the largest integer n such that 2^n divides 96?

40. The fourth root of a number is 16. What is the square root of that number?

41. Two different line segments from the set of sides and diagonals of a regular hexagon are randomly chosen. What is the probability that the line segments do not share a vertex? Express your answer as a common fraction.

42. Cindy has eight machines, and each possible pair of machines has a wire between them. She wants to remove as many wires as possible such that it is still possible to get from a machine to any other machine by going through some of the remaining wires. What is the greatest number of wires that Cindy can remove?

43. What is the smallest solution to the equation $x^2 + 8x - 105 = 0$?

44. What is the sum of the distinct roots of the function $f(x) = x^3 + 5x^2 + 3x - 9$?

45. The power level for a creature with stamina level S, defense level D, and brawn level B is given by the formula $\lfloor \frac{S^{0.5} \cdot B \cdot D^{0.5}}{10} \rfloor$, where $\lfloor x \rfloor$ equals the greatest integer at most x. Daniel's creature has a stamina level of 144, a defense level of 196, and a brawn level of 172. What is the power level of Daniel's creature?

46. The number 364807 has only two prime factors, and both of the prime factors are three-digit numbers with the same hundreds digit and tens digit. What is the sum of the two prime factors of 364807?

47. The line at the DMV is very long. Every 15 seconds, the person at the front of the line leaves. David just became the 215th person from the front once he started eating a bean burrito, and he just became the 110th person from the front once he finished eating. How many seconds did David spend eating?

48. A mebibyte is equal to 2^{20} bytes, while a gibibyte is equal to 2^{30} bytes. Charlie has a world game that takes up 0.5 mebibytes and a maker game that takes up 3 gibibytes. How many times greater is the number of bytes for the maker game than the world game?

49. The table below shows the input and output for $f(x, y)$, $g(x, y)$, and $h(x, y)$.

(x, y)	f(x, y)	g(x, y)	h(x, y)
(0, 0)	0	0	0
(0, 1)	0	1	1
(1, 0)	0	1	1
(1, 1)	1	1	0

How many tuples of the form (a, b, c, d) are there such that each of a, b, c, d is either 0 or 1 and that $f(g(a, b), h(c, d)) = 1$?

50. What is the sum of all positive whole numbers less than 30 that are divisible by either 3 or 5, but not both?

51. What is $(a + 4)(b + 2) + a^2b$ if $a = 2$ and $b = 8$?

52. Eight congruent squares that each have a perimeter of 28 are put together to form the twelve-sided polygon shown below. What is the perimeter of the twelve-sided polygon?

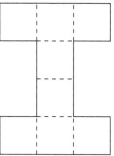

53. What is the tens digit of 9346.214?

54. Let $f(x) = x^2 + 4x - 2$. What is $f(3) + f(4)$?

55. Three fair six-sided dice are rolled. What is the probability that the sum of the numbers showing is even? Express your answer as a common fraction.

56. If $X = 25$ and $Y = 16$, what is the value of $\sqrt{X} \times \sqrt{Y}$?

57. If $\frac{1}{32} = 2^a$, what is a?

58. Three times a number plus 7 is equal to seven times that number plus 15. What is that number?

59. If a 2-digit number is increased by 45 when its digits are reversed, what is the positive difference between its digits?

60. One mile is equal to 5280 feet. How many feet are in 4 miles?

61. What is the range of the list $23, 17, -1, 8, -14, 15$?

62. In a grid of 49 unit squares, three rectangles that each have area 12 are drawn, as shown below. How many unit squares are in exactly two of the three rectangles?

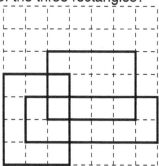

63. What is $\frac{4240}{212}$?

64. What is the volume of a right circular cylinder with base area 16π and height 5?

65. The area between two concentric circles is 36π. Given that the circumference of the inner circle is 16π, what is the radius of the outer circle?

66. 14 is 7% of what number?

67. Express in scientific notation: $(2.6 \cdot 10^2)^2$.

68. The following bar chart depicts the number of hours of screen time that Curtis spent over the past seven days. Curtis spends 90 minutes of screen time per day on social media. On how many days is the screen time spent outside of social media less than 2 hours?

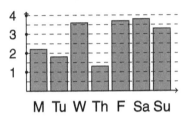

69. What is the greatest 3-digit number divisible by 37?

70. If the lengths of two sides of a right triangle are 20 and 21 units, what is the least possible length of the third side? Express your answer in simplest radical form.

71. What is $\sqrt{28} \cdot \sqrt{175}$?

72. What is the product of the digits of the second-largest two-digit prime number?

73. Two circles with the same center have radii of 20 and 23. To the nearest whole number, what is the area of the region that lies within exactly one of the circles?

74. Lani's school has 500 students. Nineteen percent of the students do robotics, 87% of the students do CS, and only 2% of the students do neither. Lani and 15 other students do robotics and CS and join the net battle club. How many students not in the net battle club do robotics and CS?

75. What is $35 \cdot 73 + 6 \cdot 73 + 41 \cdot 27$?

76. Which of the following numbers is divisible by 7? 125 126 127 128 129

77. How many 1 × 1 squares must be added to a 7 × 8 rectangle to form a 9 × 9 square?

78. Jacob inserts the numbers 2.202, 2.022, 2.020, 2.22, 2.2, and 2.1 into an empty priority queue, which sorts the numbers in increasing order after each insertion. After all the sorting, what is the sum of the number appearing before 2.1 and the number appearing after 2.1? Express your answer as a decimal without trailing zeroes.

79. A right cylinder has radius 4 and height 7. Express its surface area in terms of π.

80. The *ping time* is the average time data take to go from the client to the server and back. Elli recorded how long it takes to process five inputs for an online game in the table below. How many milliseconds is the ping time across Elli's five inputs?

Input Number	Time from Client to Server (milliseconds)	Time from Server to Client (milliseconds)
1st	43	64
2nd	38	58
3rd	36	42
4th	63	37
5th	62	57

Sprint Round

1. 8
2. 29
3. 640
4. 16
5. 73
6. 9
7. 24
8. 4
9. $\frac{49}{2}$
10. $\frac{7}{500}$

11. 5
12. 4
13. 140
14. 175
15. $\frac{11}{40}$
16. 8003
17. 24
18. 22
19. -11
20. 30

21. 19
22. 2352
23. 153
24. 4041
25. 15
26. $\frac{17}{22}$
27. 4083
28. $\frac{13}{25}$
29. 23
30. 1012

Target Round

1. 26
2. 152
3. 4
4. 96
5. 32
6. 149
7. 144
8. 845

Team Round

1. 22
2. 34
3. $\frac{20}{3}$
4. 22
5. 27300
6. 3696
7. 36
8. 128
9. 44
10. 270000

Countdown

1. $26\sqrt{3}$
2. 785
3. 7
4. 60
5. 26
6. 7
7. $\frac{4}{45}$
8. 104
9. 39
10. 12
11. 30600
12. 144
13. $\frac{5}{2}$
14. 30
15. 0
16. -6
17. 2
18. 36
19. 60
20. 76

21. 126
22. 11
23. 10
24. $\frac{3}{5}$
25. $\frac{718}{7}$
26. 11
27. $\frac{1}{9}$
28. 960
29. 3
30. $\frac{17}{20}$
31. 16
32. 2025
33. 4
34. $\frac{2}{5}$
35. 6
36. 10032
37. 14
38. $50\sqrt{2}$
39. 5
40. 256

41. $\frac{3}{7}$
42. 21
43. -15
44. -2
45. 2889
46. 1208
47. 1575
48. 6144
49. 6
50. 180
51. 92
52. 126
53. 4
54. 49
55. $\frac{1}{2}$
56. 20
57. -5
58. -2
59. 5
60. 21120

61. 37
62. 7
63. 20
64. 80π
65. 10
66. 200
67. $6.76 \cdot 10^4$
68. 4
69. 999
70. $\sqrt{41}$
71. 70
72. 72
73. 405
74. 24
75. 4100
76. 126
77. 25
78. 4.222
79. 88π
80. 100

Sprint Round Solutions

1. Juliana has two ways to pick a winner from the upper pair of teams, two ways to pick a winner from the lower two teams, and two ways to pick which of the initial winners wins the bracket. Each pick is independent, so we multiply the possibilities to get $2 \cdot 2 \cdot 2 = \boxed{8}$ possible brackets.

2. Since $200 \cdot 0.15 = 30$ tomatoes are rotten, Andy has $200 - 30 = 170$ tomatoes that are not rotten. Then 170 divided by 6 is 28 with a remainder of 2, which means that Andy needs $\boxed{29}$ containers.

3. Dividing a square into nine equally-sized squares produces smaller squares with side lengths $\frac{1}{3}$ those of the larger square. Then the four larger shaded squares have a side length of $\frac{36}{3} = 12$, and the four smaller shaded squares have a side length of $\frac{12}{3} = 4$. Adding the areas of all 8 shaded squares together yields $4 \cdot 12^2 + 4 \cdot 4^2 = \boxed{640}$.

4. Let J be Jeri's paddleboarding speed in meters per second, and let $B = 2J$ be Brandi's paddleboarding speed in meters per second. Since they take 150 seconds to reach each other, we have $150J + 150B = 120$. Substituting $2J$ for B, we get $150J + 300J = 120$, or $J = \frac{4}{15}$ meters per second. This means that Jeri, the slower paddleboarder, paddleboards at a speed of $\frac{4}{15} \cdot 60 = \boxed{16}$ meters per minute.

5. We recognize 576 to be 24^2, so we factor it as $(2^3 \cdot 3)^2 = 2^6 \cdot 3^2$. Since the desired two numbers are relatively prime, they must be $2^6 = 64$ and $3^2 = 9$, which sum to $64 + 9 = \boxed{73}$.

6. Regular hexagon $ABCDEF$ has 6 sides and $\frac{6 \cdot (6-3)}{2} = 9$ diagonals. Quadrilateral $ABDE$, a rectangle, has 4 sides and 2 diagonals, all of which are shared with hexagon $ABCDEF$. Thus, the number of sides and diagonals of $ABCDEF$ that are not colored red is $6 + 9 - (4 + 2) = \boxed{9}$.

7. The squares of 4 and 8 are 16 and 64, respectively. Since $4^2 + 8^2$ is divisible by 10, the multiples of 4 can be $\{4, 4, 8, 8\}$, which sum to 24. This is the smallest possible sum as $4 \cdot 4^2$ is not divisible by 10, and neither is $3 \cdot 4^2 + (4k)^2$ for any positive whole number k since no perfect square has a units digit of $50 - 3 \cdot 16 = 2$. Thus, the answer is $\boxed{24}$.

8. Let $\{t_n\}$ be the arithmetic sequence, and let d be the common difference. Then $d = \frac{t_{10} - t_3}{10 - 3}$, which is $\frac{28}{7} = \boxed{4}$.

9. The area of a semicircle with radius 10 is $\frac{1}{2} \cdot \pi \cdot 10^2 = 50\pi$, and the area of a semicircle with radius 7 is $\frac{1}{2} \cdot \pi \cdot 7^2 = \frac{49}{2}\pi$. Since the hole can just fit a sphere with volume $\frac{4}{3}\pi$, the hole has radius 1, so the area of the hole is $\pi \cdot 1^2 = \pi$. Therefore, the area of Aidan's ball course is $50\pi - \frac{49}{2}\pi - \pi = \frac{49}{2}\pi$, or

$$a = \boxed{\frac{49}{2}}.$$

10. Since $4^4 = 256$ and $3^5 = 243$, all integers from 243 to 256, inclusive, satisfy our conditions for a total of $256 - 243 + 1 = 14$ positive whole numbers. The desired probability is then $\frac{14}{1000} = \boxed{\frac{7}{500}}$.

11. The ball hits an edge for the first time at $(3, \frac{9}{4})$, the second time at $(2, 3)$, and the third time at $(0, \frac{3}{2})$. By symmetry, we conclude that the ball will reach a corner on the sixth would-be hit, meaning that it will have hit the table's edges $\boxed{5}$ times before that.

12. The middle two pages of the book must have page numbers ending in 2 and 3 or 7 and 8 as these are the only pairs of consecutive single-digit whole numbers that multiply to yield a units digit of 6. In the first case, the total number of pages in the book has a units digit of $2 \cdot 2 = 4$, and in the second case, a units digit of 4 as well since $7 \cdot 2 = 14 \equiv 4 \bmod 10$. Either way, the number of pages in the book ends in $\boxed{4}$.

13. Any term following a term with units digit d will itself have units digit d. This is because, in reading out the last digit of the previous term, we will always say "n [copies of] d," where n is at least 1. Thus, the requested sum is simply $7 \cdot 20 = \boxed{140}$.

14. The smallest set of such numbers is clearly 6, 7, and 8. By the Chinese Remainder Theorem, we obtain the next-smallest group of whole numbers by adding $\text{lcm}(6, 7, 8) = 168$ to 6, 7, and 8 to obtain 174, 175, and 176, the median of which is $\boxed{175}$.

15. After two marbles are moved from the first to the second bag, the expected number of red marbles that the second bag contains is $2 + 2 \cdot \frac{3}{3+5} = \frac{11}{4}$ by linearity of expectation. Since there are 10 marbles in the second bag, this yields a probability of $\frac{\frac{11}{4}}{10} = \boxed{\frac{11}{40}}$.

16. Let h be the horizontal and therefore vertical distance covered by the the climber during the first ascent stage. Then $8000 - h$ and $10000 - h$ are the horizontal and vertical distances, respectively, covered by the second section of the climb. Thus, we have $10000 - h = \sqrt{3}(8000 - h)$. This gives us $h(\sqrt{3} - 1) = 8000\sqrt{3} - 10000$, or $h = 7000 - 1000\sqrt{3}$, so the desired sum is $7000 + 1000 + 3 = \boxed{8003}$.

17. We have $2(a_n + a_{n+1}) = 3^{n+1} + 3^n + 2$, so it suffices to consider this modulo 20. As the values of $3^n \bmod 20$ are $3, 9, 7, 1, \ldots$ with period 4, we have possible values $14, 18, 10, 6 \bmod 20$, hence $7, 9, 5, 3 \bmod 10$. The requested sum is therefore $\boxed{24}$.

18. By difference of squares, $\frac{(s+2)^2-(s+1)^2}{(s+3)^2-(s+1)^2} < \frac{49}{100}$ simplifies to $\frac{2s+3}{4s+8} < \frac{49}{100}$. Note that $\frac{2s+4}{4s+8} = \frac{1}{2}$, so we equivalently have $\frac{1}{4s+8} > \frac{1}{100}$ or $4s + 8 < 100$. Then $s < 23$, so the number of positive whole numbers that satisfy the given inequality is $\boxed{22}$.

19. The parenthetical polynomials factor to $(x^2 + 8x + 9)(x + 2)$ and $(x^2 + 8x + 9)(x + 1)$, respectively. We identify $x = -1, -2$ as roots and apply Vieta's formulas to find the desired sum to be $-1 - 2 + \left(-\frac{8}{1}\right) = \boxed{-11}$.

20. No whole number less than $4 + 7 + 9 = 20$ is a member of this set, so we want the sum of 20 and the largest whole number unattainable with non-negative multiples of 4, 7, and 9. All of 11 to 14, inclusive, but not 10 are possible, so by extension, all whole numbers greater than 10 can be expressed as $11 + 4k$, $12 + 4k$, $13 + 4k$, or $14 + 4k$ where k is a non-negative whole number. It follows that the largest whole number outside the numerical semigroup of $\{4, 7, 9\}$ is $20 + 10 = \boxed{30}$.

21. Selena has 25 digits, so ignoring the fact that some of them are the same, she would be able to arrange them in 25! ways. However, the 18 threes and the 6 ones are the same, so she must divide 25! by 18!6! to get $\frac{25!}{18!6!}$. Talar also has 25 numbers, but the 19 threes and the 6 ones are the same, so her number is $\frac{25!}{19!6!}$. Since we want to find Selena's number divided by Talar's number, we can cancel out common factors without actually calculating their individual numbers. Notice that both of their numbers have the factor $\frac{25!}{6!}$, so we can cancel it out. Then the quotient of their numbers is $\frac{1/18!}{1/19!} = \frac{19!}{18!}$. Since $19! = 19 \cdot 18!$, the desired quotient is $\boxed{19}$.

22. Let the length and width of the garden be ℓ and w, respectively. Then $\ell w = 24(\ell + w)$, or by Simon's Favorite Factoring Trick, $(\ell - 24)(w - 24) = 576$. Since $\ell \neq w$, we want to minimize $|\ell - w|$ without having $\ell - w = 0$. This occurs at $(\ell - 24, w - 24) = (18, 32)$ or $(\ell, w) = (42, 56)$, giving us $\ell w = \boxed{2352}$.

23. Let $\overline{AO}$ and $\overline{BO}$ intersect circle O at P and Q, respectively, and let $\overline{AB}$ be tangent to the circle at point C. Then extend $\overline{AO}$ and $\overline{BO}$ past O to intersect the circle again at X and Y, respectively. By Power of a Point, we know that $AC^2 = AP \cdot AX$ and $BC^2 = BQ \cdot BY$. Plugging in $AP = 6$, $AX = 18$, $BQ = 3$, and $BY = 15$, we get $AC^2 = 108$ and $BC^2 = 45$. As a result, $AB = \sqrt{108} + \sqrt{45}$, so $m + n = \boxed{153}$.

24. The smallest whole number that has exactly 2023 digits to the left of the decimal point is 10^{2022}. This means that n must be at least $(10^{2022})^2 = 10^{4044}$, the cube root of which is 10^{1348}. Since the square root of n cannot be a whole number, we let $\sqrt[3]{n} = 10^{1348} + 1$ and $n = (10^{1348} + 1)^3$. Note that $10^{1348} + 1$ is not a perfect square, so $(10^{1348} + 1)^3$ cannot be a perfect square, and $\sqrt{n}$ is not a whole number. Therefore, $(10^{1348} + 1)^3$ is the smallest possible value of n. By the Binomial Theorem, this equals $10^{4044} + 3 \cdot 10^{2696} + 3 \cdot 10^{1348} + 1$. Excluding leading and trailing zeroes, this number has $4044 + 1 = 4045$ digits, with only four of them non-zero. Thus, n has $4045 - 4 = \boxed{4041}$ digits that are zero.

25. As $108 = 2^2 \cdot 3^3$, either all of x, y, and z are multiples of 3 but not 9 or exactly one of x, y, and z is 9 and another is 3 or 6. In the first case, we have the 3 permutations of $(6, 6, 3)$ since x, y, and z cannot be $3 \cdot 4 = 12$. In the second case, we have the $2 \cdot 3! = 12$ combined permutations of $(9, 6, 2)$ and $(9, 4, 3)$. Altogether, the number of ordered triples (x, y, z) of single-digit positive whole numbers satisfying $xyz = 108$ is $\boxed{15}$.

26. Instead of thinking about the problem as painting dots and then rolling the dice, we can switch the order of events and apply complementary counting. If the top two faces have no dots, then all six dots are on the other ten faces. The probability of this happening is $\frac{\binom{10}{6}}{\binom{12}{6}} = \frac{6 \cdot 5}{12 \cdot 11}$, or $\frac{5}{22}$. Therefore, the probability that at least one of the two top faces has a dot is $1 - \frac{5}{22} = \boxed{\frac{17}{22}}$.

27. These numbers can only include the digits 0, 1, 2, 4, and 8. The expected value of the first digit is $\frac{1+2+4+8}{4} = \frac{15}{4}$ as it cannot be zero, and the expected value of each of the other three digits is $\frac{0+1+2+4+8}{5} = 3$. The average of all such four-digit numbers is then the sum of these expected values, which yields $\frac{15}{4} \cdot 1000 + 3 \cdot 100 + 3 \cdot 10 + 3 \cdot 1 = \boxed{4083}$.

28. The sum of $b - a$ and $c - b$ is $c - a$, so we seek the probability that $c - a \leq 2$. We perform casework on the value of $c - a$.
    - If $c - a = 0$, then a, b, and c are all equal. This yields 5 possibilities.
    - If $c - a = 1$, then (a, c) could be $(1, 2)$, $(2, 3)$, $(3, 4)$, or $(4, 5)$ while b equals either a or c. There are 4 choices for a and c, two choices for b, and $\binom{3}{1} = 3$ ways to order a, b, and c. There are $4 \cdot 2 \cdot 3 = 24$ such cases.
    - If $c - a = 2$, then (a, c) could be $(1, 3)$, $(2, 4)$, or $(3, 5)$. Then $b = a$ or $b = c$ gives us two possibilities for b and $\binom{3}{1} = 3$ ways to order the three numbers whereas $a < b < c$ sets all three numbers and leaves $3! = 6$ orders in which thse numbers could have been picked. This yields $3 \cdot 2 \cdot 3 + 3 \cdot 6 = 36$ more possibilities.

    Altogether, $5 + 24 + 36 = 65$ of the $5^3 = 125$ possible combinations of numbers satisfy $c - a \leq 2$, which represents a probability of $\frac{65}{125} = \boxed{\frac{13}{25}}$.

29. There are $\binom{6}{4} = 15$ ways to choose four of the six points. Three of these cases involve two diameters, which intersect at the center of the circle, so the distance from O to P is 0. There are two other configurations, each contributing six cases: two chords each creating a minor arc measuring $120°$ or a diameter and one such chord. In the first configuration, P is two-thirds of the way from O to the midpoint of one of the sides of the regular hexagon formed by all 6 points. The distance from O to any such side is $\frac{\sqrt{3}}{2}$, so $OP = \frac{\sqrt{3}}{3}$. In the second configuration, P is the midpoint of the non-diameter chord, so $OP = \frac{1}{2}$. Thus, the expected value of OP is $\frac{3}{15} \cdot 0 + \frac{6}{15} \cdot \frac{\sqrt{3}}{3} + \frac{6}{15} \cdot \frac{1}{2} = \frac{3+2\sqrt{3}}{15}$, so $a + b + c + d = \boxed{23}$.

30. Since $\sqrt{n - \sqrt{n^2 - 2022}} \cdot \sqrt{n + \sqrt{n^2 - 2022}} = \sqrt{2022}$, if we substitute $u = n + \sqrt{n^2 - 2022}$, we obtain $u + \sqrt{\frac{2022}{u}} \geq 2022$. For $n = 1011$, we have u equals $1011 + \sqrt{1011^2 - 2022} = 1011 + \sqrt{1011 \cdot 1009}$, and $\frac{2022}{u} = \frac{2022}{1011 + \sqrt{1011 \cdot 1009}}$. Simplifying the latter expression gives us $\frac{2022(1011 - \sqrt{1011 \cdot 1009})}{2022} = 1011 - \sqrt{1011 \cdot 1009}$. Thus, $n = 1011$ yields $u + \sqrt{\frac{2022}{u}} = 1011 + \sqrt{1011 \cdot 1009} + \sqrt{1011 - \sqrt{1011 \cdot 1009}}$. As $(1011 + \sqrt{1011 \cdot 1009}) + (1011 - \sqrt{1011 \cdot 1009}) = 2022$, but $\sqrt{1011 - \sqrt{1011 \cdot 1009}} < 1011 - \sqrt{1011 \cdot 1009}$, $n \geq \boxed{1012}$.

Target Round Solutions

1. Let's try to work backwards. If we split a large rectangle into three smaller rectangles, one of them will share a side length with the larger rectangle, and the other two rectangles will have one side length each that sum to that shared side length. If we combine the 2×3 and 2×8 rectangles, we end up with 2×11 and 3×6 rectangles, which share no dimensions. Therefore, we must combine the 2×3 and 3×6 rectangles into a 3×8 rectangle. We now have 3×8 and 2×8 rectangles, so the large rectangle has side lengths 8 and $2 + 3 = 5$, yielding a perimeter of $2 \cdot (5 + 8) = \boxed{26}$.

2. Let the smallest number be n. Then the largest number is $\frac{6n}{5}$. If two distinct multiples of 3 fall strictly between n and $\frac{6n}{5}$, the difference $\frac{6n}{5} - n = \frac{n}{5}$ must be at least 5, so $n \geq 25$. Since $\frac{6n}{5}$ is a whole number, n must be a multiple of 5. Testing $n = 25$ gives us $\frac{6n}{5} = 30$, but the only multiple of 3 strictly between 25 and 30 is 27. Similarly, testing $n = 30$ yields $\frac{6n}{5} = 36$, but only 33 is between them. Finally, testing $n = 35$ gives us $\frac{6n}{5} = 42$, and both 36 and 39 are strictly between 35 and 42. The sum of these four numbers is $35 + 36 + 39 + 42 = \boxed{152}$.

3. Note that all problems with diagrams must be geometry problems. To maximize the number of problems without diagrams, we minimize the number of problems with diagrams to be 3. These 3 problems are all geometry problems, so the number of geometry problems without a diagram is at most $7 - 3 = \boxed{4}$.

4. Note that four squares touch only one other square. We will ignore these for now. For the other 36 squares, any three squares in a row must contain each color once. Having two squares of one color on either side a square of a second color would imply that the adjacent pair(s) of squares in the rows above and/or below must all be the third color, which is impossible. This randomly chosen group of 3 then sets the colors for the rest of the 36 squares. There are $3! = 6$ ways to order the three colors, and each of these four ignored squares has two possible colors for a total of $2^4 = 16$ colorings. Thus, Rita can color the squares in $6 \cdot 16 = \boxed{96}$ ways.

5. Let this number n be four less than the perfect square k^2 so that n equals $k^2 - 4 = (k + 2)(k - 2)$. Then note that n leaves a remainder of 2 when divided by 3. If k were not divisible by three, then either $(k + 2)$ or $(k - 2)$, and therefore n, would be divisible by three, a contradiction. Thus, k is a positive multiple of 3. We test $k = 3$ and get $n = k^2 - 4 = 5$, which is $0 + 5 = 5$. However, n must exceed a *positive* multiple of 3 by 5, so $k > 3$. Consequently, we use $k = 6$ to find n, or $k^2 - 4 = \boxed{32}$.

6. The coefficient of a given term x^k in this expansion is the sum of the products of the coefficients of all pairs x^m and x^n for which m and n are whole numbers between 1 and 100, inclusive, that sum to k. If k is odd, then the number of ordered pairs (m, n) is even by symmetry, so the resulting coefficient is even as each product mn is added twice. However, if k is even, then the number of ordered pairs (m, n) is odd, and the coefficient is only even when k is divisible by 4 as the sum includes the unpaired term mn with m and n equal to $\frac{k}{2}$. Thus, we count all of the odd whole numbers and the even whole numbers divisible by 4 between 2 and $100 + 100 = 200$, inclusive, which yields $(100 - 1) + \frac{100}{2} = \boxed{149}$.

7. Note that we must alternate between even and odd numbers. Furthermore, since the first 7 positive whole numbers include four odd numbers and three even numbers, we must start with an odd number. There are then $4! = 24$ ways to order the odd numbers and $3! = 6$ ways to order the even numbers, for a total of $24 \cdot 6 = \boxed{144}$ orderings.

8. Note that we have $AC^2 = AB \cdot AD$, or $\frac{AB}{AC} = \frac{AC}{AD}$. Since $\angle ABC$ and $\angle ACD$ are both right angles, $\triangle ABC \sim \triangle ACD$ by hypotenuse-leg similarity. This also means that $\angle BAC = \angle DAC$ and $\angle BAE = \angle DAE$. Thus, we see that $\overline{AE}$ is an angle bisector of $\triangle BAD$. By the Angle Bisector Theorem, $\frac{AB}{AD} = \frac{BE}{DE} = \frac{4}{9}$, so we have $AB = 4x$ and $AD = 9x$ for some real number x. Substituting back into the equation $AC = \sqrt{AB \cdot AD} = 6$ yields $6x = 6$ or $x = 1$. Therefore, $AB = 4$ and $AD = 9$. We then use the Pythagorean Theorem to find that $BC = 2\sqrt{5}$ and $CD = 3\sqrt{5}$. By the base-height area formula, the areas of $\triangle ABC$ and $\triangle ACD$ are $\frac{1}{2} \cdot AB \cdot BC = 4\sqrt{5}$ and $\frac{1}{2} \cdot AC \cdot CD = 9\sqrt{5}$, respectively. Therefore, the area of $ABCD$ is $4\sqrt{5} + 9\sqrt{5} = 13\sqrt{5}$, the square of which is $\boxed{845}$.

Team Round Solutions

1. Since TJ forgot to set his clock one hour ahead, he actually woke up at 8 AM. This means that TJ has 45 minutes before school starts. Since TJ spends 23 minutes getting dressed and eating breakfast before going to school, the number of minutes he can spend getting there is at most $45 - 23 = \boxed{22}$.

2. From the key, we identify that Point A, Kay's Cafe, and Point B, Restaurante de Excellente, are 6 unit spaces apart, so each unit space represents 15 meters. We then plot Ellen's current location as point E.

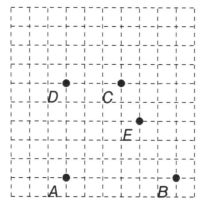

The closest restaurant to Ellen is then Ruben's Types Tacos at Point C. Ruben's Types Tacos is 15 meters west and 30 meters north of Ellen, which means that the distance between them is $\sqrt{15^2 + 30^2} \approx \boxed{34}$ meters.

3. Let Ivy and Griff's walking speed be s, and let the distance that they walk together before Ivy runs back be d. Since Ivy sprinted to school in $\frac{15}{3} = 5$ minutes after getting her homework, the walk with Griff and the jog home take $15 - 5 = 10$ minutes together. Thus, $\frac{d}{s} + \frac{d}{2s} = 10$, or $\frac{3d}{2s} = 10$, so the amount of time that Ivy walks before realizing that she forgot her homework is $\frac{d}{s} = \frac{2}{3} \times 10 = \boxed{\dfrac{20}{3}}$ minutes.

4. We can factor 314628 as $314 \cdot 1002$, which further simplifies to $314628 = 157 \cdot 167 \cdot 12$. Since both 157 and 167 are prime, $\overline{PIE}$ and $\overline{TAU}$ must be of the form $157 \cdot k$ and $167 \cdot \frac{12}{k}$, where k is a positive factor of 12. In addition, $\overline{PIE}$ and $\overline{TAU}$ are each three-digit numbers, so k cannot be 1, 2, or 12. Testing the remaining factor pairs yields $471 \cdot 668$ for $k = 3$, $628 \cdot 501$ for $k = 4$, and $942 \cdot 334$ for $k = 6$. The only pair of values for $\overline{PIE}$ and $\overline{TAU}$ with all distinct digits is $314628 = 501 \cdot 628$, which yields a sum of $P + I + E + T + A + U = 5 + 0 + 1 + 6 + 2 + 8$, or $\boxed{22}$.

5. The first unoccupied chair can be chosen in $5 \cdot 15 = 75$ ways. Then the second empty seat can be chosen in $(5 - 1) \cdot (15 - 1) = 56$ ways, and the last seat with flowers can be in $(5 - 2) \cdot (15 - 2) = 39$ places. Since the order in which these seats are chosen does not matter, the locations of the decorated seats can be chosen in $\frac{75 \cdot 56 \cdot 39}{3!} = \boxed{27300}$ ways.

6. We have $AC^2 = CF^2 + 20^2$ and $BC^2 = CF^2 + 23^2$, so $BC^2 = AC^2 + 129$. Then AC^2 and BC^2 must be perfect squares that differ by 129. By the Difference of Squares formula, $BC + AC$ and $BC - AC$ are positive integer factors of 129 multiplying to 129. Since the case $(BC + AC, BC - AC) = (43, 3)$ yields $BC = 23$, $AC = 20$, and $CF = 0$, which is impossible, we have $(BC + AC, BC - AC) = (129, 1)$. Thus, $BC = 65$ and $AC = 64$, so $CF^2 = \boxed{3696}$.

7. The condition that $\gcd(a, b)$ has 5 divisors implies that it is of the form p^4, where p is a prime. Thus, p^4 must divide both a and b, so without loss of generality, let $a = p^4 \cdot A$ and $b = p^{4+k} \cdot B$, where $\gcd(A, B) = \gcd(p, A) = \gcd(p, B) = 1$ and k is a non-negative whole number. If A has c divisors and B has d divisors, then $a \cdot b = p^{8+k} \cdot A \cdot B$ has $(9 + k) \cdot c \cdot d = 52$ divisors, and $\text{lcm}(a, b) = p^{4+k} \cdot A \cdot B$ has $(5 + k) \cdot c \cdot d$ divisors. We want to minimize $\frac{5+k}{9+k} = 1 - \frac{4}{9+k}$, so we minimize k, noting that 52 must be divisible by $9 + k$. The smallest possible value of k is thus 4 since 13 divides 52. Then $c \cdot d = 4$, so $\text{lcm}(a, b)$ has a minimum of $(5 + k) \cdot c \cdot d = \boxed{36}$ divisors.

8. Based on the shading instructions, we can divide the problem into two cases.
   - If exactly one shaded square shares an edge with the 5×5 square, then there is exactly one possible location for the second shaded square given the first one. The first square cannot be in a corner, so there are $(5 - 2) \cdot 4 = 12$ shadings in this case.
   - If both shaded squares share an edge with the 5×5 square, then picking any two of the 16 squares on the border of the 5×5 square to shade yields $\binom{16}{2} = 120$ possibilities. However, if the two border squares immediately next to a corner square are shaded, the unshaded square in the corner does not border another unshaded square. Thus, we have to exclude 4 possibilities, for a total of $120 - 4 = 116$ possible shadings.

   Altogether, Josh can shade two unit squares in $116 + 12 = \boxed{128}$ ways.

9. The amount of money that Lily has must be divisible by 4 and be 2 more than a multiple of 6. Thus, she must have at least 8 dollars, and $\text{lcm}(4, 6) = 12$, so she can have any number of dollars representable by $n = 8 + 12k$ where k is a non-negative whole number. Then let x be the number of orchids that Lily buys, and let y be the number of roses that Lily buys. That gives us the equation $4x + 6y + 8 = n$, which we rewrite as $4x + 6y = n - 8$.
   - Having 8 dollars gives her the sole option of buying 0 roses and orchids after buying a tulip. Testing larger values of k, we see that there are $4 + 2 + 1 = 7$ ways for Lily to buy roses and orchids if she brings \$20, $4 + 2 + 1 + 3 \cdot 2 + 4 + 2 = 19$ ways to buy roses and orchids with \$32, and $3 \cdot 4 + 4 + 2 + 19 = 37$ ways, our target value, if Lily brings 44 dollars.
   - Alternatively, we can take advantage of whole-number vertices and the area bounded by $4x + 6y = n - 8$ and the x- and y-axes to solve this problem using Pick's Theorem. Note that the x-intercept is $3k$, and the y-intercept is $2k$. The area enclosed by $4x + 6y = n - 8$ and the coordinate axes is $\frac{1}{2} \cdot 3k \cdot 2k = 3k^2$, and the number of boundary points is $(3k + 1) + (2k + 1) + (k + 1) - 3 = 6k$. This means that there are $37 - 6k$ internal points, and applying Pick's Theorem yields $3k^2 = 36 - 3k$ with the unique positive solution $k = 3$, or $n = 12k + 8 = 44$ dollars.

   Notably, whichever way we approach the problem, we find that Lily brought $\boxed{44}$ dollars to the flower market.

10. Reflect D over the perpendicular bisector of diagonal $\overline{AC}$ to a point D'. Then we see that M reflected over this perpendicular bisector gives us N, so $\angle CMD = \angle AND'$. We also have that $\angle BNC = \angle CMD$, so the angles $\angle BNC$, $\angle CMD$, and $\angle AND'$ are congruent. We also have congruent angles $\angle ANB$ and $\angle AMD$, which gives us $\angle ANB = \angle CND'$. We thus conclude that B, N, and D' are collinear. By reflections, we have that $\angle AD'N = 30°$ and that $\angle ABN = 60°$, so $\angle BAD' = 90°$. Thus, $\triangle ABD'$ is a 30-60-90 triangle. We are given that $AB = 20$, so $AD' = 20\sqrt{3}$, and the area of $\triangle ABD'$ is $\frac{1}{2} \cdot 20 \cdot 20\sqrt{3} = 200\sqrt{3}$. Finally, we see that the area of $\triangle ABD'$ is the sum of the areas of $\triangle ABN$ and $\triangle AND'$, noting that $\triangle AND' \cong \triangle CMD$ by reflections and that $\triangle ABN$ and $\triangle CMD$ take up $\frac{2}{3}$ of $\triangle ABC$ and $\triangle ACD$, respectively. Thus, the area of $ABCD$ is $\frac{3}{2} \cdot 200\sqrt{3} = 300\sqrt{3}$, the square of which is $\boxed{270000}$.

Sprint Round
12317

Place ID Sticker
Inside This Box

Name _____

Grade _____

School _____

1.	2.	3.	4.	5.
6.	7.	8.	9.	10.
11.	12.	13.	14.	15.
16.	17.	18.	19.	20.
21.	22.	23.	24.	25.
26.	27.	28.	29.	30.

1. What is the greatest number of y-intercepts that the graph of a function can have?

2. Below is a grid of circles, each of which is tangent to 3, 4, or 6 other circles. Some of the circles are shaded. What fraction of the circles in the grid are unshaded and not tangent to a shaded circle? Express your answer as a common fraction.

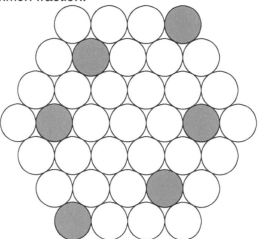

3. Isabel collects a whole number of hearts from each of six isolated isles. On each isle after the first, she collects one more heart than she did from the previous isle. If she collects no less than 250 hearts in total, at least how many hearts did she collect from the first isle?

4. Claudia has a loaf of banana bread, which is a rectangular prism with a volume of 225 cubic inches. One of the faces of the loaf is a square with an area of 25 square inches. Claudia makes 11 equally-spaced cuts parallel to the plane of the square face to form identical slices of banana bread. How many square inches is the surface area of each slice?

5. Jeremy is trying to read a 1001-page book for his English class. He cannot read more than 100 pages in any 3 consecutive days due to a lack of focus. At least how many days will it take Jeremy to finish reading the book?

6. On the city map below, each unit represents 100 meters. Brad is currently at the location marked *A*, and points *B*, *C*, and *D* denote the locations of banks. Brad travels to the closest bank by walking in 100-meter blocks in the up or right directions on the map. Given that he stops traveling after reaching this bank, how many different paths can Brad take?

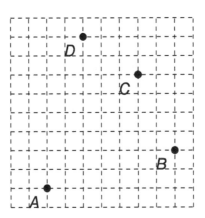

7. Let *a*, *b*, and *c* be whole numbers greater than 1 satisfying the equations $a^2 = b^3$ and $b^3 = c^6$. What is the smallest possible value of $a + b + c$?

8. Jason has 60 marshmallows and some number of pieces of spaghetti of length 1. He uses these materials to make tetrahedrons (triangular pyramids whose faces are all equilateral triangles) and cubes by using one marshmallow at each vertex and one piece of spaghetti for each edge. Jason finds that he can use all of the marshmallows and spaghetti pieces without any of either left over. How many pieces of spaghetti did Jason start with?

9. How many three-digit whole numbers with a nonzero tens digit have the property that the sum of their hundreds and units digits is at least 5 times their tens digit?

10. Claude and Maude are expert joggers who have perfected the art of running at a constant rate, with Claude running 0.25 meters per second faster than Maude. They start at the same point on a circular track with circumference 400 meters and run in opposite directions. When they next meet, Maude has jogged 192 meters. How many meters does Maude jog in a second?

11. A 5×8 rectangle and a 5×13 rectangle are drawn inside a 13×13 square such that the sides of the rectangles are parallel to those of the square, the rectangles touch but do not overlap, and there is one contiguous region inside the square and outside both rectangles. What is the sum of all different possible perimeters of this region?

12. Ken labels each of twelve lily pads with a number. Eleven of the pads are labeled with distinct integers from 1 to 11, inclusive, and the last pad is labeled with 258. Ken randomly selects three of the pads to remove one at a time. What is the expected value of the number on the third pad he removes?

13. For every hour that Patrice walks on a flat surface, he burns 100 calories. For every hour that he walks uphill, he burns p percent more calories than he does walking on a flat surface, and for every hour that he walks downhill, he burns p percent fewer calories than he does walking uphill. Suppose Patrice burns 316 calories after walking 1 hour on a flat surface, 1 hour uphill, and 1 hour downhill. What is the product of all possible values of p?

14. Two congruent circles inside square $ABCD$ are each tangent to two adjacent sides of the square and each other. In addition, every side of the square is tangent to at least one of the circles. If $AB = 10$, then the circles' radius can be expressed in the form $a - \sqrt{b}$ for positive whole numbers a and b. What is $a + b$?

15. If $(x^5 - 2)^{30} = (x^{15} - y + 1)^{42}$ and $(x^{15} - y + 1)^{42} = 0$, then what is the value of y?

16. How many ways are there to write the first six positive whole numbers in some order such that no two consecutive numbers multiply to a perfect square?

17. Jon chooses a base-10 number and writes down its binary representation. Jon observes the following properties of the binary number he writes down. Note that the *parity* of a number denotes whether it is even or odd.
    - The binary number is 7 digits long.
    - The first digit from the left has the same parity as the sum of the third, fifth, and seventh digits from the left.
    - The second digit from the left has the same parity as the sum of the third, sixth, and seventh digits from the left.
    - The fourth digit from the left has the same parity as the sum of the three rightmost digits.
    Jon then changes one of the digits in the binary number and obtains the binary number 1011101. What is the base-10 value of Jon's original number?

18. Let f be a function defined by $f(x) = \frac{x^2 + 7x + 8}{12 - x^2 - 7x}$ for all real numbers x for which $f(x)$ is defined. Given that d is the positive difference between the two values of x at which $f(x) = \frac{3}{2}$, what is d^2?

19. Regular octagon $ABCDEFGH$ has center O. Let square $IJKL$ with $\overline{IJ} \parallel \overline{AB}$ and $\overline{JK} \parallel \overline{CD}$ have center O and side length equal to that of the octagon, with L being the farthest point from $\overline{BC}$ on square $IJKL$. Then the ratio of the area of $ABCDL$ to the area of $IJKL$ can be written as $\frac{p\sqrt{q}+r}{s}$, where p, q, r, and s are positive whole numbers, $\gcd(p, r, s) = 1$, and q is not divisible by the square of any prime number. What is $p + q + r + s$?

20. A *palindrome* is a sequence of letters that spells the same thing when read forwards or backwards. For example, *NOON* is a palindrome, but *HAT* is not a palindrome. How many palindromes with at least one letter can be made by arranging some of the letters in *MATHEMATICS*?

21. In Tanya's asteroid game, each blast targets exactly one asteroid. The blast can destroy an asteroid of size 1 or 2 or split a size n asteroid with $n \geq 3$ into an asteroid with size $n - 1$ and another one with size $n - 2$. If Tanya starts with a size 5 asteroid, how many blasts does she need to completely destroy all asteroids?

22. Triangle ABC has $AB = 3$, $BC = 4$, and $AC = 5$. Side $\overline{AB}$ is extended past B to D such that $BD = AB$, side $\overline{BC}$ is extended past C to E such that $CE = 2BC$, and side $\overline{CA}$ is extended to past A to F such that $AF = 3AC$. What is the area of triangle DEF?

23. For every positive whole number n, let $f(n)$ be the value of the sum $(1 + n) + (2 + n) + (3 + n) + \cdots + (100 + n)$. What is the remainder when $f(1) + f(2) + f(3) + \cdots + f(2023)$ is divided by 1000?

24. Let $f_n(x)$ be a series of functions from the real numbers to the real numbers such that $f_0(x) = x$ and $f_n(x) = 2^{f_{n-1}(x)}$ for all $n \geq 1$. Given that a and b satisfy $f_2(a) = 512$ and $f_2(b) = 1024$, respectively, what is the remainder when $f_2(a + b)$ is divided by 100?

25. Three students each pick an integer between 1 and 5, inclusive, that is not necessarily distinct from the other students' integers. What is the probability that each of the three pairwise positive differences between the chosen numbers is less than or equal to 2? Express your answer as a common fraction.

26. Triangle MAT has $MA = 3$, $AT = 4$, and $TM = 5$. Point H lies in the interior of $\triangle MAT$ such that quadrilateral $MATH$ has area 4. What is the minimum possible value of AH? Express your answer as a common fraction.

27. Let k be a positive integer. A positive integer N is k-free if N is not a multiple of k and does not have k as its units digit. How many three-digit positive integers are both 2-free and 3-free?

28. Rowan is shooting free throws and has made exactly 55 percent of his attempts so far. If he makes all but one of his next N free throw attempts, he will then have made exactly 90 percent of his total free throw attempts. What is the sum of all possible values of N less than or equal to 1000?

29. Three circles of radius 1 are each tangent to both of the other circles. Triangle T is the smallest equilateral triangle tangent to all of the circles, and triangle U is the smallest equilateral triangle that can fully contain them. The ratio between the area of T and the area of U is equal to $\frac{p - q\sqrt{r}}{s}$, for positive whole numbers p, q, r, and s such that $\gcd(p, q, s) = 1$ and r is not divisible by the square of any prime. What is $p + q + r + s$?

30. A gumball machine contains 7 red gumballs and 3 blue gumballs. Each time a quarter, a coin worth 25 cents, is placed into the machine, the machine randomly dispenses one of the remaining gumballs. What is the expected number of cents that must be spent to dispense all of the blue gumballs? Express your answer as a common fraction.

Target Round
12317

Place ID Sticker
Inside This Box

Name _____

Grade _____

School _____

Problems 1 & 2

1. A store sells sets of 4 tennis rackets for $4.99 per set and sets of 6 tennis balls for $2.99 per set. Skye is buying the fewest possible whole sets of both items so that she ends up with the same number of rackets and balls. How many dollars does she spend? Express your answer as a decimal to the nearest hundredth.

1.

2. What is the sum of the terms in the increasing sequence $1, 20, 38, 55, 71, \ldots$ in which the difference between each pair of consecutive terms decreases by 1 from left to right, and the last two terms differ by 1?

2.

Place ID Sticker
Inside This Box

Name _____

Grade _____

School _____

Problems 3 & 4

3. Lois and Serena play a word game with 100 single-letter tiles, which cannot be reused. Lois goes first and uses 7 tiles to make a 7-letter word. Every turn after that, each player makes a word using exactly one fewer tile than the number of letters in that word. The number of letters in their first few words shown in the table below. After Serena's fourth turn, there are 58 unused tiles left. How many letters are in Serena's fourth word?

3.

	Total Letters in Lois's Word	Total Letters in Serena's Word
Turn 1	7	8
Turn 2	6	8
Turn 3	4	6
Turn 4	5	

4. Ted finds five apartments on the apartment-searching site Willow. Their mean and median monthly rents are $2000 and $2300, respectively. No apartment costs more than $2500/month or less than $1300/month, and all monthly rents are multiples of $100. How many possibilities are there for the set of 5 rents?

4.

Place ID Sticker
Inside This Box

Name _____

Grade _____

School _____

Problems 5 & 6

5. Jeremy simulated several battles and recorded the results in the table below. No monster won more than once. In addition, 5 monsters appeared in exactly 3 simulations, 69 appeared in exactly 2, and the rest each appeared in only 1. What is the probability that a randomly chosen monster from all distinct participants is a winner? Express your answer as a common fraction.

5.

Simulation	Participating Monsters	Winners
1	728	1
2	71	2
3	18	1
4	46	1
5	32	1

6. Let $ABCD$ be a parallelogram with $AB = 13$, $AC = 21$, and $AD = 20$. Let E be a point such that lines AC and BE are perpendicular and lines BD and CE are parallel. What is BE? Express your answer as a common fraction.

6.

Place ID Sticker
Inside This Box

Name _____

Grade _____

School _____

Problems 7 & 8

7. Olivia is folding a three-dimensional figure from a net that consists of two congruent regular hexagons and six congruent rectangles. One dimension of the rectangles is the same as the side length of the hexagons, with the other dimension twice as long. In addition, all six rectangles share a side with one of the hexagons in the unfolded net, but only one of them shares a side with the other hexagon. The surface area of Olivia's folded figure is $300\sqrt{3} + 1200$ square centimeters. Given that its volume is then $\sqrt{n}$ cubic centimeters, what is the value of n?

7. [_____]

8. How many ordered triples of integers (x, y, z) satisfy the inequality $x^4 + y^6 + z^8 \leq 2022$?

8. [_____]

School or Team

Name _____

Name _____

Name _____

Name _____

Place ID Sticker
Inside This Box

Place ID Sticker
Inside This Box

Place ID Sticker
Inside This Box

Place ID Sticker
Inside This Box

1.

2.

3.

4.

5.

6.

7.

8.

9.

10.

1. A vertical pole has two arrow signs attached to it: a red one pointing due north and a blue one pointing due east. The blue sign is correctly placed, but the red sign is not. Chelina corrects the direction of the red sign by rotating it 300° counterclockwise about the pole. Before Chelina adjusted the red arrow, how many degrees was the obtuse angle formed by the two arrow signs?

2. For each positive whole number n, let $f(n)$ be the sum of the n consecutive whole numbers beginning with n. For example, $f(2) = 2 + 3 = 5$ and $f(10) = 10 + 11 + 12 + \cdots + 19 = 145$. What is the value of $f(2023) - f(2022)$?

3. Below are five statements about an unknown number. What is the largest three-digit number that satisfies at least half of these statements?
    1. The number is not prime.
    2. The number has at least three distinct digits.
    3. The number has at least one non-zero digit that is even.
    4. The sum of the number's digits is odd.
    5. The positive difference between the number and its nearest perfect square is less than 10.

4. A social media app sends Phil a notification every day at a random time between 10 AM and 8 PM. Phil can post on the app at all times except for those shaded on his schedule below. What is the probability that he can post at some point in the two minutes immediately after the notification? Express your answer as a common fraction.

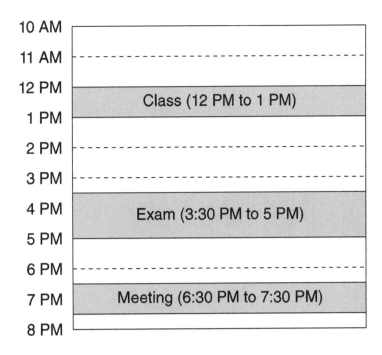

5. How many positive multiples of 125 less than or equal to 10000 have exactly twelve positive whole-number divisors?

6. If x is a real number such that $(x^2 + 4x + 1)^2 + 1 \le x^2 + 4x + 2$, then the set of possible values for x is a union of intervals $[a, b]$ and $[c, d]$ for some real numbers a, b, c, and d. What is $a + b + c + d$?

7. A semicircle has diameter $\overline{AB}$. Let points X and Y be on arc AB such that points A, X, Y, and B fall on arc AB in that order. Then let P and Q be the feet of the perpendiculars from X and Y to $\overline{AB}$, respectively. If $PQ = 5$, $PX = 6$, and $QY = 4$, what is AB^2?

8. The number $2021 = 47 \cdot 43$ has the property that the digits in its distinct prime factors sum to 18. What is the smallest positive whole number such that the digits in its distinct prime factors sum to 18?

9. In a right triangle, the altitude to the hypotenuse divides it into two segments a and b with whole-number lengths. If four times the square of the triangle's area is equal to the product of two positive whole numbers that differ by 19, then the minimum possible area of the triangle is $\frac{m\sqrt{n}}{p}$, where m, n, and p are positive whole numbers such that $\gcd(m, p) = 1$, and n is not divisible by the square of any prime. What is $m + n + p$?

10. Kenny rolls three fair six-sided dice. If the sum of the results is even, he writes down the sum of the results, and if the sum of the results is odd, he writes down the product of the results. What is the probability that the number Kenny writes down is a multiple of 4? Express your answer as a common fraction.

1. What is the square root of the product of 9 and 25?

2. A triangle has side lengths 41, 15, and 52. What is its area?

3. Ava and Michael want to order Big Plate Chicken at a Uyghur restaurant. They can order the small 20-ounce portion for $25 or the large 48-ounce portion for $36. How many cents per ounce would they save by ordering the large portion instead of the small?

4. Each person in a group of 20 people shakes hands with at most 18 other people in the group. What is the maximum possible number of handshakes, given that any pair of people shakes hands at most once?

5. There are 168 prime numbers between 1 and 1000. What proportion of composite numbers less than or equal to 1000 are even? Express your answer as a common fraction.

6. Two circles of radius 6 are drawn such that their centers each fall on the other circle. Then their overlapping area can be expressed in the form $a\pi - b\sqrt{c}$ for positive whole numbers a, b, and c such that c is not divisible by the square of a prime. What is $a + b + c$?

7. In the box plot below, Kathleen keeps track of the number of gears in each of the 9 legendary vehicles for her kingdom. What is the range in number of gears used?

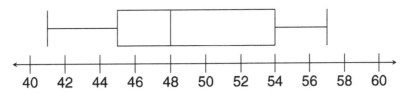

8. What is 237_8 in base 3?

9. How many ways can you select 2 books from 20 differently named books given that the order of selection does not matter?

10. The *harmonic mean* of two nonzero real numbers a and b is defined to be $\frac{2}{\frac{1}{a}+\frac{1}{b}}$. What is the harmonic mean of $\frac{5}{3}$ and $\frac{5}{12}$? Express your answer as a common fraction.

11. The side lengths of an isosceles triangle are x, $x + 1$, and x^2. What is the value of x? Express your answer as a common fraction in simplest radical form.

12. Suzy and Beth both run at constant rates. In addition, Suzy runs 2 miles in 21 minutes, and Beth runs 3 miles in 34 minutes. How many fewer minutes does it take the faster person to run a mile than the other? Express your answer as a common fraction.

13. How many rearrangements of the letters in the word *HAMLET* contain the four consecutive letters *MATH*, in that order?

14. Below are the graphs of the quadratic functions $f(x)$, $g(x)$, and $h(x)$, each of which have vertices with integer coordinates. Their leading coefficients, in some order, are -2, 1, and $\frac{1}{2}$. Given that the vertex of $f(x)$ is in the second quadrant, what is $f(7)$?

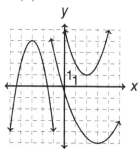

15. In base 12, A and B represent the values for 10 and 11, respectively. What is the remainder when $ABBA_{12}$ is divided by 11?

16. Anna wants to invite four friends to the movies. She selects four from the eight that are in town this week. In how many ways can she choose the four friends to invite?

17. The net below is folded into an octahedron, which has 8 triangular faces. What is the sum of the numbers on the faces sharing an edge with the shaded face?

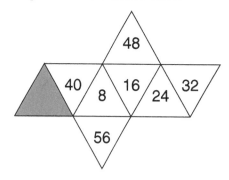

18. Mahiro and Mihari play several matches on a console game. They each start with 10 points. In each match, the winner gains 5 points while the loser loses 4 points. The game ends when one player has at most 0 points. At the end of the game, Mahiro has 0 points, and Mihari has 36 points. How many matches were played?

19. Let p and q be two prime numbers such that $(p+1)(q+1)$ is not divisible by the square of any positive whole number greater than 1. Find the smallest possible value of $p+q$.

20. Paul takes 40 minutes to answer all 30 problems on a test. On average, how many seconds does he spend on each problem?

21. In square $ABCD$, let E and F be the midpoints of sides $\overline{AB}$ and $\overline{BC}$. What is the ratio of the area of triangle DEF to that of the square? Express your answer as a common fraction.

22. A fair six-sided die is rolled 198 times. What is the expected number of times that a composite number is rolled?

23. Round $\sqrt{3\sqrt{3\sqrt{3\sqrt{3\sqrt{3\sqrt{3}}}}}}$ to the nearest positive whole number.

24. In the decimal expansion of 100!, how many trailing zeroes are there?

25. Wentinn and Taman refuse to tell Kendra how many college classes they are taking. Kendra knows that they are taking a total of 52 credits and that Taman is taking a prime number of credits more than 20. What is the greatest number of credits that Wentinn can be taking?

26. Two sides of a triangle have lengths 3 and 19. The open interval (a, b) denotes all possible values for the length of the third side. What is $a + b$?

27. Madison polled a group of people about their favorite type of apple. The results are in the picture graph below, where each full circle represents 4 people. In how many ways can Madison choose a group of 4 people if 2 picked the most popular apple and 2 picked the least popular one?

Fuji	○○◖
Gala	○○○○
Granny Smith	○○○◖
Red Delicious	○○○○○◿

28. In his dresser, Ryan has many pairs of socks: 20 blue, 7 yellow, 1 red, and 14 white. Each pair of socks, including those of the same color, is unique. Given that Ryan draws randomly without replacement, how many socks must he draw until he has a matching pair of both blue and white socks?

29. Eugene is trying to rearrange windows on his 18×11 computer screen. All of a sudden, two-thirds of the area of his screen goes black and cannot be used anymore! What is the area of his screen that is still usable?

30. Let $f(x)$ be a polynomial of degree 3 with leading coefficient 1 for which $f(1) = 19$ and $f(-1) = 7$. What is $f(2) - f(-2)$?

31. The sum of three perfect squares is 35. What is the square root of their product?

32. Owen and David are eating calzones at Brian's Bombastic Burritos. To make a calzone, they each choose one of 16 crust flavors, two of 11 different toppings, and one of 7 sauces. How many different calzones can each person make?

33. A rectangle with whole-number side lengths has a diagonal of length $\sqrt{65}$. What is the maximum area of the rectangle?

34. Lily is making 10 liters of a 25% salt water solution. She mixes 4 liters of a 30% salt water solution with 6 liters of a mystery salt water solution of unknown concentration. To the nearest whole number, what is the percent salt concentration of the mystery solution?

35. A mailman has four letters, each of which has a different recipient. He randomly hands each recipient a different letter. What is the probability that all four people received the wrong letter? Express your answer as a common fraction.

36. The sum of the divisors of 30 is N. What is the sum of the divisors of N?

37. What is the sum of all values of x such that $\frac{49}{x^2+3x-4} + \frac{64}{x^2+10x+24}$ is undefined?

38. A palindrome is a number that reads the same forwards and backwards, like 343. Mark picks a random positive whole number less than 1000. What is the probability Mark picks a palindrome? Express your answer as a common fraction.

39. The angle bisectors of equilateral triangle ABC intersect at D. What is the ratio of the area of the circle with diameter $\overline{AD}$ to the area of the triangle's circumcircle? Express your answer as a common fraction.

40. What is the sum of the prime factors of 2022?

41. How many ways are there to rearrange the letters of $BAMBOO$, given that the first letter is B or M?

42. The *Lucas numbers* are a sequence of numbers with first term 2 and second term 1. Each term after that is the sum of the previous two terms. What is the third smallest positive composite Lucas number?

43. A triangle has side lengths 11, n, and $3n$, for some whole number n. What is the greatest possible perimeter of this triangle?

44. Five contestants compete on the game show "Who Wants To Be a Thousandaire?", which has 5 identical $1000 bills as prizes. At the end of the show, the bills are distributed among the contestants. In how many ways can this happen such that exactly one person receives no bills?

45. How many divisors of 36 are perfect squares?

46. Let $f(x) = x^2 - 2x$. How many integer roots does $f(f(f(x)))$ have?

47. Shelly picks a random two-digit positive whole number. The tens digit is not a 1 or a 2. What is the expected value of Shelly's number? Express your answer as a common fraction.

48. Edward is baking cookies, but he forgot how many he baked! His friend Chinmay reminds him that the number of cookies that he baked leaves a remainder of 4 when divided by 5 and a remainder of 3 when divided by 7. What is the least number of cookies that Edward could have baked?

49. Parallelogram $ABCD$ in the xy-coordinate plane has vertices $(5, 5)$, $(10, 20)$, $(25, 5)$, and $(30, 20)$. What is its area?

50. The perfect squares starting from 1 up to and including 1600 are written consecutively as a sequence of digits $14916\ldots1600$. How many digits are in the sequence?

51. Three fair standard dice are rolled. What is the probability that the sum of the results exceeds 10.5? Express your answer as a common fraction.

52. In 2022, Thanksgiving was observed in the United States on Thursday, November 24, and Christmas was observed on December 25. How many Mondays were there between these two holidays?

53. What is the surface area of the largest sphere that can be inscribed in a cube of side length 6? Express your answer in terms of π.

54. A nonzero perfect square less than 200 is selected at random. What is the probability that it is divisible by 9? Express your answer as a common fraction.

55. Freya is taking the MKITTEN exam in her local hamlet and needs 50 out of 56 points to pass. She earns distinct positive whole number scores on each of the four 14-point sections. What is the lowest score that Freya can get on one section and still pass the MKITTEN?

56. What is $123 + 456 + 789$?

57. Tom cuts a stick that is 10 inches long into three pieces, each of which is a whole number of inches long. How many sets of sticks can he create such that he can use them to create a triangle?

58. Lucy's sugar cookie recipe makes 12 cookies from $1\frac{1}{4}$ cups of flour. She buys flour in 3 kilogram bags, and 1 cup of flour weighs 120 grams. How many cookies can she make from one bag of flour?

59. When Sally was born, her mother was two-fifths as old as her grandmother. On the day Sally turned twelve years old, her mother was one-half as old as her grandmother. On this same day, what was the sum of the ages of Sally, her mother, and her grandmother?

60. James randomly selects two different whole numbers between 1 and 10, inclusive. What is the probability that their least common multiple is greater than 35? Express your answer as a common fraction.

61. Hannah and Brian are doing a puzzle. They work together to finish the whole puzzle in 3 hours. Hannah assembles 4 pieces per minute, and Brian places a total of 450 pieces himself. What fraction of the puzzle did Hannah complete? Express your answer as a common fraction.

62. What is the units digit of 3^{111}?

63. How many diagonals does a 20-sided convex polygon have?

64. Sherry's grade is the average of two scores, both of which are two-digit positive whole numbers. However, the professor accidentally swapped the digits of Sherry's first score. If her grade is 27 points lower than it should be, what is the positive difference between the digits of Sherry's first score?

65. On the stacked bar chart below, the number of creatures in each of eight regions is shown. The white and shaded bars represent the native and foreign creatures, respectively. In how many regions are less than half of the creatures native?

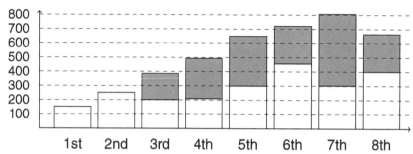

66. Addie is thinking of a number. She gives you 3 hints:
    • Her number is between 50 and 100.
    • Her number has an odd number of divisors.
    • Her number is odd.
    What number is Addie thinking of?

67. Kyle and Jimmy are running an 800 meter race. Kyle runs at 10 meters per second and finishes the race 30 seconds after Jimmy. At how many meters per second does Jimmy run the race?

68. The graph below has 15 points. The integer a minimizes the positive difference between the numbers of points on each side of the line $y = a - x$. What is a?

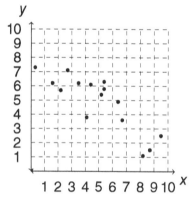

69. The prism below contains some number of identical $2 \times 2 \times 2$ cubes. What is the volume of the prism?

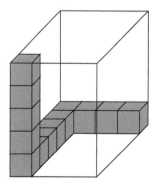

70. What is $50 \times 44 \div 100$?

71. Eugene wants to go from point *M* to point *W* on the 5 × 5 grid below by repeatedly going up one unit or going right one unit. He insists on staying on the bolded lines, but a super adaptor lets him go off the bolded lines. How many more ways can Eugene get to point W with the super adaptor than without it?

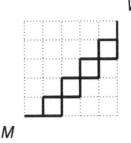

72. Eric takes 5 days to read a novel with 75000 words, reading at most one hour per day. What is the minimum average number of words per minute that Eric must have read at?

73. Ty uses a ruler to measure the length of several line segments, as shown in the diagram below. Given that four times the length of any of the segments is a whole number, how many units is the length of the longest segment? Express your answer as a mixed number.

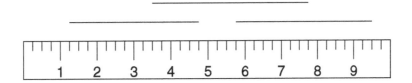

74. Angie uses a $20 gift card to buy a shirt that is 40% off. The tax rate is 10%, and the shirt originally cost $15. How many dollars remain on the gift card? Express your answer as a decimal to the nearest hundredth.

75. A unit cube is removed from each corner of a 3 × 3 × 3 cube. What is the surface area of the resulting figure?

76. Taiki can drink 20 ounces of soup in 6 minutes. Given that he drinks soup at a constant rate, how many seconds does Taiki take to drink 1 ounce of soup?

77. What is the tens digit of 1234^2?

78. Anya averaged 12 points per game in the first 5 games of an 8 game season. She wanted to average 15 points per game for the entire season. How many points, on average, must she score in each of the remaining games?

79. Meri uses the Venn diagram below to sort certain two-digit numbers by their prime factors. Each circle only contains numbers divisible by a distinct prime. What is the greatest quantity of numbers that can be in the shaded region of the Venn diagram?

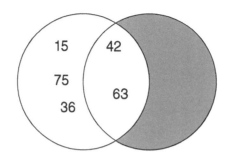

80. Lisa lives 60 miles from the beach. She drives there from home at 20 miles per hour for half the time and 30 miles per hour for the rest. On her way home, she drives at 20 miles per hour for half the *distance* and 30 miles per hour for the rest. How many minutes is the positive difference between her two commutes?

Answers
12317

Sprint Round

1. 1
2. $\frac{3}{37}$
3. 40
4. 65
5. 31
6. 36
7. 14
8. 90
9. 135
10. 3
11. 126
12. 27
13. 1600
14. 60
15. 9
16. 480
17. 85
18. 65
19. 15
20. 110
21. 9
22. 108
23. 750
24. 24
25. $\frac{13}{25}$
26. $\frac{8}{5}$
27. 240
28. 7490
29. 46
30. $\frac{825}{4}$

Target Round

1. 20.95
2. 2490
3. 5
4. 13
5. $\frac{1}{136}$
6. $\frac{252}{11}$
7. 27000000
8. 435

Team Round

1. 150
2. 6067
3. 988
4. $\frac{33}{50}$
5. 5
6. −8
7. 145
8. 158
9. 13
10. $\frac{17}{27}$

Countdown

1. 15
2. 234
3. 50
4. 180
5. $\frac{499}{831}$
6. 45
7. 16
8. 12220_3
9. 190
10. $\frac{2}{3}$
11. $\frac{1+\sqrt{5}}{2}$
12. $\frac{5}{6}$
13. 6
14. −196
15. 9
16. 70
17. 128
18. 16
19. 15
20. 80
21. $\frac{3}{8}$
22. 66
23. 3
24. 24
25. 29
26. 38
27. 11550
28. 71
29. 66
30. 36
31. 15
32. 6160
33. 28
34. 22(%)
35. $\frac{3}{8}$
36. 195
37. −9
38. $\frac{4}{37}$
39. $\frac{1}{4}$
40. 342
41. 90
42. 76
43. 31
44. 20
45. 4
46. 2
47. $\frac{129}{2}$
48. 24
49. 300
50. 117
51. $\frac{1}{2}$
52. 4
53. 36π
54. $\frac{2}{7}$
55. 11
56. 1368
57. 2
58. 240
59. 120
60. $\frac{2}{9}$
61. $\frac{8}{13}$
62. 7
63. 170
64. 6
65. 3
66. 81
67. 16
68. 10
69. 960
70. 22
71. 236
72. 250
73. $4\frac{1}{4}$
74. 10.10
75. 54
76. 18
77. 5
78. 20
79. 9
80. 6

Sprint Round Solutions

1. Every function f with 0 in its domain has a unique y-intercept $(0, f(0))$ since there can only be one value for $f(0)$. This is the concept behind the Vertical Line Test, which determines whether a graph can represent a function. Thus, a function has at most $\boxed{1}$ y-intercept.

2. There are a total of $4+5+6+7+6+5+4 = 37$ circles in the grid. We can mark all shaded circles and all circles tangent to a shaded circle with an X, as shown in the diagram below. That leaves 3 circles, so the desired fraction is $\boxed{\dfrac{3}{37}}$.

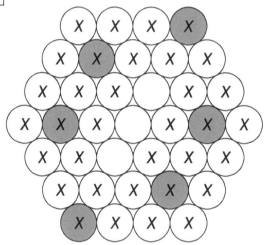

3. Let x be the number of hearts Isabel collects from the first isle. Then she collects $x + (x+1) + (x+2) + (x+3) + (x+4) + (x+5) = 6x + 15$ hearts in total, so $6x + 15 \geq 250$. Solving the inequality yields $x \geq \frac{235}{6}$. Note that $\frac{235}{6}$ is between 39 and 40. Thus, since Isabel can only collect a whole number of hearts, the minimum number of hearts she collected from the first isle is $\boxed{40}$.

4. The dimensions of the banana bread are 5 inches by 5 inches by $\frac{225}{25} = 9$ inches. By doing 11 cuts, Claudia makes 12 slices of banana bread whose dimensions are 5 inches by 5 inches by $\frac{9}{12} = \frac{3}{4}$ inches. The surface area of each slice of banana bread, in square inches, is then $25 \cdot 2 + 4 \cdot 5 \cdot \frac{3}{4} = \boxed{65}$.

5. During the first $3 \cdot 10 = 30$ days, Jeremy can read at most $100 \cdot 10 = 1000$ pages. If he does this, then he will have one page left, which he can read in one additional day. Thus, the minimum number of days he needs to read the book entirely is $\boxed{31}$.

6. By the Pythagorean Theorem, the distances between Brad and the banks at points B, C, and D are $\sqrt{7^2 + 2^2} = \sqrt{53}$, $\sqrt{5^2 + 6^2} = \sqrt{61}$, and $\sqrt{2^2 + 8^2} = \sqrt{68}$ units, respectively. Brad will then go to the bank at point B, for which he has to walk 7 100-meter blocks to the right and 2 100-meter blocks up. Therefore, the total number of paths Brad can take from point A to point B is $\binom{7+2}{2} = \boxed{36}$.

7. We know that $b = c^2$ since $b^3 = c^6$ and $a = c^3$ since $a^2 = c^6$. The least possible value of c is 2, which we pick to also minimize a and b. Then $a = 8$ and $b = 4$, so the desired sum is $a + b + c = 8 + 4 + 2$, or $\boxed{14}$.

8. A cube has 8 vertices and 12 edges, and a tetrahedron has 4 vertices and 6 edges. Then to make either of these geometric solids, Jason uses 3 pieces of spaghetti for every 2 marshmallows. Thus, the number of pieces of spaghetti that Jason started with is $\frac{3}{2} \cdot 60 = \boxed{90}$.

9. The sum of the hundreds and units digits is at most 18, so the tens digit can be no more than 3. In addition, the hundreds digit cannot be 0. We perform casework on the value of the tens digit.
    - If the tens digit is 1, the hundreds and units digits sum to at least 5. Then there are 6, 7, 8, 9, and 10 possible values for the ones digit when the hundreds digit is 1, 2, 3, 4, or at least 5, respectively. This gives us $6 + 7 + 8 + 9 + 5 \cdot 10 = 80$ options.
    - If the tens digit is 2, the hundreds and units digit sum to at least 10, so for each hundreds digit x, there are x possible ones digits. This gives us $1 + 2 + 3 + \cdots + 9 = 45$ more options.
    - If the tens digit is 3, the hundreds and units digit sum to at least 15, so both of them are at least 6. Then the hundreds digits of 6, 7, 8, and 9 give us 1, 2, 3, and 4 options, respectively, for a total of $1 + 2 + 3 + 4 = 10$.
    Altogether, the number of numbers with the desired property is $80 + 45 + 10 = \boxed{135}$.

10. Maude jogged 192 meters, so Claude jogged the remaining 208 meters. The ratio of their speeds is equal to the ratio of the distances they traveled. Let Maude's speed be s meters per second, and let Claude's speed be $s + 0.25$ meters per second. Then we have the equation $\frac{s}{s+0.25} = \frac{192}{208}$, which simplifies to $\frac{s}{s+0.25} = \frac{12}{13}$. Cross-multiplying and combining like terms yields $13s = 12s + 3$ and $s = 3$, so the number of meters that Maude jogs in a second is $\boxed{3}$.

11. The diagram below shows the 3 possible cases, with the desired region shaded. The leftmost case yields a square with side length 8 and perimeter $4 \cdot 8 = 32$. In the center case, the region is a concave polygon with a perimeter of $13 + 3 + 8 + 5 + 5 + 8 = 42$. Finally, in the rightmost case, the perimeter of the region is $13 + 8 + x + 5 + 8 + 5 + (5 - x) + 8 = 52$, where x is a number between 0 and 5, exclusive. Thus, the sum of all possible perimeters of the shaded region is $32 + 42 + 52 = \boxed{126}$.

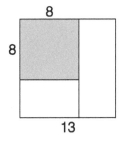 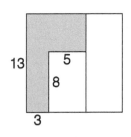 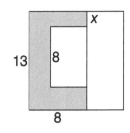

12. We can equivalently find the expected value of the label of the first pad Ken removes, which is the average of all of the pads' labels. Then the expected value is $\frac{(1+2+\cdots+11)+258}{12} = \frac{324}{12}$, or $\boxed{27}$.

13. We know that Patrice burned 316 calories, so $100 + 100 \cdot \frac{100+p}{100} + 100 \cdot \frac{100+p}{100} \cdot \frac{100-p}{100} = 316$, or $p + \frac{10000-p^2}{100} = 116$. Rearranging after multiplication by 100 yields $p^2 - 100p + 1600 = 0$, so $p = 20$ or $p = 80$. The product of these values is $\boxed{1600}$.

14. Let r be the radius of the circles. Then one circle is tangent to two adjacent sides of the square, and the other circle is tangent to the other two sides, with one possible configuration shown in the diagram below. Then the vertical distance across the square is equal to $2r + r\sqrt{2}$, which also equals the side length of square $ABCD$. Then $2r + r\sqrt{2} = 10$, so $r = \frac{10}{2+\sqrt{2}}$, or $r = 10 - 5\sqrt{2}$ after rationalizing the denominator. This can be rewritten as $10 - \sqrt{50}$, so the desired sum is $10 + 50 = \boxed{60}$.

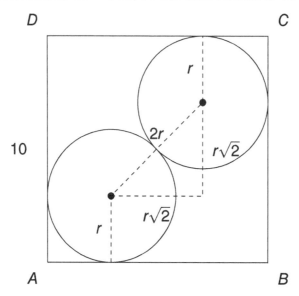

15. We have $x^5 - 2 = 0$ since $(x^5 - 2)^{30} = 0$, so $x^5 = 2$ and $x^{15} = 8$. Then $x^{15} - y + 1 = 0$ as well, and solving for y yields $y = x^{15} + 1$, or $\boxed{9}$.

16. The only way for two of the first 6 positive integers to multiply to a perfect square is if the 1 and the 4 are adjacent. There are $\binom{6}{2} \cdot 2 = 30$ total ways to place the 1 and 4 in the list of numbers, and there are $(6-1) \cdot 2 = 10$ ways to place the 1 and 4 next to each other. Thus, the number of ways to order the first six positive whole numbers without any two consecutive numbers multiplying to a perfect square is $6! \cdot \frac{30-10}{30} = \boxed{480}$.

17. If any particular digit changes, then all of the parity conditions involving that digit become false. The only condition that is now false is the last, so the digit that changed is the fourth. Then Jon's original binary number was 1010101_2, which in base 10 evaluates to $2^6 + 2^4 + 2^2 + 2^0 = \boxed{85}$.

18. Let $a = x^2 + 7x + 8$ and $b = 12 - x^2 - 7x$. Then $a + b = 20$ and $\frac{a}{b} = \frac{3}{2}$, so $a = 12$ and $b = 8$. Substituting $a = 12$ back in yields $x^2 + 7x + 8 = 12$, or $x^2 + 7x - 4 = 0$. By the quadratic formula, the difference between the two solutions for x is $\frac{\sqrt{7^2 - 4 \cdot 1 \cdot (-4)}}{1} = \sqrt{65}$, so $d^2 = \boxed{65}$.

19. Let lines $\overline{AB}$ and $\overline{CD}$ intersect at P, and let $IJ = AB = 1$. Because $IJKL$ has area 1, we now seek the area of $ABCDL$. That area is the difference between the areas of square $APDL$ and triangle BCP. Since $\triangle BCP$ is an isosceles right triangle with hypotenuse 1, $BP = \frac{\sqrt{2}}{2}$. The side length of square $APDL$ is therefore $1 + \frac{\sqrt{2}}{2}$, so pentagon $ABCDL$ has area $\left(1 + \frac{\sqrt{2}}{2}\right)^2 - \frac{1}{2} \cdot \left(\frac{\sqrt{2}}{2}\right)^2 = 1 + \sqrt{2} + \frac{1}{2} - \frac{1}{4} = \frac{5}{4} + \sqrt{2}$, or $\frac{5+4\sqrt{2}}{4}$. Thus, the desired sum is $5 + 4 + 2 + 4 = \boxed{15}$.

20. Note that the only letters that appear twice are M, A, and T, with H, E, I, C, and S each appearing once. We then perform casework on the number of letters in the palindrome.
    - If the palindrome has 1 letter, then any of the 8 distinct letters can be chosen, for 8 options.
    - If the palindrome has 2 letters, then both letters will be one of the three with two appearances, for 3 options.
    - If the palindrome has 3 letters, the first and last letters will be one of the three paired letters, and the middle letter can be any of the remaining 7, for $3 \cdot 7 = 21$ options.
    - If the palindrome has 4 letters, the outside pair of letters will be one of the three pairs, and the inside pair of letters will be one of the remaining two, for $3 \cdot 2 = 6$ options.
    - If the palindrome has 5 letters, we still need to choose two pairs of letters as with the case above, but the middle letter can be any of the remaining 6, for $6 \cdot 6 = 36$ options.
    - If the palindrome has 6 letters, all three pairs are in the palindrome, for $3! = 6$ options.
    - If the palindrome has 7 letters, all three pairs will be used, and the middle letter will be one of the remaining 5, for $6 \cot 5 = 30$ options.
    - With only 3 paired letters, no palindrome can have 8 or more letters.
    The total number of palindromes that can be made from the letters in *MATHEMATICS* is $8 + 3 + 21 + 6 + 36 + 6 + 30 = \boxed{110}$.

21. Tanya's first blast splits the asteroid of size 5 into one of size 4 and another of size 3. Her second and third blasts turn the asteroids of size 3 and 4 into asteroids of size 1 and 2 and 2 and 3, respectively. Then her fourth blast breaks the asteroid of size 3 into asteroids of size 1 and 2, leaving Tanya with a total of 3 asteroids of size 2 and 2 asteroids of size 1. These can be destroyed in 5 more blasts, so the number of blasts that Tanya needs to completely destroy an asteroid of size 5 is $4 + 5 = \boxed{9}$.

22. Let $[\mathcal{P}]$ denote the area of a polygon $\mathcal{P}$. Triangle DEF can be decomposed into triangles ABC, FCE, DAF, and EBD, so $[DEF] = [ABC] + [FCE] + [DAF] + [EBD]$. The ratio between the areas of two triangles is equal to the product of the ratios of the respective bases and heights. Thus, we rewrite $[DEF] = [ABC] + [FCE] + [DAF] + [EBD]$ as $[DEF] = [ABC] + \frac{FC}{AC} \cdot \frac{CE}{CB} \cdot [ABC] + \frac{DA}{BA} \cdot \frac{AF}{AC} \cdot [ABC] + \frac{EB}{CB} \cdot \frac{BD}{BA} \cdot [ABC]$. This factors to $[DEF] = (1 + \frac{FC}{AC} \cdot \frac{CE}{CB} + \frac{DA}{BA} \cdot \frac{AF}{AC} + \frac{EB}{CB} \cdot \frac{BD}{BA}) \cdot [ABC]$, which evaluates as $[DEF] = (1 + 4 \cdot 2 + 2 \cdot 3 + 3 \cdot 1) \cdot (\frac{1}{2} \cdot 3 \cdot 4)$, or $\boxed{108}$.

23. We can rewrite $f(n)$ as $(1+2+3+\cdots+100)+100n = 5050+100n$. Then $f(1)+f(2)+f(3)+\cdots+f(2023) = 5050 \cdot 2023 + 100 \cdot (1+2+3+\cdots+2023)$, which simplifies to $5050 \cdot 2023 + 100 \cdot \frac{2023 \cdot 2024}{2}$. Since we only care about the last three digits of this expression, we can simplify it to $5050 \cdot 2023 + 100 \cdot \frac{2023 \cdot 2024}{2} \equiv 50(20+3) + 100 \cdot 23 \cdot 12 \bmod 1000$, which further simplifies to $150 + 2300(10+2) \bmod 1000$. This is congruent to $150 + 4600 \equiv \boxed{750} \bmod 1000$.

6. Let $u = x^2 + 4x + 1$, so $u^2 + 1 \leq u + 1$. This means that $u^2 - u \leq 0$, or $0 \leq u \leq 1$. Adding 3 to the inequality $0 \leq x^2 + 4x + 1 \leq 1$ yields $3 \leq (x+2)^2 \leq 4$. Taking the square root gives us $\sqrt{3} \leq |x+2| \leq 2$, which yields $-4 \leq x \leq -2 - \sqrt{3}$ or $\sqrt{3} - 2 \leq x \leq 0$ based on the sign of $(x + 2)$. The sum of a, b, c, and d is therefore $(-4) + (-2 - \sqrt{3}) + (\sqrt{3} - 2) + 0 = \boxed{-8}$.

7. Let the semicircle have center O and radius r, so $AB = 2r$. Suppose that O lies between P and Q. Let $OP = x$ and $OQ = 5 - x$. Applying the Pythagorean Theorem to triangles XPO and YQO yields $r^2 = x^2 + 36$ and $r^2 = (5 - x)^2 + 16$. Equating the two gives $x^2 + 36 = x^2 - 10x + 41$, so $x = \frac{1}{2}$ and $r^2 = \frac{145}{4}$. If P were instead between O and Q, then we would get $x = -\frac{1}{2}$, which is impossible. The desired value is $AB^2 = (2r)^2$, which is equal to $4r^2 = \boxed{145}$.

8. We perform casework on the number of prime factors of such a number.
   - There is no prime number with digits summing to 18 because it would be divisble by 3.
   - The numbers $79 \cdot 2 = 158$, $97 \cdot 2 = 194$, $67 \cdot 5 = 335$, $29 \cdot 7 = 203$, and $7 \cdot 47 = 329$ each have two prime factors whose digits sum to 18. No number less than 158 with multiple two-digit prime factors satisfies the digit sum, so the smallest such number with two prime factors is 158.
   - No three single-digit primes sum to 18, and the smallest number with three prime factors with a digit sum of 18 is $3 \cdot 5 \cdot 19 = 285$, which is also greater than 158.
   - The smallest number with four distinct prime factors is $2 \cdot 3 \cdot 5 \cdot 7 = 210$, which is greater than 158.

   The smallest positive whole number whose distinct prime factors have digits that all sum to 18 is then $\boxed{158}$.

9. Let the right triangle be $\triangle ABC$ with hypotenuse $\overline{BC}$, and let D be the foot of the altitude from A to $\overline{BC}$. Without loss of generality, denote $BD = a$ and $CD = b$. By similar triangles, $\frac{BD}{AD} = \frac{AD}{CD}$, so $AD = \sqrt{ab}$. Taking the hypotenuse as the base, the area of $\triangle ABC$ is $\frac{(a+b)\sqrt{ab}}{2}$, four times the square of which is $ab(a+b)^2$. Then $ab(a+b)^2 = x(x+19)$ for positive whole numbers a, b, and x. The smallest value of x that yields a valid ordered pair (a, b) is $x = 6$, for which $(a, b) = (2, 3)$ or $(3, 2)$. The minimum area of $\triangle ABC$ is thus $\frac{\sqrt{ab}(a+b)}{2} = \frac{5\sqrt{6}}{2}$, yielding a desired sum of $m + n + p = \boxed{13}$.

10. We perform casework on the numbers of odd and even numbers that Kenny rolls.
    - 3 odd numbers: The product of three odd numbers is never divisible by 4.
    - 1 even and 2 odd numbers: The even number and the sum of the two odd numbers must both leave remainders of 0 or 2 when divided by 4, the probabilities of which are $\frac{1}{3} \cdot \frac{4}{9} = \frac{4}{27}$ and $\frac{2}{3} \cdot \frac{5}{9} = \frac{10}{27}$, respectively.
    - 1 odd and 2 even numbers: The product of two even numbers is always divisible by 4.
    - 3 even numbers: For the sum of three even numbers to be divisible by 4, they must leave remainders of $(0,0,0)$ or $(0,2,2)$ when divided by 4, in no particular order. The probability of this occurring is $\left(\frac{1}{3}\right)^3 + \binom{3}{2} \cdot \frac{1}{3} \cdot \left(\frac{2}{3}\right)^2 = \frac{13}{27}$.

    Then the probability in each case is multiplied by the probability of each case happening, yielding the total probability that Kenny writes down a number divisible by 4 to be $\frac{1}{8} \cdot 0 + \binom{3}{2} \cdot \frac{1}{8} \cdot \frac{14}{27} + \binom{3}{2} \cdot \frac{1}{8} \cdot 1 + \frac{1}{8} \cdot \frac{13}{27} = \boxed{\frac{17}{27}}$.

24. By the definition of $f_n(x)$, we know that $f_2(x) = 2^{f_1(x)}$, which expands to $f_2(x) = 2^{2^x}$. Then we have $2^{2^a} = 512$ and $2^{2^b} = 1024$, so $2^a = 9$ and $2^b = 10$. Thus $2^{a+b} = 9 \cdot 10 = 90$, and $f_2(a+b) = 2^{2^{a+b}}$, or 2^{90}. We then note that $2^{10} \equiv 24 \bmod 100$, $2^{20} \equiv 76 \bmod 100$, and $2^{30} \equiv 24 \bmod 100$. Thus, the remainders when increasing tenth powers of 2 are divided by 100 alternate, so it follows that $2^{90} \equiv \boxed{24} \bmod 100$.

25. Suppose a triplet of three numbers is *valid* if the pairwise positive differences are each at most 2. The probability that a valid triplet has smallest integer 1 is the probability that all three numbers are between 1 and 3, inclusive, subtracted by the probability that all of the numbers are 2 or 3. This evaluates to $(\frac{3}{5})^3 - (\frac{2}{5})^3 = \frac{19}{125}$. This probability is the same as the probability that a valid triplet has smallest integer 2 or 3 since we can add 1 or 2, respectively, to all members of a valid triplet with smallest integer 1. Finally, the probability that all integers in a valid triplet are 4 or 5 is $(\frac{2}{5})^3 = \frac{8}{125}$. Thus, the probability that a randomly chosen triplet is valid is $\frac{3 \cdot 19 + 8}{125} = \frac{65}{125}$, or $\boxed{\dfrac{13}{25}}$.

26. The area of $\triangle MAT$ is 6, so the area of $\triangle MHT$ is $6 - 4 = 2$. Using the formula $area = \frac{bh}{2}$ and taking $\overline{MT}$ as the base, we find the perpendicular distance from H to $\overline{MT}$ to be $\frac{4}{5}$. Since the length of the altitude of $\triangle MAT$ from A to $\overline{MT}$ is $\frac{12}{5}$, AH has a minimum value of $\frac{12}{5} - \frac{4}{5} = \boxed{\dfrac{8}{5}}$.

27. Such a number cannot be even or end in 3, so it must have 1, 5, 7, or 9 as its units digit. Then for each tens digit, two-thirds of the 9 possible hundreds digits will form a three-digit number not divisible by 3. Therefore, the number of integers that are both 2-free and 3-free is $4 \cdot 10 \cdot (\frac{2}{3} \cdot 9) = \boxed{240}$.

28. Converting 55% to a fraction yields $\frac{11}{20}$. Then for some positive integer n, Rowan must have made $11n$ and missed $9n$ free throw attempts so far. After Rowan takes N more free throw attempts, he will have missed $9n + 1$ and made $11n + N - 1$ attempts. With a make rate of 90%, he made 9 times as many shots as he missed, so $11n + N - 1 = 9 \cdot (9n + 1)$, or $N = 70n + 10$. Plugging in positive integer values of n yields the possible values for N to be 80, 150, 220, 290, 360, and so on. Keeping in mind that $N \le 1000$, the sum of all possible values of N is $80 + 150 + 220 + \cdots + 990 = \boxed{7490}$.

29. Denote the three circles as z_1, z_2, and z_3. The side length of U is twice the radius of the circles plus twice the length of the longer leg of a 30-60-90 right triangle with shorter leg length equal to the radius of the circles. Then U has side length $2 + 2\sqrt{3}$.

Now let the shared centers of triangles T and U be O, and let the center of z_1 be P. Let z_1 and z_2 be tangent at Q, and let OP intersect z_1 at R. Then $\triangle OPQ$ is a 30-60-90 triangle with longer leg PQ and hypotenuse OP, which has length $\frac{2}{\sqrt{3}}$. This gives us $OR = OP - PQ$, or $\frac{2-\sqrt{3}}{\sqrt{3}}$. We draw one last 30-60-90 triangle with OR as its shorter leg and its hypotenuse from O to a vertex of T to find the side length of T as $2 \cdot (\sqrt{3})(\frac{2-\sqrt{3}}{\sqrt{3}}) = 4 - 2\sqrt{3}$.

Finally, T and U are both equilateral triangles, so the ratio of their areas is equal to the square of the ratio of their side lengths, which is $(\frac{4-2\sqrt{3}}{2+2\sqrt{3}})^2 = (\frac{2-\sqrt{3}}{1+\sqrt{3}})^2$. This simplifies to $\left(\frac{3\sqrt{3}-5}{2}\right)^2 = \frac{26-15\sqrt{3}}{2}$, so the desired sum is $26 + 15 + 3 + 2 = \boxed{46}$.

30. Let a, b, c, and d be the number of red gumballs dispensed before the first blue gumball, between the first and second blue gumballs, between the second and third blue gumballs, and after the last blue gumball, respectively. As there are 7 red gumballs, $a + b + c + d = 7$. Since each possible order of gumballs being dispensed has the same probability of occurring, the expected values of a, b, c, and d are all the same. Tthe expected number of red gumballs after the last blue gumball is $d = \frac{7}{4}$, so the expected number of quarters needed to dispense all of the blue gumballs is $10 - \frac{7}{4} = \frac{33}{4}$. Converting this to cents yields $25 \cdot \frac{33}{4} = \boxed{\dfrac{825}{4}}$.

Target Round Solutions

1. The number of balls and rackets Skye buys is the same, so the quantity of each that she gets is the least common multiple of 4 and 6, or 12. This corresponds to $\frac{12}{4} = 3$ sets of tennis rackets and $\frac{12}{6} = 2$ sets of tennis balls, which have a total cost of $3 \cdot \$4.99 + 2 \cdot \$2.99 = \$\boxed{20.95}$.

2. We can rewrite the sequence as $1, 1+19, 1+19+18, 1+19+18+17$, and so on. These $19+1 = 20$ terms then sum to $1 \cdot 20 + (19) + (19+18) + (19+18+17) + \cdots + (19+18+17+\cdots+1)$. To simplify, we group terms and obtain $1 \cdot 20 + (19 \cdot 19 + 18 \cdot 18 + 17 \cdot 17 + \cdots + 2 \cdot 2 + 1 \cdot 1)$, which evaluates to $20 + \frac{19 \cdot 20 \cdot 39}{6} = \boxed{2490}$.

3. Let x be the number of tiles in Serena's fourth word. Over their first four turns, Lois used $7 + (6-1) + (4-1) + (5-1) = 19$ tiles, and Serena used $(8-1) + (8-1) + (6-1) + (x-1) = x + 18$ tiles. A total of $100 - 58 = 42$ tiles have been used, so $19 + (x+18) = 42$. Solving for x yields $x = \boxed{5}$.

4. The sum of the five apartments' monthly rent prices is $\$2000 \cdot 5 = \$10000$. Since the median is $\$2300$, the rents of the two priciest apartments are both at least $\$2300$ per month. We perform casework on the monthly rents of these two apartments.
   1. $\$2300$ and $\$2300$: The cheapest apartment costs no more than $\frac{\$3100}{2} = \$1550$ per month. This gives us $\$1300$, $\$1400$, or $\$1500$, for 3 options.
   2. $\$2300$ and $\$2400$: The cheapest apartment costs no more than $\frac{1}{2} \cdot (\$10000 - \$2300 - \$2300 - \$2400) = \$1500$ per month. All three possibilities from Case 1 still work, for 3 options.
   3. $\$2300$ and $\$2500$: The cheapest apartment costs at most $\frac{1}{2} \cdot (\$10000 - \$2300 - \$2300 - \$2500) = \$1450$ per month. This gives us $\$1300$ or $\$1400$, for 2 options.
   4. $\$2400$ and $\$2400$: The cheapest apartment costs at most $\frac{1}{2} \cdot (\$10000 - \$2300 - \$2400 - \$2400) = \$1450$ per month. This also gives us $\$1300$ or $\$1400$, for 2 options.
   5. $\$2400$ and $\$2500$: The cheapest apartment costs at most $\frac{1}{2} \cdot (\$10000 - \$2300 - \$2400 - \$2500) = \$1400$ per month. This gives us $\$1300$ or $\$1400$ yet again, for 2 options.
   6. $\$2500$ and $\$2500$: The cheapest apartment costs at most $\frac{1}{2} \cdot (\$10000 - \$2300 - \$2500 - \$2500) = \$1350$ per month. Then its monthly price must be $\$1300$, so there is only 1 possibility.

   The total number of possible sets of rents is $3 + 3 + 2 + 2 + 2 + 1 = \boxed{13}$.

5. Adding up the number of monsters in all of the simulations yields $728 + 71 + 18 + 46 + 32 = 895$ monsters. However, the monsters that appeared twice are overcounted once, and the monsters that appeared 3 times are overcounted twice. Subtracting the $69 + 5 \cdot 2 = 79$ monsters of overcount, we obtain the actual number of distinct participating monsters to be $895 - 79 = 816$. Six of these monsters won a simulation, so the probability that a randomly chosen monster was a winner is $\frac{6}{816} = \boxed{\frac{1}{136}}$.

6. We know that $BC = 20$ and $CD = 13$ since $ABCD$ is a parallelogram. Then let F be the foot of the altitude from B to $\overline{AC}$, and let M be the midpoint of $\overline{AC}$ so that $\overline{BM} \parallel \overline{BD} \parallel \overline{CE}$. We can now draw a diagram as follows.

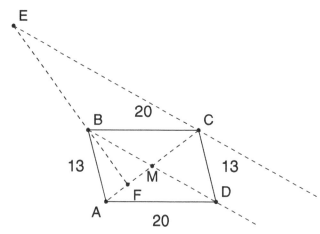

Because $\overline{BD} \parallel \overline{CE}$, $\triangle EFC \sim \triangle BFM$, so $BE = FE - BF$. From similar triangles, we have that $FE = \frac{FC}{FM} \cdot BF$, so $BE = \frac{FC}{FM} \cdot BF - BF$, which can be factored as $BE = BF\left(\frac{FC}{FM} - 1\right)$. Additionally, BF divides $\triangle BAC$ into 5-12-13 and 12-16-20 right triangles, so $FC = 16$. Then $FM = FC - \frac{1}{2} \cdot AC$, or $FM = \frac{11}{2}$, so $BE = 12 \cdot \left(\frac{16}{\frac{11}{2}} - 1\right)$, which evaluates to $\boxed{\dfrac{252}{11}}$.

7. Olivia's figure is a hexagonal prism. Let x be the side length of the hexagon, in centimeters. Then each hexagon has an area of $6 \cdot \frac{\sqrt{3}}{4}x^2 = \frac{3\sqrt{3}}{2}x^2$ square centimeters, and each rectangle has an area of $x \cdot 2x = 2x^2$ square centimeters. Since the surface area is $300\sqrt{3} + 1200$ square centimeters, we know that $2 \cdot \frac{3\sqrt{3}}{2}x^2 + 6 \cdot 2x^2 = 300\sqrt{3} + 1200$, or $3\sqrt{3}x^2 + 12x^2 = 300\sqrt{3} + 1200$. Solving this yields $x = 10$ centimeters. Then the volume of Olivia's prism is the area of the hexagon times the prism's height, or $\frac{3\sqrt{3}}{2}x^2 \cdot 2x$, which simplifies to $3\sqrt{3}x^3 = 3000\sqrt{3}$ cubic centimeters, the square of which is $\boxed{27000000}$.

8. In the inequality, every variable is raised to an even power, so none of them are confined by sign. Then we note that $6^4 < 2022 < 7^4$, $3^6 < 2022 < 4^6$, and $2^8 < 2022 < 3^8$, so $|x| \le 6$, $|y| \le 3$, and $|z| \le 2$. This would yield a total of $(2\cdot6+1)\cdot(2\cdot3+1)\cdot(2\cdot2+1) = 455$ ordered triples. However, we must ensure that combining the upper bounds still satisfies the original inequality. Indeed, both $6^4 + 3^6 + 2^8 = 2281$ and $6^4 + 3^6 = 2025$ exceed 2022. All other combinations of (x, y, z) within our bounds work, so no satisfactory ordered triples can have $|x| = 6$ *and* $|y| = 3$. This applies to $2 \cdot 2 \cdot (2 \cdot 2 + 1) = 20$ of our original triples, so the number of integer ordered triples (x, y, z) that satisfy $x^4 + y^6 + z^8 \le 2022$ is $455 - 20 = \boxed{435}$.

Team Round Solutions

1. The red and blue arrow signs are supposed to make a right angle with each other. To find the original position of the red arrow, we undo Chelina's action by rotating the red arrow sign $300°$ clockwise, or equivalently, $60°$ counterclockwise. Then the obtuse angle originally formed by the red and blue arrow signs had a measure of $90 + 60 = \boxed{150}$ degrees.

2. Evaluating $f(2023)$ and $f(2022)$ yields $f(2023) = 2023 + 2024 + 2025 + \cdots + 4045$ and $f(2022) = 2022 + 2023 + 2024 + \cdots + 4043$. The difference between these two quantities is then $4044 + 4045 - 2022 = \boxed{6067}$.

3. We work our way down from 999. Any three-digit number beginning with 99 does not satisfy conditions 2 and 5, so it would need to satisfy the other three. However, the third condition implies that the units digit is non-zero and even while the fourth condition implies that the units digit is odd. These cannot be true simultaneously. Then we proceed to 989, which only satisfies the first and fourth conditions. However, 988 satisfies the first, third, and fourth conditions, so the largest three-digit number satisfying most of these conditions is $\boxed{988}$.

4. There are 10 hours, or 600 minutes, between 10 AM and 8 PM, during which Phil has $1 + 1.5 + 1 = 3.5$ hours, or 210 minutes, of blocked time. However, if the app sends Phil a notification within the last two minutes of any blocked section, for instance at 12:59 PM, Phil can still post within two minutes. There are 3 blocked sections, so the total time that Phil cannot post within two minutes of the notification is $210 - 3 \cdot 2 = 204$ minutes. Then Phil can post on time for $600 - 204 = 396$ minutes between 10 AM to 8 PM, yielding a probability of $\frac{396}{600} = \boxed{\frac{33}{50}}$.

5. Each positive multiple of 125 can be represented as $5^3 \cdot n = 125n$, where n is a positive whole number between 1 and 80, inclusive. Let 5^k be the greatest power of 5 dividing $125n$. Since $125n$ has 12 positive whole number divisors, $k + 1$ must divide 12. In addition, k must be 3 or 5 as $5^6 > 10000$. By the formula for the number of divisors, $125n$ equals $5^5 \cdot p_1$ when $k = 5$ and $5^3 \cdot p_2^2$ when $k = 3$ for primes p_1 and p_2. Since $125n$ is at most 10000, p_1 is one of 2 or 3, and p_2 is one of 2, 3, or 7. The number of multiples of 125 less than or equal to 10000 with 12 positive factors is therefore $\boxed{5}$.